Women
and World
Religions

SECOND EDITION

Women and World Religions

Denise Lardner Carmody

University of Tulsa

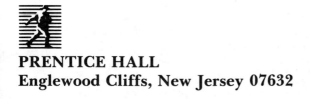

PRENTICE HALL
Englewood Cliffs, New Jersey 07632

LIBRARY OF CONGRESS
Library of Congress Cataloging-in-Publication Data

Carmody, Denise Lardner
    Women and world religions / Denise Lardner Carmody. -- 2nd ed.

    Bibliography
    Includes index.
    ISBN 0-13-962424-4
    1. Women and religion.   I. Title.
BL458.C37 1989
291'.088042--dc19   88-15580
                                           CIP

Editorial/production supervision and
  interior design: *Jenny Kletzin*
Cover design: *Ben Santora*
Manufacturing buyer: *Peter Havens*

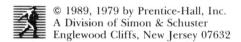 © 1989, 1979 by Prentice-Hall, Inc.
A Division of Simon & Schuster
Englewood Cliffs, New Jersey 07632

Printed in the United States of America

10   9   8   7   6   5   4   3   2   1

ISBN 0-13-962424-4

Prentice-Hall International (UK) Limited, *London*
Prentice-Hall of Australia Pty. Limited, *Sydney*
Prentice-Hall Canada Inc., *Toronto*
Prentice-Hall Hispanoamericana, S.A., *Mexico*
Prentice-Hall of India Private Limited, *New Delhi*
Prentice-Hall of Japan, Inc., *Tokyo*
Simon & Schuster Asia Pte. Ltd., *Singapore*
Editora Prentice-Hall do Brasil, Ltda., *Rio de Janeiro*

In Memory of Marie Longbottom
and for Bruce Longbottom

Contents

CHAPTER THREE: *Hindu Women*   *39*

CHAPTER FOUR: *Buddhist Women*   *67*

CHAPTER FIVE: *Chinese Women*   *93*

Preface

For some time I have wanted to revise this work. The good reception it has received from teachers of courses on women and religion has pleased me, but in the nearly ten years that separate the first and second writings, many things have changed. I wrote the first version in good part because there was no comprehensive overview of the topic. Now many studies have enriched our appreciation of the diversity of women's religious experience. The first version had to be quite succinct, due to publishing considerations. Now I have had the chance to expand the exposition to nearly double its original length. But perhaps the most significant change has been the development of feminist theory, to sharpen the focus that studies of women's religious experience ideally would have, and the collection of testimonies from women themselves about what being Jewish or Christian, Buddhist or Muslim, has meant. Where possible I have drawn on such testimony, trying to stay close to the stories women have fashioned. As well, I have tried to incorporate social-scientific studies bearing on women's images and roles, which regularly were sanctioned by the prevailing religous orthodoxy.

What has not changed from the first edition is the audience I have in mind. Once again, my main objective has been to put into the hands of undergraduates the gist of women's experiences with the world religions. My thanks to Jean Hager, my original editor at Abingdon; to Joe Heider, my editor at Prentice Hall; to the students of my women and religion courses throughout the past decade; to my many feminist friends who share my interest in religion; and to my husband, John Carmody.

Women
and World
Religions

CHAPTER ONE

Introduction

THE INFLUENCE OF WORLD RELIGIONS

The majority of the roughly 5 billion people in our contemporary world adhere to a religious tradition.[1] They are Hindus or Muslims, Christians or Buddhists, Jews or adherents of other faiths. And even the hundreds of millions of people who do not belong to a traditional religion usually organize their lives through allegiance to a worldview that operates much like a religion. For example, the more than 1 billion Chinese living in a Communist culture are guided by the thought of Karl Marx and Mao Tse-tung, as well as by the older thought of Confucius and Lao Tzu. The people of the Soviet Union continue to be shaped by the legacy of Eastern Orthodox Christianity, even when it serves their Communist leaders as part of an enemy system they have rejected. Many Africans still think of the world much as their ancestors did two hundred years ago, trying to increase the forces of fertility and avoid evil spirits. Many Americans working with sophisticated technologies think about values in fundamentalist Christian categories.

   Throughout the world, then, religion continues to play the role it apparently has played since the dawn of reflective consciousness, when "human beings" first arose. Religion is the dimension of life and thought where human beings focus on ultimate issues. It is where the mysteriousness of existence most forcefully comes home, along with the problem of why people can't get along—why injustice and warfare trouble each generation. The doctrines, ethical codes, myths, rituals, worship ceremonies, and social gatherings of religious groups the world over address such matters. Referring to God, the Buddha, Krishna, Jesus, and other sources of guidance, people East and West regularly try to renew their hopes and experience healing.

Our focus is the people who are religious, who do these things, in female bodies. We are interested in what the world religions have had to say about women, in how women have been shaped by religious experience, symbols, doctrines, and rituals. Being female or male is the first specification of one's humanity. As soon as the child emerges from the womb, the word goes out: "It's a girl" or "It's a boy." In the womb the child has developed in accord with its genes and hormones, which are specific to its sex. As soon as it is outside the womb, the child begins a social development equally stamped by its sex. All onlookers react to the new baby in sex-specific ways programmed by their culture. The religious dimension of culture is no exception. It, too, has tended to think of females differently from males. It, too, has placed on the new little person expectations specific to her or his sex.

The world religions, like the different national cultures, do these things both consciously and unconsciously. Their theologies, ethical codes, and ritual systems regularly address vices and virtues, rights and duties, considered typical of women and men, specific to one sex or the other. Thus many religious traditions have considered women more prayerful and peaceful than men. Many have reserved community leadership and authority in ritual matters to men. These attitudes shape the minds of both women and men, giving them concepts that may further or retard their development. Perhaps more significantly, these attitudes play unconsciously through the hundreds of expectations, perceptions, and judgments that both sexes make each day.

For example, if a religion thinks that women's bodies are likely to disturb men, it may well urge women to drape themselves in loose clothing. One of the interesting present-day movements in Muslim countries is for women to don more modest clothing. Countries where a generation ago women were abandoning the veil and adopting Western clothing are now witnessing a return to covered heads and floor-length robes. The motive clearly is several sided, but for many women the most pressing reason is religious: this is what Allah wants.

To stay with a Muslim example, one can further note that in Egypt, where the movement for more modest clothing for women recently has gained strength, there is a related movement to bring women into the mosque. Previously women mainly worshiped at home and had only limited opportunities for religious instruction. But some of the same dynamics that have led to a desire for more modest clothing have sparked a desire for a better understanding of the Qur'an and more opportunities for women to worship Allah together.

One could develop similar examples from the recent Roman Catholic movement to gain women the right to be ordained as priests and so exercise church leadership, or from the movement of Jewish women to gain access to the rabbinate. These religious movements flow into and out from the wider cultural currents of the nation in question, but the impact of precisely religious views cannot be doubted. What their religious traditions think of them shapes the behavior of women the world over. How they raise their children, how they think about divorce, whether they would have an abortion, whether they would work outside the home—these and other issues that determine the texture of everyday life are shot through with religious influences. So is the question of the models that women have in mind, the feminine ideals to which they aspire. In ages when Kuan-yin, the Buddhist goddess of mercy, was a leading authority figure in East Asia, many East Asian women undoubtedly thought that the ultimate force in the world was a motherly compassion. Thinking that way, they had to feel some confidence that they could bring their troubles to Kuan-yin in prayer, and they had to feel some responsibility to try to be kindly and loving themselves. The parallel to women brought up in Christian countries which greatly revered the Virgin Mary was quite exact. The case of Indian women modeling themselves on the girlfriends of Krishna naturally differed in details, but the general principle held. Women and men the world over have modeled their lives on the incarnations of divinity and the examples of virtue held out to them by their cultures.

This principle admits of various degrees of sophistication. In many cases the goddess or saint proposed to women was accepted quite literally. In some cases people clearly realized the symbolic nature of the model proposed and were more impressed by the mysteriousness, the unrepresentableness, of divinity. A third group of cases has included women who paid little attention to religion, for even in ancient times some people no doubt considered religion more hokum than help. But it seems fair to say that the vast majority of women throughout history have derived crucial parts of their identity from their religious culture. Thus it seems fair to say that if we are to understand where today's women are coming from, we need to include religion among the main objects of our study.

By feminist, egalitarian standards, the story of women's experiences with the world religions is not a happy tale. Regularly women have been represented as the weaker sex, the sex less capable of handling religious authority. This has led to women's not receiving much religious education and being few of the teachers who developed the tradition's theology and ethics. On the other hand, all of the world's religions have paid tribute to saintly and wise women. As well, many have symbolized important aspects of wisdom and divinity as feminine. So one has to read the story of women's experience with the world religions on several levels. The official doctrines about the nature of women and what roles women ought to play have been only part of the plot. As we have learned more about both the history of women's religious experience and the complexity of religious symbols, we have come to see that a phenomenon such as veiling, or a crucial decision such as abortion, sends out tendrils in a dozen different directions. Both women and men are complex religious beings. Both are communal and private, virtuous and vicious, creatures saying "both/and" more than "either/or"—all of which can make the study of women and world religions fascinating.

FEMINIST STUDIES OF RELIGION

By feminism I mean the movement to support and advance the proposition that women are as fully human as men and so should enjoy an equal measure of rights and opportunities. Working with a philosophy such as this, (or one that stresses the superiority of women's instincts), many scholars, male as well as female, have been reexamining the world religions.[2] In their studies, they have attended to the normative view of women laid out in the scriptures and authoritative traditions of the different religions. Increasingly, however, they have also attended to what women themselves have had to say. For only a little attention to the actual practice of Islam or Christianity, Judaism or Buddhism, makes it clear that often women have not accepted the designations of their nature and roles laid out in the given religion's orthodox writings. Nearly always these writings have come from men, as have the prevailing interpretations of what the writings ought to mean for daily life. Finding that male designations sometimes did not ring true to either their own experience or their own needs, women frequently have gone their own way, either paying lip service to the norms or openly disregarding them.

For example, Hindu women who in many ages were taught that the only way they could gain salvation was by first being reborn as men often laughed and went to their devotions confident that God would take care of them. Muslim women brought up on the notion that their greatest accomplishment would be giving birth to sons often crooned to their daughters serenely, telling them they were just as precious. Christian women who outwardly accepted the rules that said only men could be ordained priests or ministers often knew in their bones, and said in their women's groups, that these rules deprived the church of half its talent for leadership. Jewish women who could not lead worship services in the synagogue or teach in the seminary often reminded themselves that the crucial religious formation occurred at home, when the child was most impressionable.

It would not be accurate to paint this independence as the strongest factor in the character of the typical religious woman, or to imply that it compensated for the damages wrought by a second-rank official status. Simply by being part of their religious community and being brought up on the official doctrines, religious women took in many seeds of inferiority. Yet it also would be inaccurate to make the official, male-sponsored profiles of religious women the whole story. As they have listened to women's own interpretations of the traditions, feminist scholars have strengthened their convictions about this latter point. To get the full picture of women's experience with the world religions, one has to pay at least as much attention to the actual, concrete voices of women as to the official, usually male voices of the traditional writings and authorities. To grasp how a given tradition impacted on women's work, sexual love, prayer, education, and other realms of experience, one has to put aside preconceptions and let the variety of what women have suffered, enjoyed, thought, and done come into its own.

Probably that is the main development that feminist allegiances have brought to religious studies in the past decade. At the time I wrote the first edition of this work, there were few primary or secondary sources making available women's own voice. Today much work remains to be done, but both historical studies and contemporary case studies have more than doubled our resources. The result has been a tendency to suspend the authority of the male-generated traditional guidelines and wait for documents on what the women concerned themselves had to say. So, for example, sociologists took note of the Vatican teaching prohibiting artificial contraception but took more note of what Catholic women actually were doing. The result was a view of the sexuality of Catholic women considerably different from what the documents from Rome prescribed. Suspecting that today's women do not differ completely from their sisters of medieval or Reformation times, feminist historians have gone back to the sources with an eye for analogous ways in which the official ethics may not have matched what women actually thought and did.

Since women of the past often had little voice in official theology or culture, feminist historians frequently turn to records dealing with ordinary people and daily life. And since women often have been either illiterate or on the margins of the bookish culture of their day, feminist historians also have begun to pay more attention to painting and other nontextual sources. Working in this way, the historian Margaret R. Miles has concluded:

> If we were, for the moment, to put all of our historical literary texts back on the shelf, to shelve even our knowledge of them, and to reconstruct a history of Christianity on the evidence of visual texts alone, we would see immediately that from the earliest Christian images there is a continuous depiction of women and the development of subjects and themes based on the experience of women. For a woman whose daily life centered around the worship of a Christian community, these daily images may have been powerfully affirming

in a way that twentieth-century women find difficult to imagine, flooded as we are with exploitative commercial images of women.[3]

The study of women's images in art requires considerable sophistication, for it is difficult to interpret what a swooning Virgin Mary or a passionate Mary Magdalene probably meant to a thirteenth-century Italian or a sixteenth-century German female beholder. It also requires considerable self-criticism, as the end of the quotation from Miles signifies. Many feminists begin with a cultural bias against past ages, thinking that present cultures, despite all their signs of sexism, represent a more enlightened view of sex than past cultures. But when one allows the presuppositions of the past culture in question to have their own say, one can find them presenting current cultures a strong challenge. Similarly, one can hear a present-day Egyptian woman explain that by donning more modest garb she has given a signal to the men she meets at work and saved herself considerable sexual harassment. That does not shut the door to further questions about possible puritanism and psychological repression, but it does make a traditional position a respectable partner for dialogue. Women in both given traditions and scholarly circles have been immersing themselves in such dialogue, grateful to hear the experience of other women and fascinated by the many stories of women's ingenuity. The result has been more attention to experience and less trust of established, male-dominated authority.

Indeed, many of the women who participated in an important recent study of women's ways of knowing described coming to trust their own experience as a key moment in their growth. Thus Inez, a thirty-year-old Columbian-American woman told the researchers: "I can only know with my gut. I've got it tuned to a point where I think and feel at the same time and I know what is right. My gut is my best friend—the only thing in the world that won't let me down or lie to me or back away from me."[4] Eventually women such as Inez may realize that they enrich themselves by drawing on other sources of knowledge than pure subjectivism, but for women who previously were slaves to external, male authorities, coming to trust their own instincts can be a great liberation.

All the more so is this the case when women have suffered sexual abuse from men, and feminist scholars in all fields are starting to reckon with the possibiliity that such sexual abuse may be much more widespread than previously was thought. For example, in the sample of seventy-five women who were the subjects of the study of women's ways of knowing, 38 percent of those who were in schools and colleges told of incest, rape, or seduction by a male authority figure. And 65 percent of those contacted through social agencies told of such experiences.[5] If women in general prove to have experienced anything like such frequency of abuse by their fathers, brothers, teachers, bosses, and doctors, scholars will have to attend to women's actual religious experience with all the more sensitivity.

MOTIFS OF THIS BOOK

This book is an introduction to the full range of women's experience with the world religions. In the next chapter we begin our survey with the likely experience of prehistoric women and women who have lived in small-scale, nonliterate societies. Then, in succeeding chapters, we consider the experience of Hindu, Buddhist, Chinese, and Japanese women. The second half of the book deals with women in Western religious traditions: Judaism, Christianity, and Islam. Our last survey deals with the religious experience of American women, and we conclude with brief reflections on the significance of the overall patterns of women's immersion in the world religions.

Each of the topics we consider is unmanageably vast: the potential subject of a dozen specialized studies. Thus we shall have to content ourselves with highlighting the main trends. As much as possible, we shall focus on women's own voices, trying to hear what being Hindu or Confucian as a woman actually has felt like. On the other hand, we shall also attend to what the male-dominated authoritative texts have said about women, since these texts have shaped the cultural expectations of both women and men. As long as one remembers that things on the books are not things always practiced in the kitchen or the bedroom, studying the official views can prove highly illuminating.

In each chapter, we shall be dealing with a tradition that has many different component parts. Not Hinduism nor Christianity nor any of the other traditions has been a monolith. Indeed, some scholars find it misleading to take a tradition such as Hinduism as an integral entity, arguing that the reality is that Hinduism has embraced many different religions.[6] One might make the same argument for Christianity, if only to block any facile attempt to sweep Catholic, Protestant, and Eastern Orthodox women into one undifferentiated pile. Geographic, historical, and ethnic differences all play a part in what the women of a given religion have experienced. Class and race are other significant factors. Almost always, therefore, one is proferring generalizations that one knows fit few specific situations exactly. Almost always one is hoping that students will have the chance to study at least a few specific situations in detail, so that they may realize for themselves the limitations of introductory generalizations.

My pedagogical model has students moving from first, orientational studies to studies that go into greater depth. As any teacher of introductory courses knows, the great hope is that students will get under way on studies of their own that help them to see the richness of the inquiry in question and begin to appreciate its implications for their own lives. So while I warn students that we are only making a beginning, only doing the best we can by way of an overview, I do not apologize for the inevitable oversimplifications. One has to make a beginning somewhere, and if the beginning gets students into the process of ongoing reading and reflection, the self-corrections of that process will weed out the grosser misconceptions.

Perhaps it is worth noting explicitly that any such self-correcting process that bears on matters of personal significance has its painful moments. For example, I have observed American female students who started a course confident that they themselves had never experienced religious sexism end shaken by what their studies had revealed. Often the pattern has been that such students were intrigued and angered by what they were seeing in foreign religious cultures and then were shocked to realize that very similar patterns obtained at home. For foreign students, similar dynamics often have been at work.

The more dogmatic or fundamentalist their own religious tradition, the greater psychological tension students tend to suffer. Some leave the course at the first sign that no scripture or traditional authority is going to be exempt from what I hope is a balanced criticism. For such students the Bible or the Qur'an is an absolute, something nonnegotiable. Any kindly teacher tries to deal with such an outlook gently, but eventually one has to make it clear that the academic study of religion can grant no traditional authority an exemption from criticism. While respecting the great influence most such authorities have wielded, and trying to appreciate their deep stores of wisdom, academic studies of religion have to ask what part they played in such phenomena as war making, economic injustices, environmental destruction, racism, and sexism. True enough, one has to guard against anachronism and not expect people who lived a thousand years ago to have today's sensitivities. On the other hand, one also has to probe the part past ages played in the rise of today's problems and sensitivities, offering even-handedly such praise and blame as the data seem to warrant.

The majority of the students in most courses on women and world religions are women, but enough men enroll to merit a few comments on what they are likely to experience. First, many men find it a revelation that the canonical authorities in virtually all of the religious traditions have been patriarchal and so ill-equipped to treat women and men even-handedly. This judgment about such authorities immediately prompts the feminist scholar to qualify their claims, and such a qualification can throw male students for a double loop. Not only is the Bible or the Qur'an being studied as a human document, it is being studied as a document likely to have sexual biases.

Second, the discussions that feminist studies of religion can generate can exacerbate the often already tense relations between men and women and so seem merely to compound the sexual malaise, as Dorothy Dinnerstein has called it, warping both sexes.[7] One of the ground rules that I have found it useful to employ is a distinction between what we have inherited from the past and what we are making of our inheritance through our free choices in the present. Neither men nor women are responsible for what their grandparents did, let alone what happened at the beginning of their religious tradition. But both men and women have a responsibility to become aware of how they are treating one another today and to bring their actions into line with honesty, justice, and (I would say) love.

One of the fascinating dimensions of religious studies is the realization that most of the traditions one encounters have great resources for forgiveness and renewal. As well, they have great resources for treating both women and men kindly, supportively. The Hindu goddesses, for example, offer a wealth of symbols of women's strength and wisdom. The Christian saints offer a wealth of examples of women scaling the peaks of prayer and providing the poor heroic service. The ideal Jewish woman praised in Proverbs 31 is strong and resourceful. Muslim women such as the Prophet's wife Khadija and his daughter Fatima understandably have been influential models of faith.

Without denying the great influence that such models have had on women's experience through the centuries, numerous feminists tend to think that because religion almost always has supported a patriarchal status quo, it almost always has been more harmful to women than helpful. From their religious traditions, the vast majority of the world's women and men have gotten the message that women were less godlike than men, were required by heaven to submit to men, and could be constrained (punished, abused) by men to stay submissive. Men regularly found religious sanctions for their desire to control women's sexuality, and these ranged from relatively mild limitations on the behavior of married women to such painful, destructive practices as clitoridectomy, marriage at puberty (and sometimes betrothal before puberty), menstrual taboos that removed women from general society, and images of women as promiscuous, unreliable, stupid, and always in need of male control. Because religion has structured so much of human history, feminists who find human history a dismal story of men oppressing women have good grounds for considering religion their foe.

Without denying this feminist critique, I would add that, nonetheless, the bottom line in virtually all the developed religious traditions is a holiness equally available to women and men. Women have suffered many disabilities in the organizational dimension of religion, but when it comes to intimacy with God and helpfulness toward other people, they do at least as well as men. The stories to the effect that the Buddha hesitated to accept women into his community and thought that their acceptance would lessen its life show that misogyny began early in Buddhist history, but they do not blot out the fact that Buddhist women always have been capable of enlightenment. The Confucian orthodoxy that consistently subordinated females to males certainly deprived women of many rightful opportunities, yet nothing in the Confucian ideal of goodness (*jen*) and grace (*li*) was intrinsically foreign to women. For the wisdom of the Chinese Way (*Tao*) or the love of the Christian God, what mattered was one's character, one's self. If one's self was honest, loving, and wise, one was what God or the Way wanted. So the depths of the world religions offer an instruction as important as it is consoling. Indeed, the instruction is important precisely because it is consoling: any person may become holy and wise.

DISCUSSION QUESTIONS

1.   What does "religion" mean in this book?
2.   What does "feminism" mean?
3.   Why does the academic study of religion grant no religious authorities exemption from criticism?

NOTES

¹The *1987 World Almanac and Book of Facts* (New York: World Almanac, 1987), basing itself on the *1986 Encyclopaedia Brittanica Book of the Year*, lists the world population at 4,842,048,000 and estimates that 2,548,085,200 belong to a religious tradition. See p. 340.

²See Constance H. Buchanan, "Women's Studies," in *The Encyclopedia of Religion*, Vol. 15, ed. Mircea Eliade (New York: Macmillan, 1987), pp. 433–440.

³Margaret R. Miles, *Image as Insight: Visual Understanding in Western Christianity and Secular Culture* (Boston: Beacon, 1985), p. 11.

⁴Mary Field Belenky et al., *Women's Ways of Knowing: The Development of Self, Voice, and Mind* (New York: Basic Books, 1986), p. 53.

⁵See ibid., pp. 58–59.

⁶See Heinrich von Stietencron, "Hindu Perspectives," in Hans Küng, *Christianity and the World Religions* (Garden City, N.Y.: Doubleday, 1986), pp. 137–159.

⁷See Dorothy Dinnerstein, *The Mermaid and the Minotaur* (New York: Harper & Row, 1976).

CHAPTER TWO

Women in Primal Societies

COMMON MOTIFS

Insofar as "history" coincides with writing, both prehistoric peoples and primal or nonliterate peoples living after the rise of writing have shared certain important cultural characteristics. Both groups have relied on oral traditions and memory. Both have encountered many realities more immediately than bookish people tend to do. For both, the spoken word has tended to have a power that it can lose when writing takes hold. For both, art and song have played fuller roles in ritual and religious culture.[1]

In literate cultures, the control of tradition turns on the production and control of scrolls, manuscripts, and books. Thus the priestly scholars of many traditions have been great powerbrokers. Often women have been excluded from such priestly castes, forbidden access to the prized books as well as the altars where men presided over the holy rites. In nonliterate cultures, the control of traditional lore is more complicated. Men may claim the right to determine **canonical*** wisdom and judge present affairs in its light, but women tend to develop their own, complementary traditions. Thus many nonliterate peoples, both long past and recent, have held separate initiations for women and men and have organized two sets of secret societies.[2]

*Terms in boldface are explained in the glossary.

Both men and women have handed down lore peculiar to their sex-specific roles and needs. Both men and women have worked out schemes for the life cycle that ritualized the key transitions brought by aging. However, women's transitions have been more dramatic and physical than men's: the onset of menstruation, childbirth, and menopause. As they explained these matters to the younger generation, women have either used **myths** peculiar to themselves or adapted the general myths to their own special needs. In nonliterate societies, therefore, women often have brokered a tradition of competitive if not equal standing with men's. Since the traditional words have not been so controllable as they are when they are written down, women have had more chance to create such words or reinterpret them.

As we shall see, the association between women and fertility is both rich and nuanced, since in prehistoric times femininity meant much more than reproductive fertility. Yet it remains a regular theme of the nonliterate traditions that women have a special biological power which shapes their place in society. This theme plays in literate religious traditions too, of course, but often we see it more clearly displayed in small-scale, nonliterate cultures. From earliest times, when people lived by hunting and gathering, men have predominated in hunting bigger game and defending the tribe against aggressors. The power men needed to fulfill these roles was the power to kill. It was considered a good power, although obviously one needing great restraint. The power specific to women has been the power to create new life. If women were secluded during menstruation and childbirth, it was mainly to protect and honor this creativity. Just as the hunter or warrior who had killed would be secluded, to protect others from the power presumed still charging within him and to allow him to purify himself, so the new mother would be secluded to allow her to readjust to normal, everyday living.

In nonliterate cultures the songs sung for both mothers and warriors came from a deep well of memory and focused on powers of life and death that linked human beings intimately with the animal world. Most nonliterate peoples have developed special techniques for handling such power, and regularly women have had access to such techniques. Shamans and shamanesses have both deployed various stratagems for exiting from ordinary consciousness and gaining ecstasy or trance. Fasting, dancing, beating a drum, going without sleep, ingesting tobacco or hallucinogens, plunging into icy water, and meditating before a skull are just some of the methods investigators have documented. Many shamanic figures have employed animal helpers or familiar spirits first met in dreams or initiation ordeals. Usually the women and men who shamanized had positive ends in mind: curing sickness, guiding the souls of the dead to the place of rest, finding where the game had gone, or helping their group to settle conflicts. Sometimes the ecstatics employed their techniques for the sheer joy of it:

the exultation of flying to the gods or plunging down under the sea to encounter again the mistress of the sea animals. Sometimes they went to the
sweat lodge or engaged in the dance to feel purified: lightened in spirit,
again able to appreciate the splendors of nature, to sense the omnipresence
of spiritual powers. Other times shamans and shamanesses have tried to
turn their powers against their enemies, causing sickness or even death.
Negative witchcraft and black magic frequently are ecstatic powers set in
the service of doing harm.

Literate traditions have had their analogies to such shamanic practices. The advent of writing and textual study did not mean the end of
meditation, trance, and ecstasy. But it did change the rituals for ecstatic
healing, **exorcism**, and burying the dead. It did tend to move the ceremonies for a successful hunt, a successful harvest, a successful reconciliation of
enemies toward something less volatile, something more predictable. The
artifacts of prehistoric people, and the rituals of recent nonliterate people,
regularly suggest that they were awed by the fluid, changing character of
reality. They knew about the regularities of the sun and the moon, of the
seasons, the migrations of the animals, and the aging of human beings. But
both nature and the human psyche more impressed upon them the novelty
always waiting to jump out. Be it the thunder storm and flash flood, or the
birth pangs that took away the young mother's life, the reality of
nonliterate people has demanded respect for its sudden, unpredictable
character.

For women this no doubt honed the need to discipline their emotions
and keep their eyes sharp. The lore about conception and childbirth could
not overlook the dangers of pregnancy. The joy that came at puberty, after
which one could conceive, had to be tempered by the knowledge that conception often proved lethal. Similarly, the joy that came at childbirth had to
be tempered by the knowledge that many newborn never made it through
their first year. The women who brought ecstatic powers and mastery of
traditional lore to the tasks of conception, childbirth, and nursing were special benefactresses. The women who tested herbs, roots, and berries for
their medicinal powers often served men, but more often their ministrations went toward their sisters.

In recent societies, both nonliterate and literate, women have predominated in the role of **mediums**. Running through many different cultures has been a belief in the continued existence of the ancestors. To communicate with an ancestor or departed friend, one could commission a
medium. In trance, the medium would allow the spirit of the deceased to
speak though her, giving the living what solace or demands it would. The
rationale for this practice, like the rationale for many other shamanic practices, has been that human beings are kin to all other existents, especially
animals and the spirits of the dead. Nonliterate cultures have tended to
think of the world as a single living whole. Their religious concepts and

practices have been organic, holistic. They have distinguished among divinities, human beings, animals, plants, and departed spirits, but they have felt there was constant communication among all these different realms.

Similarly, nonliterate peoples have tended to think holistically about the human person, not separating body and spirit or matter and mind. Healing, for instance, has been holistic: for both body and spirit. Worship has been both communal and individual, and worship has employed tokens of the plant and animal worlds as signs that people wanted to dedicate all of creation to the powers that wrought it, or as signs that the needs of human beings both interlaced and conflicted with the needs of animals. Nonliterate women therefore have tended to live in situations where their receptivity and creativity was much prized (sometimes to the detriment of their initiative, though by no means always).

PREHISTORIC RELIGION: OLD EUROPE

The two principal sources for scholarly hypotheses about the religion that preexisted the rise of writing (in the ancient Near East, before the beginning of the late centuries of the fourth millennium B.C.E. [perhaps 3200 B.C.E., in Sumer])[3] are grave sites and artworks (many of which have been preserved in European caves). Prehistorians regularly note the opacity of the artifacts from which they construct their hypotheses and confess that it renders all of their speculation quite fragile.[4] Nonetheless, ornaments deposited with the dead suggest such social differentiations as that between unmarried and married women,[5] while the direction in which many prehistoric dead were laid and the bodily posture in which they were placed suggest hopes of their entering upon another phase of life, as though the earth could be for them another womb.

For our interests, however, the most striking artifacts of prehistoric people are the representations of goddesses that abound in the Old European cultures. Marija Gimbutas has argued for a gynecocentric axis throughout Old Europe, and although some have found her interpretations too bold, the richness of the archeological evidence upon which she draws makes her hypotheses more than plausible.[6] The period on which Gimbutas concentrates is the Europe that predated the arrival of Indo-European speakers from the steppes of Eurasia about 4500–2500 B.C.E. The Indo-Europeans brought a **patriarchial** culture which Gimbutas thinks supplanted, although it did not completely oust, the previous gynecocentric Old European culture. Roughly, the period Gimbutas describes ran from 7000 B.C.E. to 2000 B.C.E., depending on the locale (Northern Europe held out longest against the patriarchal invaders). This was the period when agriculture spread and Old Europeans shifted from hunting and gathering to cultivation. Prior to this period, in paleolithic times, women certainly had played an important economic role as gatherers, probably providing a steadier source of food than what the male hunters, who were tied to the vagaries of the large game, could supply. As well, they had been the focus of the human fertility through which tribes continued their life another generation. But it was in the neolithic period, from which most of the artifacts Gimbutas treats come, that the Old European divinity most dramatically assumed various female forms. Perhaps spurred by the new absorption with the fertility of the earth that agriculture entailed, these sculptures and figurines carried preagricultural motifs over into a new appreciation of female symbolisms of creativity.

For example, the three phases of the moon (growing, full, waning) were represented by the trinity of maiden, nymph, and crone. A water bird goddess, with a beak, a long neck, a crown of hair, breasts, wings, and protruding buttocks in the shape of a duck or swan seems to have stood for the divinity of moisture. Meandering patterns, streams, chevrons, and V's (probably derived from the female pubic triangle) were her principal symbols. This water bird goddess went back to paleolithic times and was associated with the number three, perhaps in token of the processive, changeable character of the vital reality over which she presided. Her sacred animal was the ram, and in the early neolithic period she became the weaver of fate and fortune. Other art forms of this goddess include the water container and figurines decorated with her pubic triangle.

A second version of feminine divinity found throughout Old Europe was the snake goddess. Her artifacts have snakelike hands and feet, a long mouth, and a crown. Spirals and coils are her emblems. She apparently was worshiped in house shrines as a symbol of fertility, well-being, and vital energy. In European folklore her crown is still a symbol of wisdom. Horns resembling a crescent moon link the snake goddess with the cycles of the moon. The megaliths (huge stone monuments) of Western Europe sometimes are decorated with winding snakes, which seem to be symbols of regeneration. (Stone itself symbolizes permanency and so resistance to extinction.)

A third aspect of the Old European goddess of life that Gimbutas discusses is the goddess who gives birth. This deity has roots in the deep paleolithic era (as early as 21,000 B.C.E.). Indeed, from 30,000 B.C.E. there are representations of the vulva that seem to signify a sacral concern with female generativity. Gimbutas links this goddess with the doe and the bear and speculates that in paleolithic times the primeval mother was pictured as a birth giver in animal form.

A fourth prehistoric representation of female divinity is the nurse or mother who holds a child. She may be depicted in hunch-backed figurines or as a bear-masked madonna with a pouch for her baby. Other faces that she presents are those of a bird and a snake.

The prehistoric goddess is not always associated with birth and fertility, however. In some important representations she seems associated with death. Thus there is the vulture or owl goddess, who is like a malignant twin of the goddess who gives birth. She comes as a carrion eater yet has qualities of regeneration (perhaps in recognition of how life feeds on life). Her images include the vulva, the umbilical cord, and the labyrinth. She also may be associated with hooks and axes—apparently symbols of energy and stimulus. A seventh millenium B.C.E. shrine excavated at Catal Huyuk in present-day Turkey shows the beaks of griffins emerging from the nipples of female breasts. The breasts of the owl goddess also decorate megalithic graves in Brittany. Another form of the goddess of death is the snowy owl, of whom there is widespread evidence from the neolithic through the bronze ages. In the bronze age, in fact, the snowy owl became the usual shape of urns. People apparently sacrificed birds of prey to this goddess, and her widespread wings figured prominently in prehistoric conceptions of how death could swoop down.

Still another association of femininity with death occurs in the so-called white lady who often has folded arms tightly pressed to her bosom, closed legs, and a masked head with a high, cylindrical crown (called a polos). The white lady has an abnormally large pubic triangle and appears in reduced images as a bone. Perhaps she stands for the closure of fertility.

Falling more on the side of female symbols of life is the goddess of regeneration, whose forms include the fish, the toad, the frog, the hedgehog, the triangle, the hourglass, the bee, and the butterfly. This woman often appears with a human head and the feet, claws, or full body of such animals. Gimbutas conjectures that most of these animals were assimilated to the uterus and were considered change-of-state beings who regenerated themselves from stage to stage. Another prehistoric symbol of the regenerative goddess was the bucranium (head and horns of a bull or ox), which resembles the uterus and fallopian tubes.

Last, Gimbutas discusses the pregnant goddess, whom she takes to represent mother earth. Usually her representation is natural: a nude with hands on her enlarged belly. She may also be presented as a bulging mound or an oven. Her sacred animal is the sow, and prehistoric grave sites at Malta, Sardinia, and Ireland suggest that in Western Europe she was the mother of the dead. In the neolithic era she became the earth mother and giver of bread, appearing enthroned and crowned.

In summary, Gimbutas writes:

> Judging by the stereotypes that recur in figures over the millennia, the religion of Old Europe was polytheistic and dominated by female deities. The primary goddess inherited from the Paleolithic was the Great Goddess, whose functions included the gift of life and increase of material goods, death-wielding and decrease, and regeneration. She was the absolute ruler of human, animal, and plant life and the controller of lunar cycles and seasons. As

giver of all, death wielder, and generatrix, she is one and the same goddess in spite of the multiplicity of forms in which she manifests herself. The prehistoric goddess survives still in folklore.[7]

In the Old European beginning, then, women had a powerful sacredness.

OTHER ARCHAIC THEMES

We know more about the prehistoric culture of Europe than we do about that of other geographical areas because of a conjunction of well-preserved sites and intensive archeological exploration. Nonetheless, other ancient cultural areas have been sufficiently explored to suggest that the Great Goddess was not limited to Old Europe. We shall meet an ancient, archetypal feminine deity in India, China, Japan, and the New World. The ancient Near East worshiped many different goddesses, and we find African female deities that seem cast in lines similar to the European Mother. However, before dealing in this section with a sampling of such other instances of ancient veneration of femininity, perhaps we should pause to indicate how such terms as "goddess" and "sacredness" should be understood.

As Gimbutas makes plain in dealing with Old Europe, the ancient religion was polytheistic. By this she means that it had many different foci and did not worship a sole, single divinity. Although female deities predominated, Old European religion did have such male archetypal figures as a sorrowful ancient who apparently represented a harvest god, and a mature male with a crosier (curled staff) who probably was a patron of hunters. Still, Gimbutas estimates that male figures represent only 2 to 3 percent of the total number of Old European statues that archeologists have recovered.[8] Hence her insistence on **gynecocentrism**.

Theoretical explanations of the religious life represented by prehistoric artifacts depend on assumptions that vary widely from scholar to scholar. Arguing from the cultures of recent nonliterate peoples, many prehistorians interpret ancient cultures as highly mythological and ritualistic. In other words, they assume that prehistoric peoples developed and enacted stories of how the world arose and how such key phenomena as birth and death were guided. Observing the growth of plants, the gestation of women, the death of animals killed in the hunt, the change of the seasons, storms and drought, they tended to personify such powers and link them to supernatural beings. The many varieties of feminine figures suggest that the cycles of birth and death were a central prehistoric interest. To call such figures representations of "goddesses" is simply to apply a term from literate religions. The intent in such application is to suggest the investment prehistoric people probably made in the somewhat personified forces they were representing. By analogy with both the religions of literate people and the religions of recent nonliterate people, it seems fair to think that prehistoric people would have petitioned the goddess of birth for healthy human children, or that they would have asked the white lady to help them contend with death. In hope, fear, gratitude, and the other emotions we find ingredient in all religions, they would have tried to make sense of their situations and gain psychological health. Such health, in Freudian terms, is the ability to love and to work. In commonsensical terms, it is the capacity to survive with enough joy and satisfaction to make one's life seem worth living.

What we find in the goddesses of Old Europe and other prehistoric cultures are probably symbols of the mystery of existence with which prehistoric people had to grapple. Of course we continue to have to grapple similarly today, for our scientific knowledge hardly has solved the mysteriousness of birth and death, of evil and beauty. To say that prehistoric people did their grappling by references to goddesses and gods is to say that they tried to give the forces they found most crucial forms in which they could contend with them. To say that most of these forms in Old Europe were feminine is to suggest that femininity, especially but not exclusively in its mothering aspects, struck Old Europeans as the most relevant or approachable form in which to conceive the "other," the mysteriousness, with which they were involved. Everywhere ancient peoples have thought that a **sacredness**, a realness and purity not found in human beings yet hinted at by both human nature and physical nature, was the key to where they had come from and where they were going. Many ancient peoples finally epitomized this sacredness as that out of which they and other creatures had arisen—as the womb of a cosmic mother.

Largely due to feminist interests, the past decade has abounded in studies of the Goddess.[9] If prehistorians have concentrated on Old Europe, historians have concentrated on the Mediterranean cultures and India. We shall deal with Indian goddesses in the next chapter, when we study how women have fared in Hinduism. Here we may indicate some of the motifs that the study of Mediterranean goddesses has exposed.

In her book on Greek goddesses, Christine Downing has studied such diverse figures as Persephone in Hades, Ariade the mistress of the labyrinth, Hera the consort of Zeus, Pallas Athene the patroness of artists, Gaia the primordial earth mother, Artemas the woman who is fearless and self-sufficient, and Aphrodite the goddess of love.[10] They and the many other goddesses of Greek religion indicate the wide range of sacredness that female nature suggested in that culture. Certainly Greek culture had many impressive male gods, and certainly Zeus was the head of the Olympic pantheon. But many of the female deities either predated the Olympic pantheon or operated at its margins. At the least one must say that pre-Christian Greek culture insisted on the two-sexed representation of ultimate, sacred forces. At the most one might say that female sacredness received a fuller, better-rounded symbolization.

The Greek goddesses had meant a great deal to Downing in her childhood, and one of the virtues of her study is the psychological significance she shows them to have had for her personal growth. Often they would appear to her in dreams, and she has used them to help her determine what her own femininity ought to mean:

> I still know the goddesses most intimately, most immediately, as I knew them as a child: Persephone, as a figure much younger than that represented at the beginning of the Homeric myth, more like myself at some pre-school birthday with a wreath of spring flowers in my hair; Athene, as the intelligent and athletic girl, proudly encouraged in all her activities by her devoted father; Hera, as my own youthfully blooming mother. Yes, I love those goddesses with my childhood—and that early love enabled me to love even those aspects which the child did not know or might not have accepted.[11]

The Book of the Goddess: Past and Present, a fine anthology of studies, can round out our suggestion of what the primordial feminine power has meant to the religious lives of people the world over.[12] In ancient Mesopotamia, the goddesses Ishtar and Inanna represented power, fertility, and charm in feminine modes. In ancient Egypt such goddesses as Isis, the great wife and mother who personified both the power of the soil and the throne of the pharaoh, and Hathor, the goddess of the sky and the cow, represented maternity, love, nursing, and the underworld. Roman civilization took in many of the Hellenistic and Mediterranean deities, including both Isis and Cybele, an Anatolian mother goddess. For the ancient Romans she was the Magna Mater—the Great Mother among the gods. Ancient Canaan worshiped such goddesses as Asherah and Anath, who presided over fertility, appeared in the key Canaanite myths, and were attacked by many writers of the Hebrew Bible, who probably saw them as threats to patriarchal powers as well as to Israelite monotheism. As we shall see, these Mediterranean goddesses had their sisterly parallels in Asian cultures. Indeed, the more we learn about the archaic roots of virtually any culture, the more likely we are to find female sexuality a potent presence.

Whatever one's hypothesis, there is an enormous amount of archaeological and mythological data collocated around the Great Goddess and awaiting explanation. There are world-creator goddesses in Sumer, Babylon, Egypt, Africa, Australia, and China. There are female divinities credited with having created specific cultural arts: India, Ireland, and Sumer, for instance, have goddesses who invented the alphabet, language, and writing. Other cultures trace agriculture and medicine back to kindly goddesses. The Sioux Indians attribute the origin of the buffalo to a sacred, beautiful, feminine divinity. All these activities, in the archaic mind-set, were associated with the sacred. For them to be ascribed to *female* divinities, then, argues that women were their principal mediators.

More complex, perhaps, is the military power implied in the Amazon myths of Libya, Anatolia, Bulgaria, Greece, Armenia and Russia. Either archaic women did indeed fight alongside men, or their sexual power and female societies' authority raised a certain militancy in the early consciousness of women's potential. Finally, perhaps the "ordinary" behavior of women, since they were valued in early societies, generated the widespread reverence for the Great Goddess' wisdom that we find. Pre-Christian Celts, for example, worshiped Cerridwen as the Goddess of Intelligence and Knowledge. The Greek Demeter and the Egyptian Isis were lawgivers— wise dispensers of good counsel and justice. Egypt also celebrated Maat, the goddess of cosmic order, while Mesopotamia's Ishtar was the Prophetess, the Lady of Vision, and Directress of the People.

Indeed, in eighth century B.C.E. Nimrod, where Ishtar was worshiped, it seems that women served as judges. For just as it is logical that societies which stress the fertile sacredness of women might worship the Great Goddess, so it is logical that such worship might enhance women's social status. And, in fact, there is evidence that archaic cultures did indeed treat women more equitably than most later societies did. Specifically, the birth of a female was often a blessing; women had prestigious religious ceremonies; they could be scribes, healers, or counselors; the tribal memory accredited many cultural gifts (for example, the Australian men's ceremonies) to feminine discovery; women could participate in communal decision making. For this reason, many scholars opine that Great Goddess cultures were more pacifist than warlike, more democratic than autocratic.

Finally, a word about one ritual associated with the Great Goddess religion, fiercely denounced by later, male-dominated religions (Judaism, Christianity, Islam): temple prostitution. The term itself, of course, is one given by the critics, who were castigating this elevation of female sexuality as harlotry and filth. (The vitriol in the attacks says as much about the critics' fears as it does about the "prostitutes' " actions.) From our distance, it seems that the goddess cultures felt very strongly that sex and sexual intercourse were holy—hierophanies: revelations of the sacred, ways to union with the sacred. If this be the case, the sexual activities of the temple women, the goddess's closest devotees, were acts of worship, not debauchery. (Both Hinduism and Buddhism developed Tantrism, where sexual intercourse was considered a religious vehicle, but Tantrism mainly served males' progress).

Moreover, the Goddess cultures appear devoid of the practice of stigmatizing some children as illegitimate. Since they were matrilineal societies (a natural outcome if women alone were believed responsible for offspring), a child's legitimacy rested with knowing its mother. All children, then, could be legitimate. Patriarchal cultures, on the contrary, had to be able to prove the paternity of each child, since their bloodlines, inheritance, and legitimacy were through the father. When the patriarchal, prophetic religions (Judaism, Christianity, Islam) met the Middle East goddess practices, powerful interests came into conflict. Masculine self-control, social authority, and theological construction (a masculine god) were all bound to see the goddess temple worship as extremely threatening. Since the patriarchal religions won the battle, their scriptural and cultural authorities became "orthodoxy," and the female-oriented fertility religion became foul deviance. The resulting social subordination of women and circumscription of their sexual activity is a major theme of our later chapters, but here we must at least enter the slim warning that the goddess devotees, far from being debauched, may simply have been expressing an experience of sacrality quite healthy and natural, because in their societies *women's* sacrality was given its due.

One cannot understand the status of women in the world religions without holding on to this background of the goddesses. With many nuances, the pattern one finds in most of the world religions is for patriarchal interests to have tried to subordinate female sacredness. In the name of male rule and the primacy of male reason, most of the world religions have tried to repress female sacredness or subordinate it to male control.

AMERICAN INDIAN WOMEN

As anthropologists, ethnologists, and scholars of religion have learned more about the native peoples of the New World, they have realized that the term "American Indians" embraces a great diversity of cultures and religious attitudes.[13] After one has noted that virtually all these cultures were holistic, assuming an intimacy between nature and human beings that many literate cultures have lost, and that virtually all of them revered the powers of life and death as supernatural and sacred, one has to proceed case by case. What tends to emerge concerning women, however, is that they have dominated a solid half of the American Indian worldviews. Just as paleolithic hunting cultures often built their towns and apparently organized their sense of reality in terms of a dimorphic, male-female set of correspondences, so American Indians traditionally tended to think of female and male powers as balancing.

At puberty women had come upon them a power that men could never know. Out of respect for this power, most tribes secluded the young woman and instructed her in the essentials of her adult tasks. As Ruth Underhill, one of the pioneer students of American Indian religion, described the puberty rites of Pacific Coast Indians:

> Therefore, a coastal girl at her first menstruation "went into the corner" of the huge, barn-shaped house, where she sat on the shelf-like bed that went

along the wall and was screened off with cedarbark mats. Here she lived on dried fish and cold water, perhaps for the usual four days, perhaps longer. Among the Makah of northern Washington, the girl sat with her knees up against her abdomen to make it flat and her back against the wall to make it straight. After four days of this, she still spent most of her time in the corner, washing her hair, anointing her face and body. Makah houses were walled with horizontal planks hung from upright posts like slats. An ambitious suitor could raise one of these slats and poke in gifts and furs. If the parents approved, this might release the girl and bring about marriage. Otherwise, the father, as soon as he could, would give a feast at which suitors might contest for the girl's hand.[14]

In Underhill's study, procreative power is not linked to a goddess of fertility, but in other American Indian lore a goddess presides over the gift of the buffalo and the tribe's rites, or she represents the corn which is central to the tribe's economy.[15] Ake Hultkrantz, a leading scholar of American Indian religions, links the goddess one finds in many tribes with their Siberian ancestry:

> However, as the producer of most living things, the great goddess might also (either as the goddess or in one of her manifestations) become the mistress of the wild animals. It is this general concept of the mother goddess that penetrated North America with the arrival of the first Siberian hunters, who became the ancestors of the American Indians. Of course we have no sources on the goddess from those early days. Our first written information on North American female divinities derives from Mexican codices [unbound manuscripts] from the days before the Spanish conquest and from ethnographic reports during the last centuries. By this time the old goddess had developed into multifarious forms, some of them retaining her original symbolism and others giving her entirely new meanings. To the former belongs the concept of the mistress of the animals that we find, for instance, among the Eskimo and the tribes of the Southwest. The idea of the goddess as Mother Earth, the producer of the vegetation in particular, derives from the same general premises. This is the most common representation of the mother goddess in North America. It is possible that the peyote religion, which has spread over North America from the 1880s, has contributed to the belief in Mother Earth among hunting tribes. However, this concept has had a natural anchoring in the areas where the collecting of plant foods by women constituted the main economic pursuit—among the tribes of the Great Basin and the Southwest that since 8000 B.C.E. belonged to the so-called desert culture.[16]

In several studies of Iroquois women, Annemarie Shimony has shown that the **matrilinear** social organization of that people was linked with women's holding important rights over their children and women's playing key roles in validating tribal decisions.[17] Anthropologists studying Andean religion have found that females as well as males play key roles as diviners. In one study a female diviner named Rosinta was called in to banish a string of bad luck one family had been suffering. She was known as a powerful spiritual figure, and the following excerpt from a complicated description of her therapies gives the flavor of her work:

Rosinta placed one cotton wad in each of our hands. We presented the offerings to the lords of the mountain and the river, and prayed that our enemies would let us alone. Rosinta burned all the wads and threw the ashes into the river. Then Carmen gave Rosinta a large black-and-white guinea pig, which she dissected to examine its viscera. The still-beating heart predicted good health. Everyone crowded around as she showed us the two pancreases, dark red with white tips. She said that this sign indicated lack of life in the Yanahuaya household and that the household had not been feeding the ancestral shrines for its lineage. If the family wanted life to grow, they should begin to offer more rituals. . . . We knelt facing the river's descent. Rosinta threw the yolk and white from a chicken egg into the waters, and then she removed the black wads from our hats, headbands, and sandals. As she had done when she took them from the house and the animals, she once again passed a llama wool thread, this time around our hands and feet, and then broke it. She put the black wads into an old coca cloth with the guinea pigs, rat, coca quids, cigarette butts, and ashes. Everyone looked away as Rosinta flung the cloth into the river, saying "Begone, misfortunes!"[18]

In her lovely account of time spent with the Iticoteri, a tribe of the Yanomamo Indians who live at the border of Venezuela and Brazil, Florinda Donner stresses a mentality quite like that of Rosinta. For the Iticoteri things are powered by spirits who often are malign. Yet Donner found the Iticoteri as impressed by the beauty of their jungle world as by its dangers. Indeed, she found herself much seduced by the ability of the Iticoteri to live in the present moment and enjoy what it offered:

I suddenly knew that it was out of choice and not out of lack of interest that the Iticoteri had never been curious about my past. For them I had no personal history. Only thus could they have accepted me as something other than an oddity. Events and relationships of my past had begun to blur in my memory. It was not that I had forgotten them; I had simply stopped thinking about them, for they had no meaning there in the forest. Like the Iticoteri, I had learned to live in the present. Time was outside me. . . . Smiling, Ritimi rocked herself gently to and fro: "One day I will collect wood and you will no longer be at my side. But I will not be sad, because this afternoon, before we reach the *shabono* [compound], we will paint ourselves with *onto* [red vegetable dye] and we will be happy watching a flow of macaws chase the setting sun."[19]

One final example of American Indian women's work and worldview completes the unfortunately only brief treatment we can offer. Maria Sabina, a Mazatec woman of Meso-America, worked as a healer who drew on both pre-Christian and Christian motifs. Important to her healing was singing songs to comfort the victim. In one healing song she sang:

With calmness, with care, with breast milk, with dew, with freshness, with tenderness, with breast milk, with dew, Saint Peter, Saint Paul, Shout, you! Whistle, you! I am going to thunder, I am going to sound, even below the water, even the sea, No one frightens you, no one is two-faced, No one comes between, no one passes.[20]

This woman, revered as a powerful shaman, did her work in distinctly feminine fashion. In most tribes she would have been trained by her mother, her grandmother, or her aunt, and she would have felt that healing was an extension of her woman's life-power.

ESKIMO WOMEN

The people we call Eskimos tend to call themselves Inuit, and their religious traditions, like those of North and South American Indians, most likely derived from Siberian or North Asian shamanic hunters who migrated into the circumpolar regions and North America more than ten thousand years ago. A full consideration of the religious traditions of arctic women would involve studying many more peoples than the Inuit, but many of the themes one finds in the religious culture of Inuit women have close parallels in the other arctic traditions.[21]

The word Inuit, which is used mainly in Canada and Greenland, means "people." A cognate word used in Alaska, Inupiat, means "real people." Traditionally these people, who were spread over a sizable geographical span, lived in groups connected by kinship ties but lacking formal leadership. They lived by hunting mammals and birds, and by fishing. For housing they built with either snow or stone, sod, and wood. Modern technology now has reached most Inuit, and most have become Christians (a small population in Siberia is the exception). Traditionally, however, they practiced shamanic rites to ensure good hunting, healing, and harmony with the rest of creation, especially the animals. In the traditional Inuit world, everything significant was ensouled. This meant that the animals hunted were to be treated with respect. Whales, seals, and polar bears were important to coastal peoples, while inland peoples interacted intimately with caribou. The polar bear apparently functioned in an arctic version of the bear veneration one finds among many archaic northern peoples.[22]

Women sometimes helped in the hunting, but their more important economic role was rendering the game caught into food, clothing, and domestic implements. Women also gathered plants in the summer, searched out birds' eggs, and helped enrich the diet with small game. In the spring many groups had their women carefully clean all hunting gear, make new clothing for the men, and separate themselves from the hunters. Inuit tended to **taboo** such phenomena as menstruation and childbirth, which dealt in blood and potential death. Being subject to such phenomena or coming in contact with them rendered one polluted—an amoral concept whose main significance was that one had to be purified if one was again to be harmonious with other creatures and souls. Women therefore tended to give birth alone, isolated in a birthing hut. Women who died in childbirth were assured of an afterlife in the sea, probably due to an association between birth and emergence from water.

One of the principal deities of the Inuit was a goddess: the mistress of the sea animals called Takanakapsaluk or Sedna. Shamans would travel to the goddess in trance and petition from her the help the group required: cure of sickness, aid in finding game. With the community gathered around, they would describe their journey, using stylized features: the opening of the earth, the passage by the realm of the dead where one could hear their sighs and experience the help of dead shamans, the ordeal of passing through cruel barriers to the realm of the goddess, the confrontation with her fierce guard dog, and the ritual act of combing out the goddess's long, disheveled hair, which testified to the effects of human beings' sins. During this combing the shaman would present the needs of the people and find out the cause of their troubles: usually a breach of taboos. The group would show that it took the injunctions of the goddess to heart by confessing its sins and reaffirming the traditional mores.[23]

In the version of the Sedna story favored by the Central Eskimos of the Canadian arctic, she lives on the bottom of the sea, having been tossed from a boat by her father (he chopped off her fingers, by which she was clinging to the boat). Her fingers became the various sea animals—seals, whales, walruses—vital to Inuit survival. In another version, Sedna and her children by a dog-husband were abandoned on an island by her father, who had caused her dog-husband's death. Sedna fashioned the soles of her boots into ships in which she sent off her children, some to become ancestors of Indians or spirits, some to become ancestors of white people. (None became ancestors of Inuit, perhaps because, like most archaic peoples, Inuit considered themselves the ordinary version of humanity and so were more intrigued by the exceptional humanity of whites, reds, or other foreigners.)

In the Sedna myths, creation occurs in several ways: biologically, volitionally, and "physically." Sedna gives birth, is the material source of the sea animals, makes ships from shoes, and, in still another version, wills a dead child back to life. Jumbled together, therefore, are Inuits' awareness of female fertility, interest in the connection of sea animals with divine generativity, sense of the kinship between animals and humans, and sense that the ultimate source of life may be willful. As well, one finds hints that females were being warned not to run foul of patriarchal authority by disobeying their fathers (although she became a powerful goddess, Sedna suffered horribly for her pride and independence). We pass over the rich psychoanalytical suggestions in Sedna's relations with her father, except to point out that many Inuit practiced female infanticide.

Scholars have pointed out that creativity by the transformation of Sedna's fingers and boots may be linked to the roles of women in Inuit society. There women still may create the waterproof clothing, tents, sleeping gear, boat covers, and so on, without which the tribe could not survive. Moreover, they make these vital necessities from animal skins—sea animal skins, in the case of tribes who live near water. Such work is shrouded in taboos, some of which amount to time restrictions as to when the women can work. The women thus do much of their creating in a frenzy, at break-neck speed, and perhaps seem to "work their fingers off." There may be a parallel, then, between female work that provides many of the tribe's neces-sary artifacts and the divine work that provided the world's living artifacts. If so, one could explain the ritualized character of much female work, adducing menstrual taboos and seasonal ceremonies as further evidences that the Inuit thought world has been lively with mythic parallels between sacral powers and human tasks. In other words, the divine creational work—fingers into animals, boots into ships—is the paradigm for human creation—animal skins into useful products.[24] (In addition, Inuit women's sacral work disputes the facile anthropological assumption that primal women pattern with nature while primal men pattern with culture.)

One gets a further glimpse of the daily life of Inuit women from the following analysis of a five-hundred-year-old mummy found at Qilakitsoq on the west coast of Greenland:

> Mummy 8, one of the 50 year old women, was notable both for her ailments and for her obvious endurance. Close examination showed that she had suf-fered from illness or malnutrition as a child, resulting in periods of arrested bone growth. In addition the woman had broken her left collarbone at some stage in life, and the bone had never knit, causing impaired function of her left arm and probable chronic pain. She had also lost her lower front teeth, doubtless from lifelong chewing of skins and from holding various items she was working on between her jaws like a vise. These ailments were minor, how-ever, compared with what we found in her skull. Destruction of its base re-vealed that a cancer in the back of the nasal passage had spread to surround-ing areas, apparently blinding her in the left eye, rendering her deaf, and no doubt causing her pain. Yet she never gave in. A series of grooves on the sur-face of her left thumbnail, caused by cutting sinew thread against the nail with a knife, showed that the woman had continued to work even during her final days. Whether she ultimately died of cancer or some other cause, one can only admire her courage and endurance.[25]

Other interesting details gleaned from examination of other mum-mies in the woman's group included extraordinarily high levels of soot in the lungs, probably due to breathing in the fumes of the seal-blubber lamps the Inuit used. One of the women's tasks was to tend this lamp. The faces of all but the youngest woman showed tattoos—apparently marks of marriage—which were achieved by the painful process of stitching beneath the skin with a needle and thread dipped in soot, ashes, plant juices, or gunpowder. The examiners also remarked on the beauty of the women's clothing. Not only was it functional for life in the brutal arctic cold, it was artful and color coordinated.

In an account of a winter he spent with an Eskimo family, the anthro-pologist Franz Boas included the following incident concerning an old woman. The woman's grandchild had recently died and she was depressed by thoughts of her own coming death:

> If only she could die away from home, and thus spare her dear ones the consequences of another sickness and death. The thought preyed on her mind and finally she resolved to end her own life. The long Arctic night had set in, and only at noon came the sun near enough to the horizon to spread the faint light of dawn over the ice and mountains. One night when it was bitterly cold and the snow was drifting, lashed by a strong wind, old Petrel left the house and walked across the ice to a small island. There in a nook of barren rocks she piled up a wall of stones, and sat down behind it, in order to allow herself to freeze to death. Her thoughts dwelled with her children, and she was satisfied that she was not going to die of sickness in bed, for then her future life would have been one of agony and torture in the lower world where there is only want and famine, where cold and struggle prevail all the year round. By choosing her own death she looked forward to a happy life in the upper world. There she was going to play ball, and her friends would see her joyful movements in the rays of the Aurora Borealis. She would enjoy comfort and plenty and the cares of this world, as well as the tortures of the lower world would be spared her. Her limbs became numb with cold and she went to sleep, her mind filled with pleasant visions.[26]

Eventually the woman's family noticed that she was missing and brought her back alive, but the force of the Arctic elements that plays in the account, as well as the conception of a good afterlife, undoubtedly shaped the lives of most Inuit women. Indeed, Robert Coles, interviewing present-day Eskimo parents and children, has found that the patterns imposed by the harshness of traditional life continue to obtain. Mothers still raise their children to be very disciplined and watchful.[27]

AFRICAN WOMEN

Like American Indian women, African women have experienced a great diversity of different religious traditions, since ways of life varied greatly from area to area and tribe to tribe. Still, scholars of African religions forced to tender a few generalizations about patterns that have obtained throughout the entire continent tend to mention such characteristics as an acceptance of the fact that the human condition is imperfect, a belief that problems may be alleviated through ritual action, a theological system that provides for both an aloof supreme deity and many lesser but more vital gods, a holistic view of the human personality that links body and spirit, and a variety of ritual officers (priests, prophets, diviners, and sacred kings) maintained by rites of initiation.[28]

A wealth of myths explains these conceptions of reality. Thus the Dinka say that death and distance from God came when a woman told to pound only one grain of millet a day disobeyed God and hit him in the eye with her pole (at that time heaven hung close to earth). Therefore God withdrew. A Nuer myth claims that originally human beings lived in heaven but descended to earth to forage. When a girl fell in love with a boy she had met while foraging and asked to stay on earth with him, her companions cut the rope they had descended and so made human beings mortal. Not all such myths explaining the current human condition blame women, but enough do to make one suspicious that male informants have been the main source of our knowledge of African mythology to date.

For African women **rites of passage** have been extremely important, and as is true in other nonliterate societies most of them have related to women's fertility: puberty, marriage, birth, menopause, and death. Africans generally have placed great emphasis on dreams, through which they might receive important revelations or commune with deceased ancestors. Rites for curing sickness or averting misfortune have operated on the assumption that the human being is a psychosomatic unity and so have offered challenges and consolations to both body and spirit. In their ritual initiations and women's societies, African women have had the chance to penetrate more and more deeply into the traditional wisdom of their group and finally attain the revered status of wise elders.

Anthropological studies of particular African peoples have revealed the great complexity of their ritual lives. Frequently a strong ritual theme is the distinctness yet complementarity of the sexes. Often women have been forbidden to attend men's rituals and supposedly have misunderstood the symbolic meaning of masks or ceremonial dances, taking them at a literal level. More recent anthropological studies suggest, however, that the women are well aware of what is happening and are freely cooperating in a poetic fiction for the sake of beneficial revelations it offers both sexes.[29]

The anthropologist Victor Turner, who gained access to Ndembu women's rituals through his wife Edith, has stressed the independence Ndembu women often show. Thus in part of a protracted puberty ritual for girls,

> the singing is loud and aggressive. As the morning advances, women from neighboring villages, and even from afar—kinswomen of the novice who have been informed of the performance by messenger—arrive, many with their babies in carrying-cloths on their backs, and join the stamping, whirling circle. The men usually gather in the village shelter and drink beer. They always make comments most critical of the female sex at such times.[30]

While one can explain such comments, and the equivalent comments that women make about men, as part of a complicated process of maintaining both sexes' sense of self-importance and equality if not superiority, they remind us that nonliterate cultures have had their own brands of **sexism**. Despite the economic importance of most women in nonliterate cultures, male powerholders often have mocked women's nature and ways. Thus Ogotemmeli, a Dogon elder whose descriptions of the colorful mythical world of his people has become a high point of anthropological discovery, explained the primordial incest ingredient in the creation of the present world order and linked it with his people's menstrual taboos:

> During these bad periods a woman has to be separated from the community. Contact with her would defile the men, and her presence in places where people live would weaken the altars. She therefore lives on the edge of the village in a round house, symbol of the womb, and only leaves it at night to wash herself. She has to go by a prescribed path to the waters she is allowed to use, for if she goes anywhere else the area would be polluted, the pools would be troubled, and the headwaters of streams would boil.[31]

No doubt Dogon women had to struggle against the negative estimate of their sexuality couched in such mythic lore, yet one can imagine plucky women noting the power conceded to their fertility and thinking that if they could make the headwaters boil, they must be people of some account. Indeed, one of the subthemes of sexual interactions among nonliterate peoples in many areas is the potency of menstrual blood. The power to give birth generally has awed such people, so even when they have raised many taboos they have been confessing the remarkable character of female nature, as primal women have not been slow to realize and make a basis for thinking themselves people of great worth.

African women had resources other than their rituals and wits by which they could judge female existence to be profoundly significant. In women's societies they handled initiations into adulthood, passed on feminine lore, and reverenced deities of their own.[32] In areas such as Nigeria they had goddess figures whose power and wit offered them heavenly reenforcement.[33] Concerning women's societies, let me repeat what I said in the first edition of this work about the Sande of Sierra Leone. Sande, the women's society, is organized into local chapters. A girl is received into her mother's chapter (matrilineal social basis), but after marriage, she joins the chapter in her husband's village, where she has gone to reside (virilocal social basis). Normally, she will return to her natal village to deliver her children, often having as midwife the woman who helped initiate her into adulthood. By this linking of their chapters, the Sande women form a support network that provides social services and civil influences far beyond individual village boundaries.

Since Sande women can expect to be co-wives (their society is **polygynous**), it is important that they develop deep sisterly ties. This is one of the purposes of clitoridectomy, the practice of excising the initiate's clitoris that is part of the initiation to adulthood. This painful process is performed amid strong group support, for the other women console the initiate with food, songs, and dances. They help her to believe that her present suffering will ensure her future fertility and be a sign to her husband of her moral and social maturity. (Sierra Leone young men have their backs lacerated at puberty, and in other African groups circumcision is part of the male puberty rite.) Some scholars conjecture that clitoridectory removes any "maleness," the clitoris being perceived as a penislike organ, and helps to sharpen the distinction of the sexes. In that case, being made less malelike, more "feminine," would be a powerful experience of subordination to the patriarchal scheme of things.

Feminist scholarship understandably has criticized clitoridectomy, pointing out the ramifications that depriving women of orgasmic pleasure can have. Worldwide, several sorts of genital operations are performed on women, the most drastic of which is infibulation, in which the clitoris, labia minora, and anterior two-thirds of the labia majora may be removed. In some version, such genital operations occur in Islamic countries of the Middle East, Africa, and Asia; in East, West, and Central Africa; in Brazil, Eastern Mexico, and Peru; and among Australian aborigines. Generally the purpose seems a combination of trying to control fertility (apparent in parallel operations on men's genitals) and of men's efforts to control women's love lives.[34] A provocative question is whether most women undergoing clitoridectomy would do so apart from cultural traditions ruled by men.

AUSTRALIAN WOMEN

The native Australian traditions naturally varied across the sizable Australian continent, but everywhere the religious lives of women were shaped by myths and rituals explaining the world they had inherited. For many Australian groups the world arose through the work of mythic beings whose existence is best understood as a kind of dreaming. The stories about the origin of creation stress the presence of the creative forces in the landscape. Relatedly, the general native Australian conception of spiritual maturation has been a progressive return to the **dream-time** in which the creative beings have existed. The ritual lives of both women and men have had the goal not only of sanctifying such phases of life as menopause and such sex-specified roles as childbearing but also of taking people deeper and deeper into the dream-time.

In the general native Australian conception, life begins when a susceptible woman passes near a site where a particular vital essence associated with the creative forces is located. In other words, conception involves the action of a spiritual force or deity who animates the potential of the woman in question. Australians usually link conception, and so such action of the animating force, with an event or sign, and by their ritual actions human beings can occasion this event or sign. For example, central desert Aborigines think that killing a kangaroo who behaves in a strange manner, or whose meat sickens the hunter's wife, is the sort of event associated with the animating action of the quickening spiritual agent. Northeastern natives think that spirit-children associated with water holes work with the animating spirits to stir conception. If an animal escapes a hunter in that area the hunter may wonder whether it was the outward form of a spirit-child and so seek in his dreams a clarification of what perhaps was being revealed. Hunting, dreaming, and sexual intercourse therefore have all been ritualized, in the sense that they have been actions that might involve ancestral or quickening spirits as co-agents.

Both women and men traditionally have belonged to groups that held secrets about the mysteries of creation and initiated members progressively deeper into religious wisdom. Moreover, both groups have prohibited the other sex from access to their ceremonies. Some rituals did have open aspects, where secrecy was not necessary, but the innermost activities tended to be veiled from outsiders. Early scholarship only applied this description to men's rituals, but more recent research has shown that Australian women maintained quite parallel restrictions. The fact that women's rituals focused on the main events of their sexual maturation—puberty, birth, and menopause—obscured the fact that the celebrations of these events were initiations into richer measures of religious wisdom.[35] Traditionally the precincts and rituals of one sex were considered dangerous to the other sex—so much so that illicit contact was expected to result in death. Relatedly, not all members of a given sex had the same access to the religious ceremonies. The uninitiated had to wait for an invitation. Again the main reason seems to have been that the mysteries to be celebrated could be lethal to those unprepared or not disposed to witness them.

Anthropological observers have remarked that women's rituals tended to be less dramatic and protracted than men's, in part because they often were structured by bodily events such as the menarche or the menopause that were unique to individuals. Another reason probably was that traditionally most of the childrearing and food gathering fell to women. A third reason may be that in the Australian division of religious labors, it fell to men to work at sustaining the fertility of creation through rituals that sometimes were extensive.

The theme of fertility could work to the mythic enhancement of both sexes. For example, in a myth of the Wulamba, a people of the Northeast, creative beings called the Djanggawul, a brother and two sisters, easily begot many human beings. The myth suggests the potency of these mythic beings by giving them genitals so large they dragged on the ground. Eventually the females left some of their sacred instruments unguarded, and the males stole them, thereby gaining superior power. This eventually led to the shortening of the female genitalia. Wulamba people would reenact this mythic story annually, the women and children wiggling under a mat like unborn children and the men poking them with sticks until they emerged as newborn. At one point the myth suggests the tender regard Australians could have for their children:

> She continued giving birth to children of both sexes; when she had finished she closed her legs, and the Djanggawul Brother said to her: "Sister, these little boys we will put in the grass, so that later, when they are grown up, they will have whiskers; those whiskers are from the grass. We will always do that when we remove male children. And these little girls we have put under the . . . mat, hiding them there. That is because they must be smooth and soft and have no body hair, and because girls are really sacred."[36]

As the part of this myth about the females' loss of sacred instruments and so sexual power suggests, one of the themes of Australian lore is that originally women had more power than they have had in latter times. There was a sexual revolution, of sorts, through which men arrogated to themselves powers originally more fully possessed by women. After menopause for women and the decline of physical and sexual power for men, the previously sharp sexual distinctions have tended to blur. (Nonliterate traditions generally consider older age a somewhat **androgynous** time.) The implication of the story of revolution, which is supposed to explain why men recently have predominated in Australian culture, may be that when human society was most creative virtually all power reposed in sexual fertility, and so through their more dramatic sexual fertility women originally possessed the predominant share of tribal power.

In the traditions of the Northeast, the Djanggawul sisters were but one of many sisterly pairs who functioned importantly in the original structuring of the land. The Djanggawul sisters provided fresh water for the local human populations by urinating, at some places making waters so powerful that access to them was restricted. They also caused important trees to grow. Other sisters were responsible for shaping plants and animals, or for the development of key food plants. On the Cape York peninsula a sacred couple were the original providers. The Hard Yam Woman dug for roots and cooked them with pieces of termite mound. She carried a dillybag (mesh container), while her husband speared fish and carried a tomahawk.

Among the most important pan-Australian myths is that of the rainbow snake, who sometimes is male but at other times functions like a Great Mother. In the interpretation of western Arnheim Land people, she traveled under the sea from the northwest, and on the mainland she gave birth to the people she was carrying within her. She did this by vomiting them out, after which she licked them with her tongue and scraped them with mussel shells. Catherine H. Berndt has reported the following interpretation of the Rainbow Serpent given her by some Gunwinggu women:

> We all call her . . . "mother's mother." We live on the ground, she lives underneath, inside the ground and in the water. She urinated fresh water for us to

drink, otherwise we would all have died of thirst. She showed us what foods to collect. She vomited the first people, the Dreaming people, who prepared the country for us, and she made us, so that we have minds and sense to understand. She gave us our [social categories and] language, she made our tongues and teeth and throats and breath: she shared her breathe with us, she gave us breath, from when we first sat inside our mothers' wombs. . . . She looks a bit like a woman, a bit like a snake.[37]

In the Rainbow Snake, the Djanggawul sisters, and the other female figures who helped to shape the Australian land and people, native women certainly could find strong role models.

RECOVERING AN ANCIENT HERITAGE

As feminists have studied prehistoric cultures and the cultures of recent nonliterate peoples, many have found religious images of women and practices for women that, by comparison with the views of women available in the orthodoxies of the main world religions, have seemed liberating. This is especially true regarding the goddesses, in whom divinity has taken female form, and regarding women's rituals, through which nonliterate women have created strong networks of support. It is also true regarding the view of nature that some ancient religious cultures have espoused, and regarding human interactions, which sometimes have been remarkably noncompetitive. In this section I'd like to probe this recent feminist movement to appropriate positive features from nonliterate women's religious cultures.

Some streams of this movement flow under the banner of witchcraft, which those who hold up the banner almost always understand in a positive, life-affirming sense. So, for example, the witch Starhawk has worked out rituals drawing on Celtic traditions about female divinity that are intended to empower women—to make them feel positive about themselves as embodiments of such female divinity. While stressing that the goddess also has positive implications for men, Starhawk understandably is most eloquent about what she can do for women:

> The importance of the Goddess symbol for women cannot be overstressed. The image of the Goddess inspires women to see ourselves as divine, our bodies as sacred, the changing phases of our lives as holy, our aggression as healthy, our anger as purifying, and our power to nurture and create, but also to limit and destroy when necessary, as the very force that sustains all life. Through the Goddess, we can discover our strength, enlighten our minds, own our bodies, and celebrate our emotions. We can move beyond narrow, constricting roles and become whole.[38]

As the quotation implies, and Starhawk makes explicit in other places, her conception of the goddess equates her with nature: she is the world.

Thus Starhawk is not proposing to replace the father god who transcends the natural world with a mother goddess equally **transcendent**. Rather she wants people to see and feel the natural world as itself the ultimate mystery. Correlatively, she wants people to accept the dualities, the coincidence of opposites, that one finds in nature: creativity and destruction, beauty and ugliness, joy and suffering. Certainly there are philosophical and theological questions one should put to this proposal. Certainly the proposal itself is close to an advocacy of classic paganism, when many naturalistic gods presented people an ultimate reality in which goodness and evil or limitation were always mixed, and so salvation was much more ambiguous then it was in either the monotheistic religions or in Hinduism and Buddhism. But one of the general virtues of the proposal is that it can help us realize the price the monotheistic religions exacted when they subordinated nature to a wholly good transcendent being—the danger of losing a vitality, a love of the earth, and an immersion in the cycles of fertility that had energized ancient peoples for millennia. And one of the specific virtues of the proposal is that women can find in its affirmation of their representation of divinity a much-needed correction to the imbalances wrought by the nearly exclusively male images of divinity proposed by the orthodox mainstream of the great historical monotheisms (Judaism, Christianity, and Islam). In addition, many women find the new witchcraft persuasive on ecological and psychological grounds, feeling that its acceptance of flux, process, unity midst diversity, and **holism** liberates them from prevailing views of rationality, maturity, and wisdom that have not been fully adequate to their experience and instincts.

The main tool that Starhawk's manual employs is an education of imagination, often in the context of group ceremonies. So, for example, after describing the powers associated with the North in traditional witchcraft or goddess religion, Starhawk suggests the following exercise:

> Face North. Ground and center [yourself]. Feel your bones, your skeleton, the solidity of your body. Be aware of your flesh, of all that can be touched and felt. Feel the pull of gravity, your own weight, your attraction to the earth that is the body of the Goddess. You are a natural feature, a moving mountain. Merge with all that comes from the earth: grass, trees, grains, fruits, flowers, beasts, metals and precious stones. Return to dust, to compost, to mud. Say "Hail Belili, Mother of Mountains!"[39]

While the psychological accent of this meditation is distinctively contemporary, much in it could come straight from an American Indian reverence for the directions of the compass. Equally, one can easily see it as a legitimate descendent of pre-Christian cultures, such as the Celtic, which considered plants, animals, and the elements both kin of human beings and potential sources of help, of power. Analytically, one notes that the main appeal is the release of energies that the psychological reorientations proposed might bring about. Women or men who feel alienated from the earth, cut off from the beauty and power of the elements, not at home in their own bodies, might do themselves a world of good by grounding themselves in the earth, getting out of the thin stratum of themselves that is their mental life and centering in their visceral connections to nature and other people.

Theologically, one can note that the monotheistic traditions actually might sanction much in such meditations, indeed much in the general proposal to restore veneration of the earth, our natural mother. Insofar as such traditions proclaim the goodness, the God-givenness of creation, they offer a license to celebrate the flesh, the energies of nature, the concrete joys and sorrows of sex, eating, sleeping, and exercise. True enough, the Western world religions proclaim a Creator beyond the world. As well, they speak of human sinfulness, weakness, or forgetfulness. But they all house historically influential subtraditions in which sensuality has had a good repute, and they all have on their consciences sins against both women and nature—disparagements, subjugations, and destructions—that suggest the propriety of their giving the new witchcraft a humble, respectful hearing.

In her challenging book *Women and Nature*, Susan Griffin has worked another shaft of this mine. Many of her reflections are ecological and epistemological: how our recent, technological Western mentality has come to regard both nature and women, how it has come to neglect and destroy both. Before modern technology, Griffin imagines, male-dominated humanity appreciated nature, regarding her as a provident, generous, although mysterious mother. Slowly, however, the will to understand and control nature dissipated the mysteriousness and maternity, making her more a set of problems to be mastered than a gracious source of gifts to be venerated and thanked. The third and current phase of this evolution has nearly obliterated the original human sense of gratitude and awe:

> And he [mankind] has devised ways to separate himself from her [nature]. He sends machines to do his labor. His working has become as effortless as hers. He accomplishes days of labor with a small motion of his hand. His efforts are more astonishing than hers. No longer praying, no longer imploring, he pronounces words from a distance and his orders are carried out. Even with his back turned to her she yields to him. And in his mind, he imagines that he can conceive without her. In his mind he develops the means to supplant her miracles with his own. In his mind, he no longer relies on her. What he possesses, he says, is his to use and to abandon.[40]

Once again, there is more to be said, and calls to appreciate the benefits of technology, and its potential for improving the lives of the world's suffering billions, are in order. But it should also be said, in echo of many ecologically minded feminists, that we are in mortal danger from our recent treatments of nature and that this treatment is linked with a loss of an ancient respect for the mother of creation.

DISCUSSION QUESTIONS

1.   What are the pros and cons of women's identification with fertility?

2.   What sort of mentality made it possible for the divinity of old Europe to be both snake goddess and white lady?

3.   How do Downing's relations with the Greek goddesses illustrate the psychological impact that images of female divinity might have?

4.   What does the excerpt from the healing song of Maria Sabina suggest about American Indian medicine women?

5.   Create a psychological profile for the Eskimo woman whose mummy was described—imagine her personality and how she thought about her life.

6.   Make the best case that you can for clitoridectomy, and the worst case.

7.   How could Australian women imagine that their witnessing the religious ceremonies of men might bring them death?

8.   Perform Starhawk's exercise about the North and then write up your two or three main questions to her.

NOTES

[1]See Margaret A. Mills, "Oral Traditions," in *The Encyclopedia of Religion*, Vol. 11, ed. Mircea Eliade (New York: Macmillan, 1987), pp. 87–92; also Sam Gill, "Nonliterate Traditions and Holy Books," in *The Holy Book in Comparative Perspective*, ed. Frederick M. Denny and Rodney L. Taylor (Columbia: University of South Carolina Press, 1985), pp. 224–239.

[2]For a bibliographical lament on the scholarly neglect of female initiations, see Henry Pernet, "Masks and Women: Toward a Reappraisal," *History of Religions*, 22, no.1 (August 1982), p. 51, n. 20

[3]See P. Kyle McCarter, Jr., "Writing," *Harper's Bible Dictionary*, ed. Paul J. Achtemeier (San Francisco: Harper & Row, 1985), p. 1147.

[4]See L. G. Freeman and J. Gonzalez Echegaray, "El Juyo: A 14,000-Year-Old Sanctuary from Northern Spain," *History of Religions*, 21, no. 1 (August 1981), pp. 1–19; Karl J. Narr, "Paleolithic Religion," in *The Encyclopedia of Religion*, Vol. 11, pp. 149–159; and Mircea Eliade, *A History of Religious Ideas*, Vol. 1 (Chicago: University of Chicago Press, 1978), pp. 3–28.

[5]See Janet E. Levy, "Religious Ritual and Social Stratification in Pre-Historic Societies: An Example from Bronze Age Denmark," *History of Religions*, 21, no. 2 (November 1981), p. 180.

[6]See Marija Gimbutas, "Prehistoric Religions: Old Europe, " in *The Encyclopedia of Religion*, Vol. 11, pp. 506–515; also her *The Goddesses and Gods of Old Europe* (Berkeley: University of California Press, 1982). For a caution about Gimbutas's interpretations, see B. A. Litvinski, "Prehistoric Religions: The Eurasian Steppes and Inner Asia," in *The Encyclopedia of Religion*, Vol. 11, p. 522.

[7]Gimbutas, "Prehistoric Religions: Old Europe," p. 511.

[8]See ibid., p. 510.

[9]See James J. Preston et al., "Goddess Worship," in *The Encyclopedia of Religion*, Vol. 6, pp. 35–59.

[10]See Christine Downing, *The Goddess: Mythological Images of the Feminine* (New York: Crossroad, 1981).

[11]Ibid., p. 223.

[12]See Carl Olsen, ed., *The Book of the Goddess Past and Present* (New York: Crossroad, 1983).

[13]See Werner Muller et al., "North American Indians," in *The Encyclopedia of Religion*, Vol. 10, pp. 469–550; Frederico Kauffmann Doig et al., "South American Indians," in *The Encyclopedia of Religion*, Vol. 13, pp. 465–512; Miguel Leon-Portilla et al., "Mesoamerican Religions," in *The Encyclopedia of Religion*, Vol. 9, pp. 390–446; Ake Hultkrantz, *The Religions of the American Indians* (Berkeley: University of California Press, 1979); and Joseph Epes Brown, *The Spiritual Legacy of the American Indian* (New York: Crossroad, 1982).

[14]Ruth M. Underhill, *Red Man's Religion* (Chicago: University of Chicago Press, 1965), pp. 55–56.

[15]See Joseph Epes Brown, *The Sacred Pipe* (Norman: University of Oklahoma Press, 1953); and Hartley Burr Alexander, *The World's Rim* (Lincoln: University of Nebraska Press. 1953).

[16]Ake Hultkrantz, "The Religion of the Goddess in North America," in *The Book of the Goddess Past and Present*, pp. 203–204.

[17]See Annemarie Shimony, "Women of Influence and Prestige Among the Native American Iroquois," in *Unspoken Worlds: Women's Religious Lives in Non-Western Cultures*, ed. Nancy A. Falk and Rita M. Gross (San Francisco: Harper & Row, 1980), pp. 243–259, and "Iroquois Religion and Women in Historical Perspective," in *Women, Religion and Social Change*, ed. Yvonne Yazbeck Haddad and Ellison Banks Findley (Albany: State University of New York Press, 1985), pp. 397–418.

[18]Joseph W. Bastien, "Rosinta, Rats, and the River: Bad Luck Is Banished in Andean Bolivia," in *Unspoken Worlds*, p. 271.

[19]Florinda Donner, *Shabono* (New York: Delacorte, 1982), pp. 163–164.

[20]Joan Halifax, *Shamanic Voices* (New York: E. P. Dutton, 1979), p. 202.

[21]See Ake Hultkrantz, "Arctic Religions: An Overview," in *The Encyclopedia of Religion*, Vol. 1, pp. 393–400; Inge Kleivan, "Inuit Religion," in ibid., Vol. 7, pp. 270–273; and Barry Lopez, *Arctic Dreams* (New York: Charles Scribner's Sons, 1986).

[22]See Carl-Martin Edsman, "Bears," in *The Encyclopedia of Religion*, Vol. 2, pp. 87–89.

[23]See Mircea Eliade, *Shamanism* (Princeton, N. J.: Princeton University Press/Bollingen, 1972), pp. 288–297.

[24]See Gail Hodges, "Sedna: Images of the Transcendent in an Eskimo Goddess," in *Beyond Androcentrism*, ed. Rita M. Gross (Missoula, Mont.: Scholars Press, 1977), pp. 305–314.

[25]Jens P. Hart Hansen et al., "The Mummies of Qilakitsoq," *National Geographic*, 167, no.2 (February 1985), p. 199.

[26]Franz Boas, "An Eskimo Winter," in *American Indian Life*, ed. Elsie Clews Parsons (Lincoln: University of Nebraska Press, 1967), pp. 372–373.

[27]See Robert Coles, *Children of Crisis*, Vol. 4: *Eskimos, Chicanos, Indians* (Boston: Little, Brown, 1977), pp. 65–228.

[28]See Benjamin C. Ray et al., "African Religions," in *The Encyclopedia of Religion*, Vol. 1, pp. 60–89, especially pp. 62–63; Noel O. King, *African Cosmos: An Introduction to Religion in Africa* (Belmont, Calif.: Wadsworth, 1986); and Denise Paulme, ed., *Women of Tropical Africa* (Berkeley: University of California Press, 1971).

[29]See Pernet, "Masks and Women: Toward a Reappraisal."

[30]Victor Turner, *The Drums of Affliction: A Study of Religious Processes Among the Ndembu of Zambia* (Ithaca, N.Y.: Cornell University Press, 1981), pp. 216–217.

[31]Marcel Griaule, *Conversations with Ogotemmeli* (New York: Oxford University Press, 1965), p. 146.

[32]See Rosalind I. J. Hackett, "Sacred Paradoxes: Women and Religious Plurality in Nigeria," in *Women, Religion and Social Change*, pp. 247–271.

[33]See Joseph M. Murphy, "Oshon the Dancer," in *The Book of the Goddess Past and Present*, pp. 190–201.

[34]On the Sande, see Carol P. McCormack, "Biological Events and Cultural Control," *Signs*, 3, no.1 (Autumn 1977), pp. 93–100. On clitoridectomy in general, see Carol P. McCormack, "Clitoridectomy," in *The Encyclopedia of Religion*, Vol. 3, pp. 535–537. For a posi-

tive African view of women's coming to maturity, see Colin Turnbull, *The Forest People* (New York: Simon & Schuster, 1962).

[35]See Rita M. Gross, "Menstruation and Childbirth as Ritual and Religious Experience Among Native Australians," in *Unspoken Worlds*, pp. 277–292; also see Ronald M. Berndt et al., "Australian Religions," in *The Encyclopedia of Religion*, Vol. 1, pp. 529–570.

[36]Barbara Sproul, *Primal Myths: Creating the World* (San Francisco: Harper & Row, 1979), p. 320.

[37]Catherine H. Berndt, "Rainbow Snake," in *The Encyclopedia of Religion*, Vol. 12, p. 206.

[38]Starhawk, *The Spiral Dance: A Rebirth of the Ancient Religion of the Great Goddess* (San Francisco: Harper & Row, 1979), p. 9. On witchcraft in general, see Jeffrey Burton Russell, "Concepts of Witchcraft," *The Encyclopedia of Religion*, Vol. 15, pp. 415–423.

[39]Starhawk, *The Spiral Dance*, p. 64. Carol P. Christ also has explored women's current need to rediscover their share in divinity. See, for example, her *Diving Deep and Surfacing: Women Writers on Spiritual Quest* (Boston: Beacon, 1980).

[40]Susan Griffin, *Woman and Nature* (New York: Harper & Row, 1978), p. 54.

CHAPTER THREE

Hindu Women

INTRODUCTORY ORIENTATIONS

The *1987 Encyclopaedia Brittanica Annual* estimates the number of Hindus in the world as almost 648 million, 644 million of whom live in South Asia. India, where Hindus are about 80 percent of the population, accounts for about 600 million.[1]

Hinduism is an umbrella term, meant to cover the traditions native to India for the past thirty-five hundred years. For perhaps a millennium prior to the coming of Aryan invaders from the Northwest around 1500 B.C.E., an Indus Valley religious culture flourished at two sites, Harappa and Mohenjo-Daro, and this culture undoubtedly contributed to the Hindu synthesis. Seals and figurines from this culture suggest early forms of the god Shiva and the generic Hindu mother goddess, including her aspect of devourer of victims.[2] The relation between the culture of the Indus Valley and the Dravidian culture of southern India is disputed, some commentators linking the two and others judging them separate. Either way, the Hindu synthesis accommodated both the Aryan culture of the invaders and the prior Indian cultures, although the Vedic literature that has functioned as Hinduism's scripture came from the Aryans.

One convenient division of Indian religious history takes the Vedic period, including the priestly religion of sacrifice, as having predominated from about 1500 to 500 B.C.E. Such powerful challenges to this Vedic religion as Buddhism, Jainism, and the **Upanishads** forced accommodations, as did later innovations and challenges, especially the Muslim challenges that increased from about 800 C.E. What some call classical and medieval Hinduism covered this period of accommodation and growth, from about 500 B.C.E. to the predominance of the British around 1800 C.E. Modern Hinduism then would cover the past two centuries and would have as its subplot the interaction between classical notions and modern Western notions.[3] While there are some indications that prehistoric Indian women enjoyed a high status,[4] from the time of the patriarchal Aryan invaders and their Vedic religion Indian women have had considerably less than equal status with men. Buddhism offered more egalitarian alternatives, while Islam offered Muslim forms of women's subjugation, but Hinduism itself fairly consistently both venerated feminine divinities and kept women's social status that of dependents.

We shall consider both feminine divinity and such dependent social status in later sections. Here it may be most useful to sketch the Hindu worldview that has prevailed throughout the past thirty-five hundred years. Although different periods placed different emphases and allowed different exceptions, since the time of the fusion of Aryan beliefs with native, pre-Aryan notions Indian culture has been shaped, if not indeed determined, by such key concepts as karma, samsara, moksha, and caste. They have not supplanted more basic concerns about fertility and death, let alone about food and shelter, but they have created the framework in which Hindus have rejoiced in their children, buried their dead, and petitioned their deities for help.

Karma is the notion that present situations are the result of past actions. One might call it a moral law of cause and effect. The key significance of karma for Indian women has been the implication that they owed their present status to their choices in past lives. Insofar as being female was less desirable than being male, the doctrine of karma pressured Indian women to accept their lesser status as wholly just. As well, it offered the prospect of one day being reborn as a man, in reward for virtuous deeds performed in one's present existence as a woman. (While the doctrine of karma seems mainly fatalistic, at least concerning the influence of the past upon the present, it allows a place for freedom concerning the future: one has choices in the present that will shape the future.)[5]

Samsara is the notion that all unenlightened creatures are involved in an ongoing, potentially endless cycle of births and deaths. Insofar as being born and dying are painful experiences, samsara is a painful, undesirable condition.[6] One who thinks seriously about it will want to escape from it, and the Indian religious traditions have devoted most of their energy to developing means of escape. The ritualistic traditions, for example, have taught that sacrifice could break the chains of samsara. The yogic traditions have counseled withdrawal from action and desire. Traditions pivoting on bhakti, devotional love, have taught that intense, selfless love of a deity such as Krishna could gain one freedom from samsara. Philosophical traditions such as the Advaita Vedanta taught by Shankara, Indian's greatest philosopher, have counseled people to drop the illusion that reality is manifold and realize that only the one divinity (Brahman) is fully real.

Moksha is the state of release from the prison of samsara. It is the state of fulfillment—being, bliss, and awareness—that comes with enlightenment and the stilling of untoward desires.[7] Those who gain moksha have given karma nothing to seize upon, no handle by which to hold them in the realm of samsara. They have realized their true potential, their identity with ultimate reality, and so departed from suffering, change, and death. One therefore could say that the various Hindu regimes have targeted moksha as their goal: getting out of samsara has meant getting into moksha.

The most poignant summary of the official status of Hindu women throughout the past thirty-five hundred years has been the core conviction that to gain moksha a woman would first have to be reborn as a man. Women had some access to the disciplines of study, yoga, and detachment that attracted many Indians as pathways to moksha. They had more access to rituals and **bhakti**. But almost always the official, canonical assumption was that their religious devotions could only improve their karma sufficiently to give them the opportunity of taking serious aim at moksha in a future life, when they had become upper-caste men.

Insofar as moksha has been the highest or most noble aim conceived by traditional Hindu culture, women therefore have been at the margins of their culture's greatest treasure. Pleasure, wealth, and duty, the other three legitimate aims of life, have made room for women, although frequently as instruments of men's prowess. Moksha, however, usually has been closed to women as women, and so female Hindus have not been full participants in their culture's symbol of ultimate perfection, despite the many goddesses who personified divinity in female garb. (The relation between moksha and divinity is complex. Lesser gods are as much victims of samsara as human beings are. Great gods and goddesses seem to symbolize ultimate reality and so could be taken as the being, bliss, and awareness implied in moksha.)

The fourth notion in the traditional framework, caste, has produced a society stratified into five basic groups. Most honored have been the priests in whose care has reposed religious action (rituals) and learning. Second have come the warriors-rulers-administrators. Third have come the merchants-farmers-producers. Males of these three upper castes have all celebrated the rite of investiture with the **sacred thread** that has signified status as twice-born men eligible for enlightenment and moksha. The fourth caste, the workers, has been told to serve the upper three and hope thereby to improve their karma, which could bring them a better rebirth. The fifth social group has been the outcastes or untouchables, who were given the lowest jobs, were considered defiling to the other four groups, and so were to be shunned.

Indian women resided in one of these five groups, depending on the family into which they were born. Their basic caste, as well as such other factors as the specific work their family traditionally did, shaped such fundamental matters as whom they could interact with and marry, and where they were to worship. Caste, like sex, was considered a function of one's karma, and so something one finally had to accept. For both its masses and its women, therefore, Hinduism's last word was acceptance.

EARLY FEMALE DIVINITY

From prehistoric times, Indians worshiped female as well as male divinities. One finds traces of this worship in the mythic structures that apparently predated the infusion of Vedic beliefs, as well as in rural traditions that have been traced to the third millennium B.C.E. The generalized form of this ancient female divinity is the power later named shakti. Shakti is the energy of both creation and destruction. It is the principle of passion and change. The goddess who brings forth life, who is a symbol of the cosmic womb, is charged with shakti. So is the dark mother whose mouth is the maw of death. The essential equation that India has made through perhaps four thousand years of worship and reflection is that this primordial femininity needs the supplement, indeed the control, of a primordial masculinity, which is pictured as passionless, constant, and cerebral. Often the notion has been that if the goddess were not controlled by her male consort, her energy would go to excess and produce chaos. Many of the social constraints that Hindu culture imposed on women found their final sanction in this fundamental conception of female nature. As the main goddesses show, women have been considered dangerously passionate, possessed of a vital energy that could destroy as well as bring forth new life.

In one myth, Adi Shakti, the primordial female divinity, existed alone in the beginning. Desiring a partner, she created the world and the new, male gods Brahma, Vishnu, and Shiva (the trinity of classical Hinduism). When Brahma came of age, Adi Shakti desired to marry him, but he was repelled by such incest. So Adi Shakti destroyed him and Vishnu, who reacted the same way. Shiva, however, accepted her proposal. In the northern variant of this myth, Shiva apprentices himself to Adi Shakti and learns the secrets of life and death. He then destroys her, promising, however, that he will later marry her in her reborn form of Sati. In the southern variant, Shiva asks Adi Shakti for her brilliant jewel crown. When she removes it she ages horribly. The entrance of time does not bother Shiva, however, for he is the Lord of Time. Analysts see in both versions of the conclusion of the myth a changing of the gods. The newer order of male deities has replaced the older order dominated by the Great Mother. Even today images of Adi Shakti, the primeval mother, are made at harvest time in rural India. Typically she has many arms, an elongated body, and hollow eyes—reminiscent of the earth mothers, whose masklike faces are stark with the secrets of life and death.[8]

In the **Vedas** one of the most prominent female deities is Usas, the daughter of heaven born in the sky. She is dawn, the lady of light, the mistress and wife of the sun, who follows her as a young man follows a girl. She is also the goddess of hope and the elder sister of night. In the Rig Veda she is mentioned more than three hundred times, often in beautiful hymns:

> The poetry of these hymns is imbued with intense luminosity. The yearning for light, the deep longing for the sun, and, by contrast, the fear of shadows and of darkness are strongly marked characteristics of the soul-strivings of the Vedic people. It is in keeping with these qualities that in the Rig Veda some twenty hymns are addressed to Usas . . . the experience of Dawn is one of the simplest and most complete of all human experiences. It unites in itself a vision of nature, an aesthetic awareness, a fresh opening for Man toward a hopeful future, and a mystical insight into the horizons beyond the rising light from where all good things come.[9]

Fashioning a medley of verses from the Rig Veda in praise of Usas, Raimundo Panikkar allows us to feel something of what ancient Hindus felt for this personification of both light and femininity:

> Now Dawn with her earliest light shines forth, beloved of the Sky. . . . Just as a young man follows his beloved, so does the Sun the Dawn, that shining Goddess. . . . Fair as a bride adorned by her mother, you show your beauty for all to see. . . . Happy are you, O Dawn. Shine ever more widely, surpassing every dawn that went before. . . . Fresh from her toilet, conscious of her beauty, she emerges visible for all to see. Dawn, daughter of Heaven, lends us her luster, dispersing all shadows of malignity. . . . Like a swift warrior she repulses darkness. . . . She drives off wicked spirits and dread darkness. . . . Usas comes carefully, fostering all creatures, stirring to life all winged and creeping things. . . . Bright Usas, when your rays appear, all living creatures start to stir, both four-footed and two. . . . Arousing from deep slumber all that lives, stirring to motion man and beast and bird. . . . This maiden infringes not the eternal law, day after day coming to the place appointed.[10]

In Rig Veda 1:113:19 Usas is called the Mother of Gods and brightness of the Godhead. In 7:77:1 and 3 she is the Lady of Light. Certainly other gods of the Rig Veda have greater prominence, but the love shown this Daughter of Heaven is quite remarkable. Perhaps even more remarkable is the association of femininity with light. Insofar as it is the light of day which creates all that happens in the day, one might assimilate Usas to the typical fertility goddess. But more typically the fertility of the goddess is dark, vegetative, centered on blood and the womb. More typically female fertility is associated with nature and is contrasted with a male fertility considered more spiritual and cultural. Here the association of female divinity with light and so mind breaks such stereotypes. It opens the way for later Indian associations between femininity and the arts, femininity and wisdom. Perhaps in contrast to the bold, blazing light of the sun, the light of the dawn seemed gentle, subtle, delicate, and so feminine. Whatever the complex psychology, the love of Usas shown in many hymns somewhat redeems the androcentrism of the Vedic religious complex.

For, despite the reverence of Usas, most of Vedic religion focused on male divinities such as Indra, god of the storm, and Agni, fire god of the hearth. As well, the most important domestic rituals centered on the conception and birth of a male child, the introduction of sons to a guru, and (for the upper three castes) the investiture of boys with the sacred thread that marked them as twice-born. Only the twice-born were eligible to hear the Vedas, participate in the priestly rites, and so obtain immortality. Women usually had to await a better incarnation.

Vedic women were honored in marriage ceremonies for their beauty, sweetness, and capacity for childbearing. The marital ideal was a long life together in which the wife was to show a good disposition toward her husband, bear him many sons, and be devoted to the gods. A wife was present at household devotions, in part to offer hospitality to the gods invited into the home.

Vedic women had the job of tending the fire, which was dedicated to Agni, god of the hearth. Probably this meant a daily gift of grains or libations. There is some evidence that Vedic women were trained to sing sacred hymns.[11] It is not clear whether early Aryan women could be rishis, the religious poets later considered the channels of the divine revelation that produced the Vedas. Some may have had this status, but the generally patriarchal cast of Aryan culture suggests that women would not have had parity in that role.

In the Vedas female divinities other than Usas are important. For instance, there is Saramya, "she who runs." Saramya rushes into creation, as untamed creative will. She is a model for human life; as mother of both Death and the Asvins (twin saviors born to heal humankind's ills), she both causes problems and creates solutions. Then there is Sarama, who outwits the demons that stole away light and reestablishes cosmic order. Vedic Indians saw a trace of her celestial travels in the Milky Way. Third, the goddess appears as Sarasvati, the daughter of lightning and voice of thunder, who grants humans flashes of insight. Like the river, she rushes into human consciousness, the well-spring of intuition and creativity. In its primal layer, then, the Vedic Great Goddess religion feminizes an explosive power to generate both death and healing, cunningly restore cosmic order, and grant intuitive flashes of knowledge.

Further, the Vedas tell of Aditi, boundless Mother of All. As boundless she is androgyne: mother, father, son, all gods, being, nonbeing, whatever is or will be born. She is also Mother of Skill—particularly ritual skill needed for perfect spells and sacrifices. As Vedism became a highly priestly religion and assumed that inerrant ritual performances guaranteed cosmic order and forced the gods' will, Aditi became very important. Somewhat related to this, as Vak, the goddess controlled all speech. Vak conceived the creator and gave birth without male help. She was the parthenogenic, womblike source of cosmic order, the godhead, and author, through revelation to seers and sages, of the Vedas—the eternal word.

Nor do these five titles exhaust the goddess's Vedic import. As Mother Earth, she has spawned all creatures. As Lotus, Sri, and Lakshmi, she possesses and bestows beauty, power, and wealth. Mother Earth, indeed, became twin goddesses: Nirrti and Prthvi. As Nirrti she was the lap of decay, death, and the cause of order's destruction—a devouring mouth consuming all beings she mothered as Prthvi. Interestingly, Prthvi herself is always conjoined with Father Heaven. Only with him is she responsive, bounteous, nurturing.

Another duality in the Vedic Great Goddess makes her the sisters Dawn and Night. Thus, she is the blushing bride of the sun, but also dark and evil—eager to head back to cosmic dark, the realm of demons. Further, Dawn is arrogant and must be conquered by the male (originally storm) god Indra. Night is both luminous with stars (her thousand eyes) and impenetrable—a viscous stain on all she touches. The Rig Veda likens this stain to sin and guilt. Night is the goddess classically ambivalent—the soothing mother shedding soft light on her sleeping children and the fierce goddess blanketing the world in a heavy darkness that may well hide horror.

The Indian Great Goddess, therefore, is clearly multidimensional and highly ambivalent. To her attaches an extravagant fertility, for she is the creative source of nature, gods, humans, wit, death, order. Yet she is a dangerous mother, by turns fierce, destructive, arrogant, a source of guilt, and ineffective unless linked with Father Heaven. What is evident even from these early sources is the traditional Indian tendency to associate the female with power, energy (*shakti*), and material nature (*prakriti*)—all of which can be either benevolent or malevolent. Significantly, though, Hindu cosmology, again from prehistoric roots, makes for the female a male counterpart of spirit (*purusha*). If the female is active nature, the male spirit is "that which gives structure." Their conjunction yields structured reality, power that is controlled and therefore benevolent. The male principle is necessary if the female principle is to be fertile and good. Alone, the female principle tends to be evil and dangerous.

This theory is only clarified by the later philosophers' elaboration of matter and spirit, but it is latent in the early notions that Mother Earth needs Father Heaven to be bounteous, that women are soil and men their fertilizing and structuring seeds. Regularly, the moral in this configuration was driven home by the myth of Shiva and Kali. At the request of the gods, Kali killed an evil giant and his army. However, she became so excited she lost control and engaged in a frenetic dancing that threatened to shake apart the whole world. The gods could not stop her, and salvation came only when her husband Shiva lay down at her feet. Kali stopped immediately, for it is unthinkable that a devout wife would step on her husband. Popularly, the masses learned from this tale that unless husbands control their wives, the world will surely collapse.

Strangely, however, the evidence seems to indicate that the Vedic period itself was a time of comparative freedom for women. At least, Vedic women were accorded higher status than their sisters of later periods, though scholars are not clear precisely why this should have been so. One hypothesis is that earlier, the Harrapan veneration of the Great Goddess had given the feminine principle prestige, while later, the Aryan patriarchalism eroded women's value. On the other hand, it is argued that the Aryans brought the notion of benevolent female deities, which the Harrapan myths of the dangerous female perhaps mottled. At any rate, Vedic women apparently were fairly well educated, and they seem to have taken part in religious rituals. In some ceremonies, not only the Brahmin priest, but also his wife, had to be present (probably from a sense of androgynous wholeness). Vedic women, in addition, had rituals of their own, and the Upanishads record female philosophers such as Gargi Vacaknavi, whose penetrating questions upset the sage Yajnavalkya. Several Vedic hymns are credited to women, and some lists of scholars, poets, and teachers include feminine names.

It is true that even Vedic women were dependent on their fathers, husbands, or eldest sons, but they had property rights qualifying this dependence. In the fourth century B.C.E., for instance, a woman could hold a set amount of money in her own name, with her husband keeping the rest of her wealth in trust for her. At her death this money passed not to her husband or sons but to her daughters. Similarly, women of this early period were freer to travel, visit temples, attend festivals unchaperoned, and associate with men, than they were in later ages.

Nonetheless, the Vedic women's most honored role was that of the docile wife. In fact, this role predominated in the canonical literature over that of mother. The reason for this exaltation of the docile wife no doubt lies in the ambiguity of the Mother Goddess that we noted. She is both fertile and good, evil and dangerous. The docile wife, by contrast, is safe, because controlled by her husband. Ideally, she is cheerful, prudent, chaste, honest, humble, resourceful. Always she bathes, sleeps and eats after her husband. She is never jealous, silly, idle, or in opposition to her husband's will. Her role models in all this are Sita, who followed her husband Rama into exile, and Savitu, whose loyalty to her husband Satyavant gained his release from death. This modeling carried over to a famous medieval story. In it a wife is sitting before a fire. Her husband is asleep with his head resting in her lap. Their infant begins to crawl toward the fire. The woman remains still, lest she awaken her husband. As the baby enters the flames, the woman prays to the fire god Agni. Agni rewards her wifely considerateness; the baby sits contented and safe in the midst of the flames until her husband awakens.

Slowly, then, Indian women were molded to wifely subservience. The good wife, indeed, is primarily docile—"half the man," source of his happiness, comfort, and courage. As such, she is cherished, feted, lavished with jewels and praise. In early times, it appears, wives had clearer rights. Just as Vedic women could study the scriptures, which later women could not, so too they had, from epic characters like Draupadi, counsel to upbraid their husbands if these failed to fulfill dharma or wreaked injustice and suffering. Later redactors made Draupadi a hysterical shrew, but originally she was fulfilling her own responsibility. In early religion, then, the wife was in some ways her husband's equal, not just his subordinate.

By the time of the Buddha (500 B.C.E.), however, women were denied access to the Vedas and had no significant involvement in orthodox ritual. Between the first Vedas and the first codes of law (1500 B.C.E. to 100 C.E.), Indian women's religious role steadily declined. A major reason for this was the lowering of the marriage age from fifteen or sixteen to ten, or even five. This both removed the possibility of education, and consequently of religious office, and fixed women's role to that of wife and mother.

CLASSICAL GODDESSES

We have mentioned the rise of the trinity of classical Hindu gods, Brahma-Vishnu-Shiva. With them arose goddesses who were their consorts. In addition, post-Vedic Hinduism venerated various forms of the Great Goddess. This Great Goddess, the Maha-Devi, often was the main deity in rural villages, where her name varied from locale to locale. She served women as their mainstay in hoping for fertility, easy childbirth, healthy children, and a long life for their husbands. (To be a young widow was the worst of Hindu fates, because one was considered to have caused one's husband's death through one's bad karma and was pressured to join him on the funeral pyre.) The many festivals of the Hindu goddesses, along with the myths in which they played prominent roles, furnished Hindus their prime images of feminine nature, their prime models of the ideal wife, and their most venerable notions of what love between men and women ought to mean. Even though the officially sanctioned religious epics supported the patriarchal social structures of the Aryan invaders, one glimpses signs that Indian women took such patriarchy with a grain of salt.

For example, in the Mahabharata, the greatest of Hindu epic poems, the god Ganesha, son of Shiva and Devi (a generic name for the goddess; often Parvati, daughter of the Himalayas, is the specific name for the consort of Shiva), explains that he got his peculiar appearance—the head of an elephant on the body of a man—because of the prickly love between his divine parents:

> I was born fullgrown from the dew of my mother's body. We were alone, and Devi told me, "Guard the door. Let no one enter, because I'm going to take a bath." Then Shiva, whom I had never seen, came home. I would not let him into his own house. "Who are you to stop me?" he raged. And I told him, "No beggars here, so go away!" "I may be half naked [as an ascetic, Shiva wore few clothes]," he answered, "but all the world is mine, though I care not for it." "Then go drag about your world, but not Parvati's mountain home! I am Shiva's son and guard this door for her with my life!" "Well," he said, "you are a great liar. Do you think I don't know my own sons?" "Foolishness!" I said. "I was only born today, but I know a rag picker when I see one. Now get on your way." He fixed his eyes on me and very calmly asked, "Will you let me in?" "Ask no more!" I said. "Then I shall not," he replied, and with a sharp glance he cut off my head and threw it far away, beyond the Himalayas.
> Devi ran out, crying, "You'll never amount to anything! You've killed our son!" She bent over my body and wept. "What good are you for a husband? You wander away and leave me home to do all the work. Because you wander around dreaming all the time, we have to live in poverty with hardly enough to eat." The Lord of All the Worlds pacified her; looking around, the first head he saw happened to be an elephant's, and he set in on my shoulders and restored me to life. Parvati was happy again, and that is how I first met my father," said Ganesha, "long, long ago."[12]

The depiction of the relations between the goddess and the god is amusing, but also instructive. Comparativists point out that there is no necessary correlation between the image of female divinity a culture may venerate and the social status of women in that culture, but in making such an important point they may be overlooking subtle influences that do not necessarily show up in the formal rights and duties assigned the sexes by the law codes of their era. Hindu women generally were urged to treat their husbands as gods, never to oppose them, always to be sweet and obedient, even to worship their big toe. Yet in stories such as this one from the Mahabharata, Hindu women could see that wives had rights, including the right to berate their husbands when the husbands neglected them or acted foolishly. Though Shiva was Lord of the Worlds, Parvati could nag at him for his neglect of her and their material welfare. She could accuse him of making her and their children pay the price of his idealism. And the god was willing to admit the rightness of her complaints. From honesty and love for her, he was moved to heal the injury he had done their child. The same tradition that would have insisted on the predominance of Shiva over Parvati, had it been asked, and that insisted that wives owed husbands complete docility, was saying in the indirect speech of mythical tales such as this that male nature often made female nature pay the price for its adventures, its ideals, even its religious pursuits. It was saying that women had the right to protest having to carry more than their fair share of the load, having to deal with the children and the daily practicalities out of meager resources, and that good men would listen to them. Indeed, good men, out of honesty and love for their wives, would comfort them and set things right. Good men, like wise women, would take male supremacy lightly.

A fine collection of studies of the Hindu divine consorts, especially of Radha the mistress of Krishna, makes this point and suggests the wealth of implications that the divine images of female nature carried.[13] In the Puranas (devotional texts from the later, c.e., era, which had less official authority than the Vedas and ranked lower than great epics such as the Mahabharata and the Ramayana but still wielded great influence among the common people), Radha even attained the status of being an essential part of the manifestation of divinity: the feminine component without which Krishna would have been incomplete.[14] What Hindu iconography often expressed through **hermaphroditic** sculptures (Shiva, for instance, regularly appears as bisexual), Hindu mythology often expressed through its union of god and consort, of a male divinity and his corresponding shakti. In more abstract terms, Indian religious art used the lingam and yoni, the phallus and vulva, to stand for the coordinated life forces on which creation depended. In the stories of Rama and Sita, Krishna and Radha, the message was the same. Divinity had to embrace both female and male virtues and qualities. Unless it did, it would not be true divinity. Moreover, Indian mythology usually taught this lesson with considerable charm. Thus Sita, for all her modeling of wifely docility, purity, and devotion, actually proves more steadfast than Rama when challenged by temptation. The patriarchalism of the classical Hindu tradition certainly had its dark sides, as we shall see. We would do the realities of traditional Indian women's lives a disservice, however, if we failed to note how the tradition itself demythologized male supremacy and made many references to subtle ways in which female strength of character or gentle wisdom regularly prevailed.

In such manifestations of the primordial Great Goddess as Durga and Kali, however, classical Hinduism also granted female divinity some powers or symbolic force independent of male counterbalance. Durga represents fierce, death-dealing creativity—the womb that not only issues life but takes it back to recycle it. Kali is a mother to her disciples, nurturing their religious progress, but she is also the grim visage of death, the goddess laden with skulls and licking blood. Male gods such as Krishna and Shiva are also associated with time, destructiveness, and death, but Durga and Kali show the persistence of the intuition that the Adi Shakti was the power of decay and mortality, as well as the power of birth and creativity.

Marguerite Yourcenar, a sensitive reteller of myths, has created a good story about Kali. In it Kali has lived as a prostitute, experiencing the full effects of female desirablility. She has come to stand for samsara itself, and so to symbolize the central question of Hindu philosophy: how to escape desire. Weary, she finally confesses to a wise man that she had been a goddess in Indra's heaven. The wise man replies:

> And yet you were not freer from the chain of things, nor your diamond body safer from misfortune than your body of flesh and filth. Perhaps, unhappy woman, dishonored traveller of every road, you are about to attain that which has no shape . . .. Desire has taught you the emptiness of desire; regret has shown you the useless of regret. Be patient, Error of which we are all a part, Imperfect Creature thanks to whom perfection becomes aware of itself, O Lust which is not necessarily immortal.[15]

Dark Kali could be a sign of hope.

CLASSICAL CONCEPTIONS OF WOMEN

Many of the primary tales from which Hindu women drew their self-image presumed an immersion of human beings in cosmic patterns of fertility and regeneration. Sexuality was a force linking gods, nature, and human beings. It was a cosmic force, close to if not identical with the divine power that kept all things in being. Therefore the control of sexuality, through such institutions as marriage and such religious practices as **celibacy**, was a matter of great importance. If celibate ascetics, male or female, had too much power, nature itself might become parched and withered.[16] If women and men were not well coordinated through sound marriages, individuals, society, and the cosmos itself would suffer.

The consistent pattern shaping the vast majority of Hindu women throughout history was that they always were under the control of a man. As children, Hindu females were controlled by their fathers. Certainly their mothers also had considerable say, but the patriarchal structure of traditional Hindu society meant that their fathers' say was greater. Parents arranged girls' marriages, and often such marriages carried burdensomely high dowry prices. In many periods of Indian history girls were betrothed long before puberty and were married soon after they attained sexual maturity. Males usually were somewhat older—at least midteens—but many couples had a cluster of children before they were twenty. The extended family in which they lived mitigated some of the difficulties of girls' marriages, but one has only to read the autobiography of Mahatma Gandhi, and reflect on his troubled relations with his wife and children, to image the sufferings immature spouses and parents could generate.[17] Girls may well have matured more quickly in traditional Indian culture than they do in today's Western cultures, but to be married to an adolescent male, or even a middle-aged man (which tended to bring different but equally sobering problems), and be the mother of several children at age 15, must always have been hard. As well, it limited many girls' education.

While married, a woman was under the control of her husband, to whom, as we have indicated, she was to show docility and even worship. No doubt many women in fact asserted themselves and resisted abusive husbands, but such official ethical codes as **Manu** (from about 100 C.E.) stipulated that wives were to be loyal and faithful even if their husbands were deformed, unfaithful, drunk, debauched, and abusive. On the other hand, Manu demands that men honor and adorn women, noting that where women are honored, the gods are pleased. Where women live in grief, the family soon perishes. It is in men's interest, therefore, to honor women, treat them well, and make them happy. Manu 9:2–3, however, suggests that in official Hinduism women's happiness was considered dependent on male control:

> Day and night women must be kept in dependence by the males (of) their families, and, if they attach themselves to sensual enjoyments, they must be kept under one's control. Her father protects (her) in childhood, her husband protects (her) in youth, and her sons protect (her) in old age; a woman is never fit for independence.[18]

As mentioned, the widow was the sorriest figure in Hindu society, all the more so when she had no sons to support her. A widow was apt to bear neighbors' suspicion that her bad karma had contributed to her husband's death. She was expected to wear mourning garb, do penance for her sins, and never think of a lover other than her deceased husband. In benign situations, she might receive kindly attention from her children, but if she were forced to continue to live with her in-laws, as many young widows were, she could find herself treated as a very unwelcome burden.

This unhappy state, along with such other considerations as the control of inheritance and a view of the afterlife in which men kept their possessions, contributed to the practice of suttee (*sati* in Sanskrit): widow burning. Supposedly this was a voluntary practice, a widow throwing herself on her husband's funeral pyre out of grief at her loss and desire to share his post-mortem fate. Sometimes, however, unwilling widows were compelled to commit such ritual suicide. The Mahabharata mentions suttee for queens. A related custom sometimes anticipated the death of warrior-husbands in battle and killed the wife beforehand. Stones commemorating victims of suttee may be found throughout India, the earliest dating to 510 C.E. The Muslim Mughal rulers tried to abolish suttee, and it was outlawed in British-controlled India in 1829. But untold numbers of Indian women suffered the threat of such a premature death, and many thousands suffered the actual occurrence.[19] To gain divine help in averting the early deaths of their husbands, many middle-aged Indian women have practiced a ritual called the *habisha*. Through ascetic practices and pilgrimages, they have tried to increase their husbands' longevity and prolong their own good standing as wives.[20]

The best way for an Indian woman to gain prestige and honor was to bear male sons. Bearing daughters was an ambivalent venture, since they would not be able to carry out the parental funeral rites necessary for a peaceful afterlife and they would require doweries for their marriages. Indeed, the announcement of the birth of a female child could be made in the pathetic, disappointed words: "Nothing was born."

Two ways in which Indian women could somewhat step outside these normative controls were through popular theism (*bhakti*) and tantra. If women belonged to a devotional group that considered the love of Krishna, Shiva, or perhaps one of the mother goddesses so powerful it relegated most social conventions to secondary importance, they might find themselves treated as the near-equals of men. In such groups both caste and sex were relativized, since the love of the deity was experienced as a reworking of one's entire sense of reality. Naturally group members continued to live in society at large and so continued to be constrained by normal mores in much of their lives, but in the inner circles of their passionate religious groups, women could experience considerable equality.

Similarly, the tantric groups that sought to employ the energies of imagination, sex, ritual, and taboo to increase one's absorption in the realm of deliverance (*moksha*) often broke with social customs. Tantric women could be counseled to identify imaginatively with a mother goddess. In some exercises they could simulate intercourse with a male deity represented by a male member of their religious group. By casting aside normal taboos on alcohol and meat, they could step into a psychological zone where ordinary thinking was seriously challenged. The danger to women in tantric circles was that their feminine creativity (*shakti*) might become merely a means to male members' advance toward moksha. That is to say, some of the tantric exercises tried to gain this power for male members, often by having the female member play the role of the consort of the god the male member wanted to become in imagination. Still, tantric groups, like bhakti groups, offered Indian women some alternatives to the generally subordinate, oppressive roles available in ordinary Hindu society. At the least, therefore, they raised the possibility that in the realm of ultimate significance female sex might not be a complete liability.

Nonetheless, the ideal wife and mother, docile to her husband and fertile in producing sons, fit a model expressed in the divine wives and symbolized in the marriage ceremony. Although Hinduism has tolerated polygamy, the morally superior course has been monogamy. In the past marriage ideally was between members of the same *jati*: a group, often focused on the same work, that could share food and marital candidates. There were about three thousand such groups. However, both classical authorities and modern trends have considered marriage within one's basic caste (*varna*) acceptable. If there was a difference in castes, it was more acceptable for the man's caste to be higher than for the woman's.

The traditional wedding ritual itself consists of six main elements. First, there is a reception at the bride's house. Second, in the presence of a sacred fire the father of the bride hands her over to the bridegroom, admonishing him to be a faithful to her in matters of duty, wealth, and pleasure (three of the four aims of life). Third, the groom takes the hand of the bride, which makes her his wife. She may then don a decorative cord to symbolize her new status. Fourth, the groom leads the bride to step on a stone placed to the north of the fire. This symbolizes her putting down foes of their happiness. The bride also offers fried grain to the fire three times, feeding the holy flame that has blessed her union. Fifth,

> then follows the more dramatic part of the ceremony, the *Saptapadi*, in which the bride and the bridegroom circumambulate the fire seven times with the ends of their garments tied together, usually with the bridegroom leading. [The significance may be] seen in the words uttered on the occasion: "May you take one step for sap, second for juice (or vigour), third step for the thriving of wealth, fourth step for comfort, fifth step for offspring, sixth step for seasons, may you be my friend with your seventh step! May you be devoted to me; let us have many sons, may they reach old age."[21]

The final part of the wedding ceremony includes a lament by the bride's family at her leaving home. Consummation traditionally was supposed to be deferred until three days after the ceremony, and many of the classical commentators described the ideal consummation quite tenderly.

The three ends achieved by marriage were dharma (fulfilling one's social responsibilities and becoming fully mature), procreation (especially of sons), and pleasure. Marriage was considered the normal estate, so that men and women who did not marry and beget children were considered less than fulfilled. For that reason, the typical Hindu wife, however subject to her husband's control, was also the means of his full maturation. Thus even when texts such as Manu (2:213–215) branded female nature as seductive and destructive, ordinary married women and men had good reason to know better.

DOMESTIC RITUALS

I have mentioned the *habisha* ritual. The menopausal women who participate in it both share in festival celebrations at distant temples and perform
devotional acts at home. In East India, October has been the preferred
month for such devotion. One anthropologist's informant began by obtaining the permission of her family to embark on the extended *habisha*
process. Then she had a barber trim her nails, bathed, and went to her local
priest, who sprinkled cow-dung water on her head. Ideally, Tila, the informant, would also have drunk the five holy substances of the cow—milk,
curds, clarified butter, urine, and dung—but in recent times this practice
has fallen out of favor. Tila then donned a new sacred cloth and gave the
priest gifts. She promised to be his disciple, follow his instructions, daily
attend his scriptural recitations, and keep her month-long vows of fasting,
purification, and sexual abstinence.

As the *habisha* period drew near, Tila would rise before dawn and join
other *habisha* women from her village in bathing in the chilly waters of the
village pond. They would face each of the four directions in turn, praying
the help of the auspicious forces each housed. For instance, facing south,
the direction of death, they would ask their ancestors to witness their observances. Then, emerging from the pond with a bit of mud, the women
would mold images of Damodar, a form of the god Vishnu as a child, over
which they would pray and sprinkle both water and flowers. They would
also pray to the rising sun, and to the basil plant (sacred to Vishnu). When
the anthropologist asked why all the women were at least middle aged, Tila
explained that to perform the ritual while menstruating would bring one
demerit.

The mood of the rituals was joyous. The women were embarking on a
period when they would only eat one meal a day, would pray and purify
themselves, and would put aside their jealousies, animosities, and gossip,
supporting one another in their devotions. Their diet would be limited to
white rice and other foods considered pure: lentils, green plantain, taro,
cucumber, ginger, custard apple. They could have no spices, had to prepare their own meals, and were to add clarified butter, holy because of the
cow, to each dish.

The rest of Tila's day consisted of many washings, prayers, and clean-
ings. She lived mainly in solitude, talking only to the god (Vishnu), but
sharing her food with the priest and her husband. She also shared with her
daughter and granddaughter, when they came to visit. During the pre-
habisha period Tila would strive for a fuller purity than usual, taking more
care to avoid contact with untouchables and lower castes and to avoid
stepping in urine or feces, whether human or animal. She tried to skirt gossip and strife, and she carried with her everywhere two nuts, which represented Krishna (the most popular *avatar* or manifestation of Vishnu) and

his brother. Throughout the day she tried to keep her mind fixed on Vishnu, praying to him and singing devotional songs.[22]

When the *habisha* month actually arrived, the women's devotions grew even more complicated. Tila and another woman had in the past made the pilgrimage to Puri, where they had participated in extensive ceremonies in honor of Krishna. Even at home, however, they filled their days with ritual observances, large and small, many of them in the Indian tradition of *puja*: making a gift to a god or goddess considered present at the family shrine to receive it.[23]

Women of Central India have long practiced domestic rituals designed to help them with childbirth. Such rituals tend to involve both the members of the new mother's family and other villagers, mainly women but occasionally also men. They constitute a religious endeavor to strengthen mother and child and affirm the new state of existence both have entered. As well, they serve to affirm women's key role in producing new human life and so perpetuating both the family and the species. Among the different phases of such rituals anthropologists have discerned an initial period, beginning with pregnancy, when the mother suffers few dietary restrictions but slowly removes herself from the full round of other women. Birth itself is considered polluting and so carries many restrictions in diet, activity, and social contacts. As well, during the birth period there is a strong emphasis on the family lineage that has been strengthened. A songfest on the evening of the birth celebrates the happy event and allows the other villagers to share in the new mother's fertility.

Three days after the birth many of the prior restrictions are lifted, there is a cleansing ceremony, and both mother and child are partially readmitted into the common social circle. Another special ceremony occurs seven to ten days after birth, when the mother and child are blessed and prayers associate her fertility with the sun and water. The villagers celebrate the child's successful passage through the most dangerous period of its life. There is a special joy if the child has been a boy, and villagers bring gifts, apparently in part to show they bear parents and child no envy. At about forty days after birth the mother is fully rejoined to ordinary society, and her fertility is symbolically extended to the village well, that all areas of the common village life might prosper similarly. Later observances include celebrating the new child's first taking of solid food, recognizing through gifts from the mother's kin the baby's ties with the female line of heredity, and shaving the child's head, which symbolizes the child's separation from the mother and introduction to life outside the home.

Perhaps the most interesting phase of this ritual cycle is the *chauk* ceremony that occurs seven to ten days after birth. This usually occurs at dusk and is attended only by the women and girls of the new mother's own household, along with the woman barber who presides. A space on the floor of the main room of the house is cleansed with cow dung. The new mother, dressed as a bride (both modest and adorned), brings her baby and sits on a platform placed over this spot. The woman barber rubs the mother's feet with tumeric and paints auspicious designs on them in red. The theme is that the mother has fulfilled the promise she carried when she came to her husband's house as a bride. The sister of the father of the child paints a swastika, an ancient Hindu auspicious sign, on the head cloths of both mother and baby. This aunt of the new child then raises a platter carrying ritual objects over mother and child, waving it in patterns of blessing. There are further symbolic actions outside the house, and by the end of the ceremony the mother emerges as solidly established in her new role and as solidly praised for having fulfilled the procreative duty she assumed when marrying. The anthropologist reporting on this Central Indian pattern notes that such ceremonies unfold rather informally, in contrast to the stylized utterances at male rites led by priests. For the women the symbols and gestures are the main thing.[24]

A final example of Hindu women's domestic rituals comes from studies of the rites of high caste women of Northern India. The women studied were much restricted in their freedom to move about. Their lives centered in their houses, and their rituals were concerned with blessings for family members. In contrast, men's rituals centered on fertility for their crops and other affairs of a larger, outside world. Even within the house men and women largely stayed apart. Of the twenty different women's rituals surveyed, three involved worship of male relatives, four involved worship of deities for the protection of family members, four others were annual petitions for general family prosperity, and nine directly sought household prosperity. Rituals addressed to Devi, the mother goddess, targeted such gains as a happy marriage for the girls of the family, family protection, and protection from rains. Lakshmi, patroness of good fortune, was asked for wealth and fruits. One special observance sought the birth of sons. Another applied soot around the eyes of children, to protect them from evil spirits.[25]

WOMEN'S FESTIVALS

We have noted the influence of Vishnu in the *habisha* ritual. One of the further motifs in the devotions of pious women such as Tila is acting out scenes from the stories they all know and love about Krishna's dalliances with the cow-girls (*gopis*). In the area of Bengal, Vaisnavas, worshipers of Vishnu, have developed other rituals in which women play key roles. Partly in virtue of this tradition, Bengali women have been more prominent as writers and singers than have women of other regions of India.

From the time of the Bengali saint Chaitanya (1486–1534), who focused on the love of Krishna and Radha, Bengali Vaisnavas have produced *kirtans* (song dances) based on stories about the relations of the god and his consort. This tradition continues in Bengal today, and among the artists who perform the kirtans are several well-known women. The audience attending a kirtan tends to become intensely involved, apparently making the action of the songs and dances contemporary, so that they feel present to the events or at one with the saint Chaitanya who so popularized the medieval songs about Krishna and Radha.

For the women in attendance, Radha offers a striking model. She is single-minded in her love of Krishna, so much so that she seems oblivious to such hardships as scorching sand, snakes, thorns, and the abuse of her in-laws. Obviously women suffering hardships in their own lives receive an object lesson in endurance. As well, they may take heart from the fact that even the beloved of the god had to put up with misunderstanding from her in-laws.

Indeed, some of the songs exalt Radha over Krishna. Where he is often fickle and unfaithful, she remains steadfast. She displays a full range of emotions—hurt, jealousy, anger, and yearning. Although she does not wrong Krishna as he has wronged her, she does reject his apologies and causes him the anguish of waiting for her reacceptance. As well, some of the songs remind the audience that Krishna is but a cowherd, while Radha is a princess. The vulnerability that the god finally shows in his quest to win back Radha's love probably adds to his attractiveness, especially for the *bhaktas*, the disciples of both sexes who approach the god with strongly emotional love.

An anthropologist who studied the differences between the renditions of these stock themes made by male singers and those made by female singers noted that the males tended to shorten the references to Radha's superiority and Krishna's sufferings, while the females tended to lengthen them. Second, the female singers went on to draw some general principles about the relations between women and men in present-day Bengali society. Two women singers, for example, noted that Radha tended to remain silent and force Krishna to plead for her acceptance. So doing, she maintained her self-respect. In fact, the singers encouraged women to use the technique known as *man*: proud sulking. This, they said, was a distinctively feminine tactic, and by using it women could dispel men's anger, since men seldom have the firmness to persevere and remain angry. Women are harder to win over.

I do not mean to endorse such advice proffered by female singers. On the other hand, perhaps in Bengali society tradition is such that women who wish to maintain their self-respect and fair share of power have to sulk and play hard to placate. What seems clear is that Bengali women take pride in the exemplifications of power they see enacted through the behavior of Radha. Indeed, in some kirtans it is only women who can enter the dance precincts, and even the gods who want to come down from heaven to attend have to be changed from male to female form.[26]

Another Bengali story set into ritual form tells of a poor brahman who became enraged when his wife gave some of the meal she had cooked to their two daughters instead of saving it all for him. The two daughters, Umna and Jumna, are named for a sacred mountain and a sacred river and so give the story cosmological overtones. Their enraged father took them from their home and abandoned them in the jungle. There they struggled through a night of various crises, including attacks by animals and ghosts. Morning found them tired, hungry, and weeping. In answer to their plight, heavenly female spirits appeared and told them to perform a certain ritualistic vow, which could guarantee their family would never again want for food.

One of the spirits taught the girls all the particulars for enacting the vow. They were to bathe, fill small clay pots with soil, plant seeds of five different plants in each pot, water the plantings each Sunday with water from the sacred Ganges River, cover the pots with clay saucers, and believe in the efficacy of the rite for fertility. The rest of the story embellishes how the girls strove to carry out their instructions and finally succeeded—for instance, although they found the river where they were to bathe dry and filled with grasses, one of the spirits gave them rings of grass which, when thrown into the dry river bed, caused water to flow again. Returned home with a magical pitcher they had found on the way, the girls were welcomed by their mother but cursed by their father, who threw their magical pitcher away in anger, only to have it come back at him like a boomerang. They dutifully performed the rite they had been taught, their mother gave birth to a handsome son, and their father became very wealthy. One day a thirsty king stopped and asked for a drink of water. Jumna gave him a small pot and was surprised to find it never ran out but satisfied both the king and his entire entourage. The king married Jumna, his prime minister married Umna, and all lived happily ever after, constantly praising the efficacy of the fertility rite the girls had been taught.

This rite, known as the Itu Vrata, is observed in present-day Bengal on Sundays of the month of Agrahayan (late November and early December). The main practitioners are married women seeking prosperity for their families and young women seeking husbands. The symbol of plant fertility obviously stands for prosperity in general. In enacting the story, participants assume the roles of the key actors and fill the little pots with soil fertilized with cow dung. Analysts note that the rite seems to have evolved historically from something performed only by women to a rite in which men took an interest, and they correlate this evolution with the introduction of Sanskrit *mantras*—a sign of official priestly interest. On the whole, however, the rite has remained another way for women to express their desires for household peace and prosperity, as well as their estimates of cruel father figures.[27]

In the town of Puri, at the temple of Jagannatha (a local version of Krishna), an annual festival called Candan Jatra (Sandal Wood) prepares the people and nature for the coming of the monsoon. The time is the premonsoon period of June to early July. The special theme of the performances by the temple singers during this time is the seduction of an ascetic. A boat is rowed around the lake of the temple grounds, probably to call attention to the desirability of water, but the main action of the drama takes place in secret, apart from public eyes. A female singer, partly disrobed, seduces the god Jagannatha and his ascetic brother Balabhadra, who is reminiscent of Shiva. The nudity of the male gods stands for their ascetical devotion, which is represented in the fire of the sun that has been scorching the earth. The nudity of the female actress represents the seductive power of sexuality and regeneration, necessary if the earth is to rebloom. The waters of the monsoon bring fertility and bear an analogy to the human fluids that flow when celibacy gives way to sexual activity. One persuasive interpretation of this ritual, and of indications in ancient texts such as the Mahabharata that it carries forward long-standing Indian themes, is that women's sexuality is inherently auspicious. Linked with the renewal of nature, it is necessary and good—not the inauspicious force stigmatized by taboos and a constant need for male control.[28]

MODERN CONDITIONS

The Hindu festivals, rites for marriage and childbirth, **iconography**, and devotional literature all express a popular religion quite at variance with the austerity modeled by yogins and *sadhus* (holy men). Certainly these latter figures carry great respect, and certainly their renunciations and meditations dovetail with the convictions of Hindu philosophy about karma and moksha. But the majority of Hindus, men as well as women, have sought to improve their karma, make a living, and prosper in healthy children by worshiping the gods and goddesses. Modern educational reforms begun under British rule have stimulated Hindu interest in questions of social justice. They have extended the Western conviction that one ought to work hard to tame nature and improve material prosperity. But even though reformers can point to remarkable achievements in agriculture, technology, and law, the majority of the vast Indian population continues to be shaped by Hindu traditions thousands of years old. The result is great cultural complexity, sometimes to the point of schizophrenia.

For example, on the one hand, there is modern legislation that permits divorce and guarantees women political rights equal to those of men. On the other hand, the force of tradition continues to make wives subordinate to their husbands. Sometimes, of course, this subordination is benign:

men taking care of women in a kindly fashion. At other times, however, the subordination is brutal. When I was in New Delhi in the summer of 1976, the English language newspapers were reporting as a burgeoning scandal the high number of suicides among women married only a few years. Police were suspicious that many of the women had been murdered by their husbands, who had grown tired of them and wanted the dowry that a new wife would bring. However, some analysts, noting the high degree of education in the typical victim's profile, speculated that many of the women had been overwhelmed by the move to a new household and the restriction that marriage and/or motherhood had entailed. Having tasted freedom and envisioned broad horizons, they had fallen into terrible depression at their loss and taken their own lives.

While these suicides tended to come from the middle and upper classes, the pressures on rural women have been comparable. In their case the pressures have tended to be quite traditional, much in the basic pattern of their lives as wives and mothers having been untouched by the independence India gained in 1947. So, for example, an ethnographic study of Hindus of the Himalayas carried out in the late 1950s and updated in the late 1960s found women still subject to long-standing sexual pressures:

> The traditional view here is that a wife's sexuality may be freely used not only by her husband but by his brothers as well. One low-caste elder drew laughter from listeners when, in providing genealogical materials, he listed his brother's wives as his own in addition to his own wives. His response was, "What's the difference? They are all like wives to me." In discussing the matter other informants said, "A woman could never refuse herself to her husband's brother because he is in the same relationship as her husband and she would not like to create discord in the family."[29]

Mahatma Gandhi was a champion of women's rights and through his influence women's capacity for both salvation and political impact won new respect. (On the other hand, his relations with his own wife were not always admirable. For example, he decided unilaterally that they should practice celibacy, and he pushed her hard to take on low-caste duties such as cleaning the toilets as a way of showing her universal love.) The Constitution of 1947 (3:15, 4:39) banned discrimination against women in social, political, and economic matters. In the compromise struck between those who wanted the state run on a secular basis and those who wanted traditional Hindu mores, health care and education for women became secular matters, while marriage, divorce, and inheritance fell under the Hindu Code Bill. Indira Gandhi stands as a model of the opportunities available to upper-class, educated women in recent decades, and she worked hard for women's advancement. Yet,

> while Indira worked for the woman's cause, as have other prominent Hindu women, the most recent assessment of the overall picture of women in India,

which was stimulated by the International Women's Year, paints a pessimistic picture with reference to such women's issues as illiteracy, life expectancy, political positions, number of women in the work force, and dowry. Not only is women's status lower than men's, but the gap between the two is widening.[30]

It is still possible for a man who wants to be rid of obligations toward his wife to declare himself bent on pursuing salvation full time and leave her behind, since moksha is much more a man's affair than a woman's.[31] It is still the general cultural expectation that a woman's main task is producing sons and providing her husband a comfortable home. This is not to deny that some Indian women have profited from educational reforms and the impact of international movements for women's liberation. It is simply to suggest that in basic matters such as education, opportunities for work, freedom to marry when and whom one wishes, contraception, and child rearing, the majority of Indian women, as the majority of women in other countries, remain greatly constrained. Hinduism continues to buttress centuries-old patterns of male supremacy, and these only obtain the more harshly when poverty and overpopulation run rampant. Women may indeed imitate Radha and sulk their way to domestic power. Certainly many of them enjoy simple pleasures and thank the deities for such blessings as health and children. Yet Indian women have more than enough problems to afford practitioners of ancient healing practices a thriving business.

Many of these practices assume that the person suffering the affliction has been possessed by a malign spirit. Sudhir Kakar's study of the psychology behind traditional Indian healing techniques suggests that people flock to renown sites, such as the Balaji temple 250 miles south of Delhi, because they want an attention and release of inner conflicts that they have been unable to obtain either on their own or from Western medicine. The pattern is for the patient to fall into a fit that commands attention and brings the ministrations of a spiritualistic healer. So a woman named Asha went to the Balaji temple because

> she had suffered from periodic headaches ever since she could remember, though her acute distress began two and a half years ago when a number of baffling symptoms made their first appearance. Among these were violent stomach aches that would convulse her with pain and leave her weak and drained of energy. Periodically she had the sensation of ants crawling over her body, a sensation that would gradually concentrate on her head and produce such discomfort she could not bear even to touch her head. There were bouts of gluttony and fits of rage in which she would break objects and physically lash out at anyone who happened to be near her. "Once I even slapped my father during such a rage," Asha told us. "Can you imagine a daughter hitting her father, especially a father who I have loved more than anyone else in this world?"
>
> Treatment with drugs (her uncle was a medical doctor) and consultations with an exorcist did not make any appreciable difference to her condition, but

what really moved Asha to come to Balaji was her discovery, six months after her father's death, that her skin had suddenly turned dark. This caused her intense mental anguish, since she had always prided herself on her fair complexion. Asha now felt that she had become very unattractive and toyed with the idea of suicide.[32]

This is a clinical case study, reported by a psychoanalyst who suggests that Asha's case in particular, and the cases of many such contemporary Indian women in general, amounts to a reaction against an upbringing that inhibits healthy sexual love. One can find artistic treatments of the situation of contemporary Indian women that move to the same conclusion.[33] Both the clinical and the literary lessons have their obvious parallels in other cultures: Muslim women suffering *sar* **possession**,[34] Western women turning anorexic and flocking to counselors in droves. Sad to say, women the world over are sisters suffering many inhibitions.

CASE STUDIES AND MODELS

While the general portrait of Hindu women, both through the ages and today, would be similar to the portrait of women from other religious cultures in stressing their fertility and docility, Hindu women are also like their sisters in other lands in evading such stereotypes and often coming through as feisty individuals. Thus Radha Bhatt, writing on social protest in the Himalayan foothills, has stressed the impact of models for resistance and social change developed by Mahatma Gandhi, the father of India's liberation from British rule. In one protest campaign against government liquor stores, a group of women who had traveled 60 kilometers to confront the district magistrate pointed out to him that they could easily set fire to the liquor stores, should he not take their protests to heart. When he promised that such an action would get them handcuffed and put in jail, the women challenged him to come with ten thousand handcuffs. They felt their lives were threatened by the liquor stores, and they were confident they could muster row after row of protestors—numbers impossible to keep in the jails. Sensing the women's implacable will, the magistrate agreed to close the liquor stores.[35]

The Gandhian legacy of nonviolent tactics for opposing injustice and organizing social change seems to have had special appeal for Indian women, partly because it agrees with their instinctive distaste for violence and partly because of the Mahatma's own model of promoting women's political participation. So it has become accepted, if not normal, for women in several parts of India to muster successful campaigns against unwanted industrial developments and projects that threaten the ecology of areas such as the Himalayas. Indian feminists have started to ponder the special contributions that this Gandhian legacy might make to feminist ethics, arguing that its basic principle of self-reliance is just the stress women need if they are to develop the changes in both themselves and repressive, sexist societies that are most needed.[36]

The late Indira Gandhi, the daughter of Jawaharlal Nehru, the first prime minister of independent India, was probably the most famous woman in India, if not the world, at the time of her assassination by Sikh extremists in 1984. Born in 1917, she was in the midst of her fourth term as prime minister when she was slain. She had been brought up on politics, learning about Gandhian tactics from the Mahatma himself and watching her father's efforts to construct a modern, secular Indian state. She was educated in both India and England, worked for the national Congress Party, and served in the government of Lal Bahadur Shastri, who had succeeded her father as prime minister. On the death of Shastri in 1966, she herself became prime minister (at the age of 49). Her various terms were marked by a turbulence not uncommon in Indian politics, but she showed herself a wily infighter and continually rebounded from defeat. Her own outlook was quite internationalist. She strove to position India as the leader of the nations not aligned with either the Soviet bloc or the West, and so she was courted by both groups. On the home front she ran afoul of various independence movements, trying to maintain the integrity of the nation against pressures in several Indian states for greater independence. The action that apparently precipitated her assassination came in June 1984 when government troops attacked Sikhs at the Golden Temple in Amritsar, the Sikhs' holiest shrine, and killed 492.

Indira Gandhi worked hard for such measures as improving Indian technology and self-reliance. She fostered campaigns for reforestation, literacy, and contraception. In many of her programs she ran afoul not only of Indian regionalism, but also of religious opposition, Hindu, Muslim, and Sikh alike. Commentators sometimes likened her typical frown to the displeasure of the Great Goddess. Whether or not they found her personality or policies appealing, however, they seldom failed to note the symbolic impact of a woman's heading the second largest national population in the world.[37]

A different sort of role model occurs in the figure of Ma Jnanananda of Madras, a present-day guru. Although much less prominent than Indira Gandhi, this leader in the Advaita Vedanta sect more clearly exhibits the religious implications of Hindu feminism. Ma Jnanananda came to her present position after having married and raised five children. From childhood she had experienced visions and feelings of being one with the cosmos. As she worked through her domestic responsibilities and searched out her vocation, she wondered whether her psychic experiences weren't signs of mental imbalance. Yet finally she found guidance through Advaita Vedanta, the philosophy of nonduality derived from the famous medieval philosopher Shankara (788–820). This philosophy teaches that all things really are one: but manifestations of the ultimate Brahman. In the religious teaching of Ma Jnanananda, the stress lies on love of the divine, which one can find everywhere. Ma is quite traditional in urging renunciation of desires other than the love of God, and quite down to earth with the many people who come asking her advice. She notes that many of them are their own worst enemies, but she continues to offer them a fine blend of demanding criticism and gentle love.

When asked about the traditional Hindu taboos and stereotypes regarding women, Ma Jnanananda is quick to reject them as unimportant. To her mind one's sex is relatively insignificant when the question is spiritual liberation. Women of course have to contend with the social roles afforded them in their culture, and they have to break with the forms of vanity and delusion urged on them by their culture. But in matters of meditation, self-restraint, and love of God, they should find their sex no obstacle. Indeed, the guru herself seems an eloquent argument that innate talent and hard work are the main determinants of spiritual progress. She has achieved the deepest levels of *samadhi*, classical yogic trance or self-possession. One of the leading authorities of her religious group has authenticated her experiences and so in effect licensed her as a *satguru*: a genuine master. The popularity of her counsel is strong evidence that many Hindus, both men and women, now have no prejudice against female religious leadership. Insofar as Ma Jnanananda becomes something closer to the rule, rather than the exception, among leading Hindu teachers, one will be able to say that the androgyny of the Hindu divinity has become fully represented in the ranks of those who teach the way to that divinity.[38]

The way that Ma Jnanananda teaches is the way of love, bhakti, although her version of this most popular Hindu path is well rooted in traditional philosophy and yogic practice. The many Hindu women who have not had spiritual gifts like those of Ma Jnanananda, nor her opportunities for spiritual development, nonetheless have agreed more times than not that bhakti is the crux of Hindu practice. Whether by reflecting on the stories about the goddesses, or participating in women's rituals, or performing **puja** (household devotions) for the well-being of their families, Hindu women have contributed strongly to the great stream of religious women who have turned their yearning for love and fruitfulness into a striking theology.

Usually the divinity they have worshiped has been more complicated or many-sided than the divinity worshiped by Westerners. It has been a divinity manifest in the capricious side of the goddesses and the gods, as well as in their acceptance and love. It has shone in the faces of Kali and Shiva, even when these destroyers have been smeared with blood or have been dancing their dances of destruction. Hinduism has taught women the centrality of sexuality to religious love, just as it has taught them that creativity and destruction are inseparably blended. It has led many contemporary leaders, such as Mahatma Gandhi, to think that by loving well, women can gain salvation, all the traditions about women's need first to be reborn as men notwithstanding. Such bhakti might enrich any one of us, and with a guru like Ma Jnanananda, we might feel it to be the fulfillment of the feminine portion of anyone's soul.

DISCUSSION QUESTIONS

1. How would moksha solve the problem of women's karma?

2. Explain the positive and negative implications of the symbolism of the Adi Shakti.

3. What might the figure of Usas have meant to Vedic women?

4. How does the traditional injunction always to keep women under the control of men relate to the feminization of shakti in earliest Hindu tradition?

5. What implications do you see in the concern of many Hindu domestic rituals to achieve purification?

6. Evaluate the model of Radha as a proud sulker.

7. What undertones might a psychoanalytic listener hear in Asha's lament at having physically lashed out at her father?

8. What are the transcultural possibilities you see in Hindu bhakti?

NOTES

[1]See *1987 Brittanica Book of the Year* (Chicago: Encyclopaedia Brittanica, 1987), pp. 338, 667. However, Alf Hiltebeitel, "Hinduism," in *The Encyclopedia of Religion*, Vol. 6, ed. Mircea Eliade (New York: Macmillan, 1987), p. 336, estimates that Hindus are about 70 percent of the roughly seven hundred million people in India.

[2]See Hiltebeitel, "Hinduism," pp. 336–337.

[3]This is the historical scheme used by Katherine K. Young in her chapter, "Hinduism," in *Women in World Religions*, ed. Arvind Sharma (Albany: State University Press of New York, 1987), pp 59–103.

[4]See Jan Gonda, "Indian Religions: An Overview," in *The Encyclopedia of Religion*, Vol. 7, p. 170; and Pupul Jayakar, "Indian Religions: Rural Traditions," in ibid., pp. 176–177.

[5]See Wendy Doniger O'Flaherty, ed., *Karma and Rebirth in Classical Indian Traditions* (Berkeley: University of California Press, 1980).

[6]See Edward L. Greenstein, "Samsara," in *The Encyclopedia of Religion*, Vol. 13, pp. 56–58.

[7]See A.M. Esnoul, "Moksa," in *The Encyclopedia of Religion*, Vol. 10, pp. 28–29.

[8]See Jayakar, "Hinduism: Rural Traditions," p. 177.

[9]Raimundo Panikkar, *The Vedic Experience: Mantramanjari* (Berkeley: University of California Press, 1977), pp. 163–164.

[10]Ibid., pp. 164–165.

[11]See Jogiraj Basu, *India of the Age of the Brahmanas* (Calcutta: Sanskrit Pustak Bhandar, 1969), p. 40; and Bhagwat Saran Upadhyaya, *Women in Rgveda* (New Delhi: S. Chand, 1974), p. 185.

[12]William Buck, *Mahabharata* (Berkeley: University of California Press, 1981), pp. 6–7.

[13]See John Stratton Hawley and Donna Marie Wulff, eds., *The Divine Consort: Radha and the Goddesses of India* (Boston: Beacon Press, 1986).

[14]See C. Mackenzie Brown, "The Theology of Radha in the Puranas," in ibid., p. 57.

[15]Marguerite Yourcenar, *Oriental Tales* (New York: Farrar, Straus, Giroux, 1985), p. 125.

[16]See Frederique Apffel Marglin, "Female Sexuality in the Hindu World," in *Immaculate and Powerful: The Female in Sacred Image and Social Reality*, ed. C. Atkinson, C. Buchanan, and M. Miles (Boston: Beacon, 1985) pp. 39–60.

[17]See Mohandas K. Gandhi, *An Autobiography: The Story of My Experiments with Truth* (Boston: Beacon, 1957); and Erik H. Erikson, *Gandhi's Truth* (New York, W. W. Norton, 1969).

[18]Sarvepalli Radhakrishnan and Charles A. Moore, eds., *A Sourcebook in Indian Philosophy* (Princeton, N.J.: Princeton University Press, 1957), p. 190.

[19]See "Suttee," in *The Encyclopaedia Brittanica*, Vol. 11 (Chicago: Encyclopaedia Brittanica, 1987), p. 420; also see Mary Daly, *Gynecology: The Metaethics of Radical Feminism* (Boston: Beacon, 1978), pp. 113–133.

[20]See James M. Freeman, "The Ladies of Lord Krishna: Rituals of Middle-Aged Women in Eastern India," in *Unspoken Worlds: Women's Religious Lives in Non-Western Cultures*, ed. Nancy A. Falk and Rita M. Gross (San Francisco: Harper & Row, 1980), pp. 110–126.

[21]Arvind Sharma, "Marriage in the Hindu Religious Tradition," *Journal of Ecumenical Studies*, 22, no. 1 (Winter 1985), p. 74.

[22]See Freeman, "The Ladies of Lord Krishna," pp. 113–116.

[23]See Nancy E. Auer Falk, "Hindu Puja," in *The Encyclopedia of Religion*, Vol, 12, pp. 83–85.

[24]See Doranne Jacobson, "Golden Handprints and Red-Painted Feet: Hindu Childbirth Rituals in Central India," in *Unspoken Worlds*, pp. 73–93.

[25]See Susan S. Wadley, "Hindu Women's Family and Household Rites in a North Indian Village," in ibid., pp. 94–109.

[26]See Donna Marie Wulff, "Images and Roles of Women in Bengali Vaisnava *Padvali Kirtan*," in *Women, Religion and Social Change*, ed. Yvonne Yazbeck Haddad and Ellison Banks Findly (Albany: State University Press of New York, 1985), pp. 217–245.

[27]See Sandra P. Robinson, "Hindu Paradigms of Women: Images and Values," in ibid., pp. 181–215.

[28]See Marglin, "Female Sexuality in the Hindu World."

[29]Gerald D. Berreman, *Hindus of the Himalayas: Ethnography and Change*, new, ext. ed. (Berkeley: University of California Press, 1974), pp. 171–172.

[30]Young, "Hinduism," p. 97.

[31]See Alaka Hejib, "Wife or Widow? The Ambiguity and Problems Regarding the Marital Status of the Renounced Wife of a Samnyasi," *Yoga Life* 13, no. 11, pp. 3–14.

[32]Sudhir Kakar, *Shamans, Mystics and Doctors: A Psychological Inquiry into India and Its Healing Traditions* (New York: Alfred A. Knopf, 1982), pp. 70–71.

[33]See Mohan Rakesh, "Miss Pall," in *Modern Hindi Short Stories*, trans. and ed. Gordon C. Roadarmel (Berkeley: University of California Press, 1974), pp. 105–131.

[34]See I. M. Lewis, *Ecstatic Religion* (Middlesex, England: Penguin, 1971).

[35]See Radha Bhatt, "Lakshmi Ashram: A Gandhian Perspective in the Himalayan Foothills," in *Speaking of Faith: Global Perspectives on Women, Religion and Social Change*, ed. Diana L. Eck and Devaki Jain (Philadelphia: New Society, 1987), pp. 180–181.

[36]See Devaki Jain, "Gandhian Contributions Toward a Feminist Ethic," in ibid., pp. 275–291.

[37]See "Gandhi, Indira," *The Encyclopaedia Brittanica*, Vol. 5, p. 109.

[38]See Charles S. J. White, "Mother Guru: Jnanananda of Madras, India," in *Unspoken Worlds*, pp. 22–37.

CHAPTER FOUR

Buddhist Women

INTRODUCTORY ORIENTATION

There are now about 307.5 million Buddhists in the world, the vast majority of them in Asia (equally divided between East Asia and South Asia).[1] Buddhism began with Gautama (536–476 B.C.E.), a member of a warrior caste called the Shakas from Kapilavastu in Northeast India, at the foothills of the Himalayas. According to the legends, Gautama grew up protected from all hardships, married, begot a son, but in his late twenties was afflicted by questions about the meaning of life—questions prompted by encounters with sickness, old age, and death. He left home to pursue answers, studied with Hindu gurus, practiced various austerities, and still was unsatisfied. Choosing a middle path between laxity and harsh austerity, he concentrated on meditation and vowed to attain understanding of the human condition. In his experience of enlightenment he discerned what later became known and preached as the Four Noble Truths: (1) All life is suffering. (2) The cause of suffering is desire. (3) If one removes desire one can remove suffering. and (4) The way to remove desire is to follow the noble eightfold path of right views, right intention, right speech, right action, right livelihood, right effort, right mindfulness, and right concentration. In practice this has meant an integration of philosophy, ethics, and meditation.

Gautama, who became the Buddha (Enlightened One) through his visionary experience, supposedly was undecided whether to teach others what he had learned but was persuaded by the entreaties of the god Brahma. In addressing his first listeners, women as well as men, he would explain the Four Noble Truths, stressing how they provided a program for escaping from the sufferings inevitable as long as people were trapped in samsara. Like Hindu teachers, the Buddha believed that one had to improve one's karma and then finally escape from the karmic cycle completely. He differed from the Hinduism of his day in denying that there was a substantial self and paying little attention to either the Vedic gods or the absolute (Brahman) that was the focus of many of the Upanishads (contemporary poetic/philosophical writings.)

Not only did the Buddha include women among those to whom he preached, wealthy women supported his work. Apparently he did not accept the Hindu prejudice against women's capacity for salvation and did not consider contact with women dangerous. On the other hand, traditions gathered after the Buddha's death portray him as being reluctant to admit women into the Sangha, the Buddhist community whose heart has been those who chose celibacy and monastic life. The fact is that the Buddha did allow women to enter the Sangha and follow him in his itinerant ministry. The legend is that he predicted that because of the admission of women the Sangha would decline much sooner than it would have had he restricted membership to men.

One formally becomes a Buddhist by "taking refuge" in the three "jewels" that Buddhists most treasure: the Buddha himself, the **Dharma** (Teaching), and the Sangha. The historical pattern has been for men to hold authority in the Sangha and predominate among Buddhist teachers. Even when women have run their own monastic houses, they have always in principle been subject to men. Nonetheless, women have sometimes become influential teachers, especially of other women, and Buddhism virtually always has granted that women could gain enlightenment and nirvana (the Buddhist state of release analogous to the Hindu moksha).

Buddhism flourished in India from the time of Gautama to the seventh century C.E. In some periods it was more influential than Hinduism, due to royal patronage. From the third century B.C.E. it existed in several forms, the major distinction being that between the Theravada schools and the **Mahayana**. The Theravadins gave greater centrality to monks, while their laity became more interested in acquiring merit for a good rebirth than in gaining enlightenment and **Nirvana**.

The Mahayanins developed new philosophical emphases that gave the Buddha many existences and a cosmic body. They concentrated on an enlightenment that would lead directly to nirvana, broadened the profile of the ideal Buddhist to include greater mercy for other suffering creatures, and paid more attention to the religious needs of the laity. Both Theravada and Mahayana sent missionaries outside of India. In the third through sixth centuries c.e. virtually all of South and East Asia learned about Buddhism. After the decline of Buddhism in India, Theravada was strongest in such countries as Sri Lanka, Burma, and Thailand. Mahayana predominated in China, Vietnam, and Japan. Tibetan Buddhism was more influenced by Indian traditions than Chinese, especially the Indian tantrism that stressed the place of the imagination and libidinal energies in gaining enlightenment. Needless to say, Buddhist women were always influenced by the social traditions of their particular country. For example, in East Asia, where Confucian views structured family life and male-female relations, they were brought up on an ideal of reverence for their parents and the aged, deference to their husbands, and gaining power by the production and influence of sons. Even Chinese Buddhist nuns were shaped by such an ideal, having to contend with the suspicion of Chinese husbands that contact with nuns would destroy the docility of their wives and having to deal with monks who assumed male supremacy.

A key ingredient in the treatment of women wherever Buddhism was strong was the suspicion easily raised by both the general teaching about desire and the particular practice of monastic celibacy. A dialogue supposedly held between the Buddha and his favorite disciple Ananda suggests early forms of such suspicion:

"How are we to conduct ourselves, Lord, with regard to womankind?"
"As not seeing them, Ananda."
"But if we should see them, what are we to do?"
"No talking, Ananda."
"But if they should speak to us, Lord, what are we to do?"
"Keep awake, Ananda."[2]

The general Buddhist psychology regarding desire led to an ideal of restraining all of one's senses, but of course the power of sexual desire led to special emphasis on sexual restraint. Both monks and nuns were to practice celibacy, not simply because the responsibilities of family life could impede their spiritual progress but also because physical contact with objects of desire was thought to keep the person enmeshed in samsara. Samsara and karma, perhaps inevitably, carried physical overtones. The more one was living "spiritually"—eating little, speaking little, having no sexual intercourse—the less one was giving karma handles by which to keep one in thrall.

Although monks and nuns were held to special rules and precepts, some of which specified how they were to interact with the opposite sex, they were more fundamentally held to the five general precepts incumbent on all Buddhists. These five precepts, known as **sila** and still in force for Buddhists today, are (1) not to kill, (2) not to steal, (3) not to lie, (4) not to commit unchaste acts, and (5) not to take intoxicants. Positively, sila has inculcated an attitude of respect for all life, freedom from material possessions, honesty, freedom from lust, and sobriety. When animated by a meditational practice and a philosophical understanding that stressed the intrinsic goodness of all people and things, their innate **buddhanature**, the precepts of sila could be guides to graceful, joyous living.

Last, we should note that both lay Buddhists and monks and nuns have usually celebrated a full liturgical year of ceremonies and observances. New Year's Day and the Buddha's birthday have been but two of the special holidays. Pious Buddhists also have followed monks and nuns in taking some parts of the year as an annual time for penance and special vigor in pursuing enlightenment. Householders have regularly prayed at domestic shrines, in effect offering a Buddhist version of Hindu home prayers (*puja*).[3] Buddhists concerned with gaining merit have added special weekly and monthly devotions, and many such Buddhists of course have been women.[4]

NUNS

Although women have had a checkered career as followers of the Buddhist monastic life, occasionally being well honored but more often getting little support, it is useful to study the evidence about the establishment of women's right to the monastic life. Within five years of founding the Sangha for men, the Buddha had completed his attack on the Hindu orthodoxy of his day by allowing women to "go forth" from their homes and join the wandering life of the Sangha. Hinduism had long sponsored a celibate life for men, including their gathering in ashrams (religious communities). But it had frowned on celibacy for women, thinking that women's physical fertility was their main reason to be. The Buddha attacked this assumption, along with Hindu assumptions about caste and animal sacrifice. In this new synthesis, women responsive to the Dharma (Teaching of the Enlightened One) deserved the right to pursue **enlightenment** and **nirvana** full time.

The chief champion of women's rights in early Buddhism was Ananda, the disciple we have already mentioned. According to tradition, the first woman disciple granted access to the Sangha was the Buddha's aunt, Pajapati. When she proposed to the Buddha that women's going forth from home would be a good thing, he showed himself very cautious. Pajapati therefore was discouraged and left crying. Through the intercession of Ananda, however, the Buddha finally granted permission. His reluctance supposedly was shown in his making the declaration, previously noted, that this step would shorten the life of the Sangha. As well, some traditions say that he enjoined on nuns eight special precepts.

They were to request ordination as nuns in the presence of monks, to seek instruction from the monks every half month, to spend no rainy season (the time of settled living and intense meditation) apart from the guidance of monks, to have monks as well as nuns participate in the penitential ceremonies that ended the rainy season, never to accuse a monk of defects (but to allow monks to accuse and correct them), not to be angry with a monk or scold him, to do penance every half month for infractions of the rules, and even if one hundred years old to reverence the youngest of monks.[5] In the eyes of most commentators, these rules reflect Buddhist nuns' having had a second-rate status from the beginning of their admission to the monastic life.

Despite these special rules, and the fears attributed to the Buddha and other elders that the presence of women would both complicate the life of the Sangha and weaken it, women flocked to the Sangha in large numbers. Some women quickly established their ability to withstand the rigors of the sparse, wandering regime, while others soon were honored for their grasp of the Dharma and their spiritual progress. There are records of early nuns gaining enlightenment and nirvana, and the text known as the *Psalms of the Sisters* (*Therigatha*) records other triumphs of the first nuns. Those who showed understanding and proficiency could teach other women, but there are no indications that the first nuns ever became teachers of men.

The nuns actually proved less troublesome and threatening to the monks than the lay women who supported the monastic establishment. The nuns had accepted the discipline of celibacy and knew both the letter and the spirit of the rules that safeguarded the monks from worldliness. As celibate they were thought to have entered a neutral state, or even to have taken on male attributes (a male cast of mind being assumed necessary for spiritual development). The laywomen retained their feminine sexuality and power. Forced into contact with them by the rules requiring monks to beg their food, and by the need of the Sangha for financial and practical support, monks often found laywomen unconverted to monastic modesty, still inclined to be attractive if not seductive. How much such danger usually was in the mind of the monk rather than the mind of the woman filling his begging bowl is hard to say, but the practical upshot was that monks soon came to think of laywomen as their greatest temptation or obstacle. Thus meditation masters such as Buddhaghosa (fifth century c.e.) wrote graphic descriptions of what women "really" were made of: flesh that would soon decay, bodies that would rot in the grave and be foul-smelling. The objective was to make women, like food or fame or other potential seductions away from monastic austerity, as repulsive as possible. Buddhaghosa did not hesitate to concentrate on pus, phlegm, blood, urine, and feces. The inevitable result was a degradation of female humanity, even though it was partially redeemed by the fact that Buddhaghosa wrote the same way about a man's stomach and offal.[6]

In Mahayana tradition, nuns occasionally entered the canonical lists of great teachers, even being accounted *bodhisattvas*: buddhas-to-be. Diana Paul has translated a text about a nun named Lion-Yawn (the roar of the lion is a Buddhist symbol for enlightenment). Probably Lion-Yawn is a fictional character rather than an actual historical woman, but even so she testifies to a positive strain that appreciated women's religious possibilities. In the text a merchant's son named Sudhana goes in search of Lion-Yawn, probably because he is a genuine seeker and has heard good things about her. He enters a lovely park, symbol of the natural harmony wrought by the merits of bodhisattvas, and finds Lion-Yawn seated on a throne, tranquil as a still lake. Actually, he sees many images of her, for she is teaching many different groups: sons of Shiva, gods, great serpents, and human disciples. Sudhana resolves to walk around her several hundred thousand times, both to honor her and to take in her teaching. Finally addressing her and asking about her teaching, he receives a full discourse, replete with standard Mahayana doctrine about meditation and the status of enlightened beings.

The only surprising aspect of the response by Lion-Yawn occurs at the end of her exposition. She bids Sudhana visit a woman named Vasumitra, whom he should ask about the training of a bodhisattva. Commentators point out that unenlightened people accounted Vasumitra a prostitute. Lion-Yawn therefore is indulging in the tendency of advanced Mahayana teachers to equate samsara and nirvana (both, as names or terms, are empty of ultimate significance) and conclude that enlightened people often judge things differently from unenlightened people. What might seem vice to the unenlightened could seem virtue to the enlightened, and vice versa. Diana Paul notes that both prostitutes and nuns fell outside the ordinary circumscription of women. Ordinarily, women were associated with family life. As independent women, both nuns and prostitutes could raise anxieties, especially among men who thought women always ought to be under male control.[7]

A few other nuns are commemorated in the scriptures. In the Theravada **canon** Dhammadinna preaches to her former husband, the lay disciple Visakha.[8] Her preaching includes both such standard fare as the Four Noble Truths and subtle insights into meditation. The Buddha himself praises her work, calling it learned and full of spiritual understanding. On the whole, however, female teachers receive much less attention than male, and throughout history women's monasteries received much less support from the laity than men's. No doubt the cultural expectations of Indian, Chinese, and other Asian lands that men would be the main doers and teachers while women would tend the home and raise the children contributed to this lesser support. Nuns were going against stronger social conventions than monks were, even in countries such as China where monasticism strictly so called had little native tradition. Simply by providing periods of retirement from public life and organizations for men's study, Taoism and Confucianism had furnished Chinese society precedents for the withdrawal of Buddhist men from ordinary society. But nothing similar had existed for women. In addition, throughout Asia wealth tended to be in the hands of men, and many men were too ambivalent about monasticism for women to support it generously. To be sure, there were wealthy women, and both they and some men supported nunneries. But the laity seldom perceived nuns to be the great benefactors they perceived monks to be, and seldom were they as devoted to nuns' support.

LAYWOMEN

We have noted some of the liabilities that laywomen suffered in the view of monks and meditation masters. Because they were still fully sexual beings, laywomen presented monks potentially formidable temptations. On the other hand, as we have also noted, laywomen—at least those married and managing children—were under the control of men and fit a social status Indian society had long sanctioned. To be a wife and mother was a valid, praiseworthy vocation. It is true that Buddhism carried out the general Indian tendency to subject women to men's control by insisting that nuns always be in the charge of monks. Still, by establishing the possibility of a monastic vocation for women, Buddhism gave Indian women an option previously not available. The result, interestingly enough, was that Buddhist married women came to have more rights than did Hindu married women.

In the first place, there was the fact that marriage was now a genuine choice rather than an inevitability. Even when one agrees that most Indian families probably continued to expect their daughters to marry and continued to bargain about the dowry and other parts of the marital arrangement, the mere fact that Buddhist nuns existed proved that marriage was not the only path a devout Buddhist woman could choose. Second, perhaps as a result of this fact Buddhist mothers came to have more say in the fate of their children than had Hindu mothers. For example, one who wished to enter the Sangha, as either a nun or a monk, required the permission of both parents. For another example, Buddhist teachers elaborated the mutual responsibilities of wives and husbands, and while the wife's service of the husband and docility toward him stand out, one also notes that she was to manage the household prudently and handle his money well. In return, he was to show her affection and consideration, in addition to providing for her material well-being. Certainly one probably found these traits in good Hindu marriages, but the Buddhist sense of women's spiritual potential seems to have raised Buddhist marriage to a more explicit goal of partnership, even equality, than what one finds in the Hindu codes.[9]

One way in which laywomen, like laymen, suffered in the common Buddhist estimation was that by immersing themselves in the world they were thought to have chosen a less noble and efficacious path than those who had chosen monastic life. The celibacy intrinsic to monastic life cast a pall over marital sexuality, and the fact that monks were the primary teachers and spiritual authorities further contributed to a two-tiered Buddhist community. In many periods, monks, and to a lesser extent nuns, were considered the real Buddhists, fully engrossed in spiritual work and intent on attaining nirvana, while laypeople, however sincere, were considered amateurs or part-timers. The trade-off often made between those in monastic life and those in the world was that the monks and nuns would instruct the laity and help the laity gain merit, while the laity would support the monks and nuns financially (and so gain merit). Indeed, lay Buddhism in many periods became mainly a matter of gaining merit: bettering one's karma so that in a future existence one might have a better chance of gaining nirvana. Buddhism was not so specific as Hinduism about the need to be a man existing in a high caste (the Buddhists, having theoretically if not always practically abolished caste, might have made living as a monk the equivalent of being a Hindu brahman). In principle it allowed that anyone could gain enlightenment and nirvana. But most Buddhist schools, and lay Buddhism generally, tended to picture enlightenment as having come to people who were well positioned because they had gained considerable merit and good karma.

An important qualification to this thesis was the promotion of the lay state by some Mahayana groups. For example, in the Vimalakirti Sutra, the householder Vimalakirti appears as the ideal Buddhist, the one who is going to become a bodhisattva. This sutra won great favor in East Asia, where the strength of Chinese and Japanese family traditions, and the absence of native traditions of permanent celibacy, made the monastic life suspect. Certainly monastic life came to flourish in both countries, but both countries also developed a lay Buddhism that carried more prestige than lay Buddhism had carried in India. So, for further example, the Japanese saint Shinran, founder of one of the most important devotional sects, won permission from his teacher to renounce celibacy and minister to the common people as a fellow householder. His rationale was that in the present, difficult age, people needed to rely on the mercy of Amida, the Buddha of Light, rather than on their merits or on austerities such as celibacy.[10]

In a well-received study of Burmese (Theravada) Buddhism, the anthropologist Melford Spiro has stressed the focus on gaining merit that has predominated in most households and so has shaped the rituals of popular Burmese Buddhist faith. Concerning the shift from the classical goal of gaining nirvana (*nibbana* in the Pali used by the Theravada texts) to a religion concerned with improving karma through meritorious deeds, Spiro writes,

> Typically, instead of renouncing desire (and the world), Buddhists rather aspire to a future worldly existence in which their desires may find satisfaction. Contrary to nibbanic Buddhism, which teaches that frustration is an inevitable characteristic of samsaric existence, they view their suffering as a temporary state, the result of their present position in *samsara*. But there are, and they aspire to achieve, other forms of samsaric existence which yield great pleasure.[11]

As is true of other religions and cultures, the effect of Buddhist religious doctrine on Burmese views of women is hard to specify. Spiro finds women in fact accorded a high status, but this seems to hold despite negative judgments deeply rooted in Burmese males' **misogyny**:

> It is true that women enjoy a high status in Burma—although it must be remarked that it is high in fact, rather than in principle. "Males are much nobler than females," the Burmese say; so much so that "a male dog is nobler than a female human." It would be difficult to attribute the genuinely high status of Burmese women to Buddhism, since there have been other Buddhist societies where the status of women was low. Conversely, as the Mother of God and the Queen of Heaven, the Virgin occupies a much higher place in the Catholic sacred hierarchy than any female follower of the Buddha ever has held, without this having affected the relatively low status of women in traditional Christendom.[12]

One of the strengths of Spiro's study is his delineation of the many rituals through which Burmese laypeople seek to ward off evil and improve their karma. Women participate in most of these rituals, especially those celebrated at home or performed in the vernacular at local chapels. The devotional world such rituals open up is reminiscent of the Hindu wealth of ceremonies for important occasions in the life cycle and throughout the calendrical year, although the Buddhist liturgical cycle seems considerably poorer in symbolic power and mythological resources. Throughout Asia Buddhism has established especially impressive funerary rites, and once again we have to include the impact of such rites on women when we try to imagine the religious life of the typical Buddhist female.

For example, I have visited the shrine to Kannon, a goddess of mercy, in Tokyo and seen the pictures of children affixed in appreciation for the help Kannon gave in securing their conception and healthy birth. When one imagines the perils of childbirth in the premodern era, recalling the figures on infant mortality and the loss of women in childbirth, the right to petition Kannon becomes a very powerful resource. Indeed, as we shall see when considering Buddhist goddesses, one has to challenge Spiro's assertion that Buddhism never gave females high status in the sacred hierarchy. That might be strictly true regarding human female disciples, but when it came to images of ultimate help and sacredness, many female figures played strong roles, offering the laity motherly sources of spiritual help.

GODDESSES

I have referred to Kannon as a mother goddess, using the perspective of a comparativist. In such a perspective, which tends to stress how a figure actually functions in the devotional life of the common people, a Hindu goddess such as Mahadevi, the Christian Virgin Mary, and the Buddhist Kannon seem quite similar. Each has received the prayers, the heart-felt trust, of many of the ordinary people. Each has come close to being worshiped: accounted a kindly face of the ultimate sacredness people believe guides the world and promises help. In this comparative perspective, it is somewhat secondary that orthodox Christian theology always affirmed the creaturehood of Mary and never allowed the faithful to offer her worship strictly so called (*latria*). Many of the ordinary faithful certainly knew this and distinguished between the veneration they offered Mary and the worship they offered Christ, the Spirit, and God the Father. In practice, however, the mother who went to Mary when her child was worrisomely sick often made of the Virgin a kindly, comforting symbol of the divine compassion. In practice, the differences between her attitude and the attitude of a Japanese woman in similar circumstances praying to Kannon probably were quite small.[13]

The doctrinal question in Buddhism, parallel to the Christian doctrinal question about the status of Mary the Mother of God, is whether there are any official gods or goddesses. When the Buddha surveyed the Hinduism of his time, he decided that the Vedic gods were inefficacious. To solve the existential questions absorbing him, he turned to detachment, meditation, and self-reliance. In early Buddhist philosophy, the gods were relegated to the samsaric realm and so were accounted as much in need of nirvana as human beings. In some later Buddhist syntheses, the Dharma was considered atheistic, either in the practical sense of ignoring the help of the gods or in the speculative sense of denying that there were any entities called gods.[14] Nonetheless, as buddhas and bodhisattvas came to proliferate in Mahayana lands, popular Buddhist religion in fact furnished numerous foci for petitionary prayer and devotional praise. Sophisticated Buddhists may well have thought that these foci were only symbols of an ineffable ultimacy: ways to pin down the imagination and rouse the affections. Many common people probably took the symbols fairly literally, believing that Amida Buddha presently resided in his Western Paradise the way a king resides in the land he rules, or believing that Kannon had to gather her gown as she bent down to hear the worries of her children.

Diana Paul, contributing a Buddhist chapter to *The Book of the Goddess*, has stressed the role of Kuan-yin, the Chinese equivalent of Kannon, in the search of adherents of the Pure Land sects for salvation.[15] Students of Mahayana philosophy are familiar with the *Prajnaparamita*, the Wisdom-That-Has-Gone-Beyond, who functions as the Mother of All Buddhas.[16] She represents enlightenment, the experience and wisdom that enable buddhas and bodhisattvas to see reality as it truly is. In such texts as the *Heart Sutra*, calling upon her becomes a great mantra, a spell thought efficacious for gaining enlightenment.[17] Many traditions associate wisdom with femininity. The biblical Wisdom (Hokma, Sophia), the Chinese Tao, the Jewish Shekinah, and the Christian Holy Spirit all carry feminine over-tones. In the Buddhist case, the associations between wisdom and medita-tion suggest that whenever one verges upon reasons of the heart, insights that engage the affections and come from love as much as knowledge, one spotlights modes of knowing which in cross-cultural stereotype are more feminine than masculine.

One might call such modes of knowing intuitive or holistic, as long as these terms carried no dismissive, pejorative overtones, for all the religious traditions, Buddhism most definitely included, consider that what happens in meditation, contemplation, and mysticism is more basic and central for an adequate appreciation of ultimate reality and human nature than what happens in scientific or academic understanding. Such religious, unitive experience is the prime source of wisdom, while logical, argumentative forms of intellection are considered secondary. To the religious mind, the more profound and creative human beings become, the more they fuse mind, heart, soul, and strength. In the great saints, shamans, prophets, and sages, knowing and loving intertwine, as do faith and understanding.

Both female and male religious adepts tend to speak in such holistic terms, giving the lie to the many cultural stereotypes, East and West, that oppose women and men as emotional and rational, as concerned with love and concerned with logic. One great utility of religious experience, there-fore, is that it can help people overturn the stereotypes that would keep women out of scientific laboratories and would keep men out of poetry and child rearing. Inasmuch as the sexes agreed that the mystery of existence, the holy presence of God, are the great treasure of life, they would have less inclination to fight about whose stereotypical way of dealing with every-day, worldly matters should hold pride of place.

Another Buddhist version of the appreciation of the femininity of re-ligious wisdom and creativity that comes through contemplative experience is the Tathagatagarbha: the womb of suchness or reality. In texts beloved of such schools as the Mahayana Yogacarin, which tried to correlate its met-aphysics with yogic experience, the ultimate source of reality is pictured as a cosmic womb. Creatures come from this source, in the mysterious ways of creation. It is the matrix of all that exists, and the entire symbolism of how the manifest world stands in being is rooted in a primal affinity to human birth. Once again, therefore, ultimate experiences and insights have taken Buddhists toward conceiving of the ultimate as feminine. Sophisticated Mahayana philosophers no doubt knew very well the limits of all symbols and regularly recalled the Buddha's own reluctance to speculate about nirvana and other matters pertaining to the wisdom that has gone beyond samsara. Yet both the Prajnaparamita and the Tathagatagarbha functioned for significant intellectuals as the metaphysical equivalents of motherly goddesses—sources of insight and being who were both subtle and ever-fertile.[18]

In Tibetan Buddhism the great feminine figure has been Tara, of whom Stephan Beyer has not hesitated to use the words goddess and worship:

> The worship of the goddess Tara is one of the most widespread of Tibetan cults, undifferentiated by sect, education, class, or position; from the highest to the lowest, the Tibetans find with this goddess a personal and enduring relationship unmatched by any other single deity, even among those of their gods more potent in appearance or more profound in symbolic association.[19]

Beyer offers several illustrations of the goddess's appearance. In one picture of her as the White Tara she sits in the lotus position, is adorned with auspicious marks, and has her hands in a stylized position (mudra). Her head inclines slightly to her right, she wears a crown of flowers and is surrounded by plants and flowers, and her expression seems a slight, gentle smile. The Green Tara sits in something less than a full lotus position, is considerably less adorned (only a few flowers), and wears a countenance no less serene than that of the White Tara but perhaps more severe. In both iconographies Tara is beautiful—slim, graceful, wonderfully hipped—but the Green Tara has less luxuriant hair (perhaps even is shaved like a nun) and is less girlish. Both Taras would serve well as mandalas—figures to use in meditation. Both are unthreatening, cool, and radiate peace. In summarizing the cult of Tara Beyer writes,

> To her devotees, however, Tara is an abiding deity, her constant availability perhaps best symbolized by the daily repetition of her ritual rather than by any great ceremony taking place only once a year. She is a patron deity in a second sense of the word, a personal deity rather than a monastic patron, a mother to whom her devotees can take their sorrows and on whom they can rely for help . . . The popular cult of the goddess is one of trust and reverence, of self-confident reliance upon the saving capacity of the divine and upon the human capacity to set in motion the divine mechanism of protection.[20]

The Buddhist Great Goddess, we might say, has brought home to the faithful the compassion with which Gautama often has been credited. He decided to preach the Dharma from compassion for all those suffering the pains of samsara. When Buddhism thought about the wisdom of this decision, it often projected a motherly kindness upon the ultimacy the Enlightened One had understood.

QUEENS

In comparative perspective, distinctions among Buddhas, bodhisattvas, and divinities may be more matters of convenience than hard and fast separations. One might add to this list of Buddhist worthies princesses and queens who functioned in some of the significant devotional literature as models of enlightenment and virtue. One must remember that traditional Buddhism, like the traditional version of most other faiths, thought theocratically. That is, it made no natural distinction between what we now call secular affairs and affairs of religion. For example, Buddhists have considered the reign of King Ashoka (273–232 B.C.E.) a golden era in Indian history. Converted to Buddhism, the king apparently tried to mold his government according to Buddhist ethical ideals, including the ideal of nonviolence. In many periods of Chinese history Buddhism had the ear and allegiance of the emperor. Few Chinese emperors were as pious as Ashoka, but mixed with their appreciation of the political advantages that Buddhism offered often was an apparently sincere personal commitment. Thus when we find kings, princes, queens, and princesses introduced into Buddhist sutras (authoritative texts), we should suspect that they are functioning as leading figures in what ideally would be a Buddhist commonwealth. Further, we should suspect that the authors thought that if people at the top of the social order were enlightened, the rest of the realm would probably be in good shape.

In the figure of Queen Srimala, we find these ideas pushed to the point where one can ask whether the text isn't in fact presenting a female buddha. Whereas other buddha figures tend to be either male, asexual, or females who have changed their sex to become male, Queen Srimala remains female throughout. (Interesting variations on the general predominance of maleness or asexuality in the presentation of buddhas occur in both the Tantric schools, which have had great influence in Tibet and often present divinity androgynously, and in the figure of Kuan-yin/Kannon, who is a female bodhisattva in East Asia but began in India as the male bodhisattva Avalokiteshvara.)

Queen Srimala is the featured player in a sutra known as *The Sutra of Queen Srimala Who Had the Lion's Roar*. This is perhaps the most popular of the sutras that teach about the Tathagatagarbha, the cosmic womb. The queen is portrayed as the ideal layperson whose teaching about the Tathagatagarbha greatly helps those desiring Buddhist salvation. Her instruction clarifies how individuals carry buddhanature within them as their best potential and how they may give birth to this buddhanature by realizing what they most are. Such teaching dovetailed with the stress many Mahayana schools placed on emptiness—the conditioned, nonultimate character of all realities. When people came to appreciate emptiness, their false identities would fall away.

The historical identity of Queen Srimala is obscure. Some traditions associate her with Mallika, wife of the Indian king Prasenajit, while the sutra itself identifies her as the daughter of Prasenajit. *Srimala* means "Beautiful Flower Garland" and refers to her custom of wearing flowers in her hair. A story in her honor tells how she became the wife of the king. He was visiting in the palace precincts, and she ordered the gates closed during his stay. This foiled enemies who had planned to assassinate him, and out of gratitude he asked Srimala to be his queen and rule with him. How historical any of the traditions about Srimala are is quite debatable. More significant is her status as an esteemed teacher of the Dharma—so esteemed that she seems the equivalent of a buddha.[21]

Another Buddhist scripture that uses royal imagery to portray female nature advancing toward enlightenment is the section of the *Lotus Sutra*, a very influential text, that deals with the Naga princess. Nagas were lovely beings with the face of a human but the body of a snake. They were thought to live in watery paradises and to renew themselves endlessly by shedding their skin. The princesses among them were the acme of wit and beauty, so that to be said to have the beauty of a Naga princess was a great compliment. In Buddhist folklore they became entrusted with the Prajnaparamita, the Buddha's most precious teaching about ultimate wisdom.

In the episode recorded in the *Lotus Sutra*, an eight-year-old Naga princess is proposed as the one best capable of understanding the Buddha's preaching and gaining enlightenment. Called before the Buddha to demonstrate her abilities, the princess hears from the disciple Sariputra that because of her sex she will never attain buddhahood, even if she perseveres perfectly through thousands of eons. The princess offers to the Buddha the jewel she carries on her head, the sign of her femininity. In making this sacrifice, she symbolizes her willingness to undergo any transformation necessary for enlightenment. Implicit in the transformation of the princess from female to male was the Buddhist conviction that only males were detached from sexuality and possessed full self-control. The story therefore shows the perdurance in Buddhism of the Hindu convictions about the limitations of female nature and the necessity for it to stay under male control.[22]

Another female figure who contends for high status, here buddhahood, is the daughter of the householder Vimalakirti, who himself sometimes is portrayed as an ordinary layman and other times has the authority of a kingly personage. Candrottara, the daughter, is described in the sutra carrying her name as a child born in exquisite form. Before her birth, her wealthy, pious parents had awakened in her the thought of enlightenment. At her birth prodigies suggested her wonderful destiny: bright light shone all around, the earth trembled, and flowers tumbled from heaven. She got her name, which means "On Top of the Moon," from the light that shone whenever anyone touched her body. She grew quickly, and wherever she walked the earth would glisten, the air would fill with perfume. So desirable was she that princes threatened her father with horrible violence if she did not agree to be their wife. She consoled her terrified father by explaining that no violence, hatred, or foolishness dwelt within her, so there was nothing anyone could do to harm them. Her virtue would be a sufficient shield. To give herself some time in which to maneuver, she promised to announce her choice of a husband in one week.

Having promised to observe all the precepts incumbent on lay Buddhists, Candrottara received a messenger from the Buddha and then flew through the air to meet the Enlightened One himself. In an audience before him she explained the most profound dimensions of the Dharma and then argued that her sex was irrelevant. In the perspective of **emptiness**, being female or male didn't matter. Despite this strong argument, which won her the promise that she would become a buddha, Candrottara did change her sex. Diana Paul thinks that this move, which contradicted the principles Candrottara herself had just exposed quite brilliantly, was a concession to Indian mores of the text's time. Thus Candrottara changed her sex to allow herself greater freedom. Another interpretation might be that the editors of the text worried about the liberationist thrust of Candrottara's main argument and contrived her change of sex as a way to appease traditional male sensibilities.[23]

From these sketches of royal or prominent female figures who contended for buddhahood, we sense the ambivalence that early Buddhism felt about female nature. Indian traditions counseled the subjugation of females to males and the separation of femininity from buddhahood. In their view one could no more have a female buddha than could have a female Brahman or king. On the other hand, Buddhism had brought liberation from sexual restrictions, at least to the extent of allowing women to become disciples and admitting that some women showed a fine grasp of the Dharma. But prejudices against a woman's mind tended to prevail sufficiently to keep full enlightenment a male preserve.

ADEPTS

Whether or not women in theory could attain full enlightenment and become buddhas, in practice many women gained fame as holy and wise. One such woman was the Tibetan Ayu Khandro, who was born in eastern Tibet in 1839 and died in 1954, having spent the last 50 of her 115 years in meditation. Ayu was a youngest child and was brought up by a pious aunt who taught her the Buddhist religious practices. She was betrothed at the age of fourteen, despite her objections, but won a partial reprieve: she would be allowed to continue studying Dharma with her aunt until she was nineteen. The goddess Tara was one of the first subjects of her meditations.

The marriage occurred as contracted, but after three years Ayu came down with a form of paralysis. A lama (upper-echelon monk) analyzed her condition as the result of her having interrupted her religious studies. Ayu's husband agreed to her returning to live with her aunt (they had begotten no children). When the lama who had befriended her family died, Ayu and her aunt attended his funeral, losing themselves in deep meditation. As Ayu surfaced from her meditation, she realized that her aunt had died. The aunt remained in her meditational posture for three days after her last breath—a sign of her high level of religious accomplishment.

Now age thirty, Ayu spent fifteen years traveling throughout Tibet, sometimes alone and sometimes in the company of other Buddhists. She grew in her meditational prowess, favoring a technique in which she would leave her body to enter the form of a fierce goddess. From this new position she would then transform her human body into food for all hungry beings—deities, ghosts, and humans alike. In their travels, Ayu and her companions would chant the liturgy for cutting attachments to worldly things and would beat drums and sound bells to ward off evil influences.

When she was forty-four, Ayu returned to her husband's household, where she was supported in her practice and gave religious instruction to both him and other members of his family. The husband built a hut where she could retreat into solitude. She reported meditating on great travels and waking up to find herself physically transported to the place she had imagined. After some years of regular retreats into solitude, Ayu decided that she wished to spend the rest of her life in meditation. Occasionally she would give students instruction, and her reputation grew as a mistress of specialized Buddhist rituals. Most of her practices came from the tantrist tradition and involved meditative union with a colorful deity, usually one in feminine form.

At age 115 Ayu still showed no signs of ill health. One day she called her students and told them that in three weeks she would die, so they should prepare for her funeral. The times were changing and she felt it was well for her to depart. Like her aunt, she died in meditational posture. Reports went about that after her death she had retained this posture for two weeks, her body steadily becoming smaller and smaller. The weather turned surprisingly hot and trees and flowers bloomed. Her reputation was such that many thought her a living form of the Great Bliss Queen (a high Tibetan Buddhist deity).[24]

Certain formulaic features suggest that the life of Ayu Khandro has been assimilated to Tibetan traditions about the features of saints who in-carnate high deities. Nonetheless, she must have been a remarkable woman to have so impressed those who knew or remembered her. Anne Klein, the author of the study I have been using, speculates that Ayu profited from the presence in Tibetan Buddhist tradition of powerful female deities such as Tara and the Great Bliss Queen. Tibetan Buddhism, in contrast to the Indian traditions we viewed in the last section, did not separate sexuality from enlightenment.

The tantrist traditions on which Tibetan schools often drew, and which they further developed, thought that libidinal energies should be put in the service of enlightenment. The meditations of Ayu Khondro ap-parently limited themselves to imaginative identification with queenly dei-ties and did not dwell on sexual intercourse. In "left hand" tantrist tradi-tions, disciples sometimes have simulated sexual intercourse (or actually engaged in sexual intercourse) as an enactment of full union with divinity. This of course broke strong taboos, as did such related practices as eating meat and drinking alcohol. When not simply licentious, tantrists engaging in such practices were under the instruction of a guru and were trying to realize, as vividly as possible, the Mahayana doctrine that nirvana and samsara are one. The wisdom that went beyond ordinary living to enlight-enment had to transcend ordinary morality. Many tantrist groups, Hindu as well as Buddhist, broke with sexual stereotypes and gave women equal footing with men. As well, many Hindus dismissed considerations of caste. In some ways, therefore, women profited from tantrist venturousness and iconoclasm. In other ways, however, women suffered liabilities, because In-dian tantrism thought of women's shakti as a power to be tapped for men's enlightenment, and women could become mere instruments of men's struggles for liberation.

In the Vajrayana ("Thunderbolt") school of Buddhism, which was es-pecially influential in Tibet, tantric convictions led to women becoming gurus or masters. Such women were called *siddhas*, and they were believed to be perfectly enlightened. Since Vajrayana tradition depended upon transmission through a line of masters, the siddhas had a quasi "institu-tional" importance. One of the striking features of the siddhas' teaching was that, pushing Mahayana notions of emptiness, they counseled their fol-lowers to stop thinking of themselves as anything definite enough to be bound by social convention. Their "crazy wisdom" was expressed through bizarre and eccentric behavior, as well as through trampling on social ta-boos. In addition, Vajrayana developed the notion of *Taras*, goddesses or savioresses who were consorts of the buddhas, and this had great influence on popular piety.

Nonetheless, the inbuilt sexism of Indian social formation made it difficult for women to become gurus, even in Vajrayana. This is illustrated in the case of Laksminkara, a famous siddha born in Northwest India in the eighth century C.E. Since Northwest India was at that time a stronghold of Vajrayana, Laksminkara had access to tantric teachings from early childhood. Because she was of royal blood, however, she was betrothed at age seven to the Hindu ruler of a neighboring kingdom. For nine years, Laksminkara remained in her family home, studying the tantras and being initiated, until it came time for her marriage. Then everything started to go wrong. Her reception at her husband's castle was very cold, because the harem, as well as the general populace, resented her as a Buddhist outsider. As she waited outside the castle, Laksminkara saw the royal hunting party returning with their catch, a newly slain deer. This so shocked her Buddhist soul that she fainted dead away. Upon reviving, she gave away her dowry and all her jewels. Then she locked herself in a room, to go naked and feign insanity. After many tribulations, she wandered in abject poverty for seven years, all the while pretending to be insane, a favorite tantric ruse for rejecting common values. Eventually her suffering won her deep enlightenment and many disciples, among them her former husband and her brother. Much in Laksminkara's life story, no doubt, is legendary, but it testifies to the possibility of a female tantric guru.

The enlightenment experience of an American woman, aged fifty-one, can suggest the openness of the Zen school of Buddhism to accrediting the spiritual potential of women. Zen stresses the primacy of meditation, and the experience, which occurred in Pennsylvania in the mid-1950s, is typical of Zen reports. The woman, an artist, had worked as a sculptor, experienced marriage and motherhood, and become a member of Alcoholics Anonymous to try to deal with her troubles. She felt bruised by life, unable to cope, and so had sought solace in drink, despite her mounting feelings of guilt at neglecting her husband and children. When she joined Alcoholics Anonymous she took the first step on a quest for understanding that might change her life.

This quest took her to books on Eastern religions, and finally to Japan, where she attended a sesshin (meditational retreat). In Japan she was befriended by some Zen Buddhists and introduced to the rudiments of Zen practice. After four years of practice, at a sesshin in Pennsylvania, her struggles came to full fruition. She was working on the koan mu (a famous meditational exercise concerned with grasping the significance of the exclamation "mu" [no]. The objective was to identify with her **koan** and penetrate its essence with her whole being, not just her mind. More and more she lived with mu, thought only about mu, walked and breathed and ate mu. Against fatigue and feelings of despair about her still troubled family life, she mustered the energy to keep attacking.

> " 'Go deeper,' the roshi [guru] said. 'Question "What is this Mu?" to the very bottom.'
> Deeper and deeper I went . . .

My hold was torn loose and I went spinning . . .
To the center of the earth!
To the center of the cosmos!
To the Center
I was There
With the sound of the little kinhin bell I suddenly knew."[25]

The rest of the woman's report on her experience stresses the roshi's confirmation of her enlightenment and her feelings of cleanliness, freedom, and readiness to live with zest. She had come to feel reoriented, reconstituted, no longer restless and dissatisfied. In other accounts of *satori*, the Zen version of enlightenment, similar descriptions arise. People experience the unity of existence, the falseness of distinctions and dichotomies. They feel liberated from the alienations and divisions they previously had experienced, feel suffused with peace, joy, and light. Such descriptions seem to vary little from men to women. Both sexes usually have been suffering from either personal problems or simply the sense of living with only part of their energy, only part of themselves. Some roshis, at least, now have no prejudice against female disciples, and in some sects female roshis are now an ordinary occurrence. Indeed, one can read endorsements of women's aptitude for Zen that praise the holism and sensitivity to which women have been socialized in many cultures. Prior to World War II, women would seldom have been welcome in a male monastic setting, but now their presence is nothing extraordinary.

FURTHER IMAGES OF WOMEN

We have seen something of the range of attitudes toward women evidenced in the Buddhist scriptures and practices. It remains in this section to fill out this description and further communicate its feel or flavor. For example, there is the story of two monks traveling through the forest who came to a river swollen by spring rains. A woman stood at the river's edge, debating how to cross. One of the monks offered her a ride on his back, which she gladly accepted. One the other side of the river, she departed and the two monks continued their journey. Some miles further along the second monk broke their silence and criticized the first for having been so intimate with the woman. The first monk said, "I put the woman down hours ago. Why are you still carrying her?"

The story suggests not only the fear of women evidenced in many monastic texts, but also the antidote Buddhist spirituality readily offered. As monks or laymen grew in detachment, in the purification of their desires, they could gain a more positive view of women, food, work, and other staples of daily life. When they were confident enough of their own ability to follow the basic precepts of sila, they did not have to worry about every decision or see every attractive creature as a threat. One finds this same possibility in other religious traditions. Alongside the prudishness that sometimes soured relations between the sexes in Judaism, Christianity, and Islam, for instance, lived a commonsensical freedom. Blessing women, children, good food, and laughter, some rabbis, priests, and mullahs praised God for the beauty of life and kept their disquisitions about temptation and sin minimal. Consequently, one learns to consider diatribes against women and lust as much expressions of the inner anxieties of the writers as objective reactions to objective cultural abuses. Religious people, men or women, who are content, who feel at ease with their practice, don't see the devil behind every tree. They are like the first monk, happy to be of service and encumbered with neither useless longings nor vain regrets.

A text from fourth- or fifth-century C.E. Kashmir, which at the time was a leading center of Buddhist studies, illustrates the less balanced approach to lust that meditation masters sometimes indulged. Instead of concentrating on how to heal the meditator afflicted with lust for women, the text blames female nature, which it characterizes as producing words that seem honeyed but flow from a poisoned heart, as appearing like a cave full of treasures but actually housing a lion, as ruining the clan and destroying the family, and as being like a fine-meshed net that catches fish for a fisherman who then rips out their entrails.[26]

Offsetting such a textual attack on women was the living example of a woman such as the Chinese nun Miao-yin, the abbess of a leading monastery at the end of the fourth century C.E. She was esteemed for her diplomacy as much as her learning, and her tact won her the trust of several emperors. She became a regular at the literary discussions of the royal court, and other Chinese women certainly could see in her living proof that the Dharma, femininity, and political influence all could harmonize.[27]

The twofold character of all human beings, their potential for both evil and good, naturally made a strong impression on Buddhist commentators, and even when classical texts seem to stress the problematic character of women's ways they often at least indirectly make it clear that women also can be singularly virtuous. So, for example, a story of the Buddha supposedly relayed by the disciple Ananda describes a powerful king with at least two influential queens. The Buddha was visiting the royal court and the chief queen, Syamavati, heard his preaching with great approval. Consequently, she spread good reports about him throughout the palace and supported the Buddha and his monks with generous alms. A second queen, Anupama Magandika, was jealous and required flattery. She attacked both the Buddha and the chief queen. The king believed this second queen and shot an arrow at the first, virtuous queen. She, forgiving him this evil deed, entered meditation. The arrow stopped in midair above the king's head. There it blazed brilliantly, instilling fear in all who beheld it. The king was confused and in turmoil, and he addressed the chief queen as though she were a goddess or a Naga princess. She modestly denied any superhuman status and attributed all her powers to her having accepted the Buddhist Dharma and followed the Buddhist ethical precepts. She also assured the king that, despite his being disposed against her, she wished him no harm, only compassion. If he were wise, he too would take refuge in the Buddha.

Thinking that it would be good to consult the source of such power, the king went to the Buddha and prostrated himself. He then expressed repentance for having listened to the evil queen and asked forgiveness for his offenses. The Buddha accepted the king as a disciple and bade him concentrate on important things, that he might experience no future births and transgress no more.

The king complained that his faults were due to women, and he asked the Enlightened One to explain women's faults. The Buddha told him that he ought first to understand the faults of men, which explain why men have trouble with women. The faults disturbing men included: addiction to **desire**, which led them to look upon women as objects for their own self-indulgence; the lack of a close relation with monks and those who kept the moral precepts; foolishness, related to association with evil friends; disregard of parents; abuse of the rights of animals; and neglect of the Buddha, the Dharma, and the Sangha. Other faults included forgetting the mortality of their bodies and using their money for pleasure rather than the support of good causes like monasteries. Some of the Buddha's images for men enslaved to desire were graphic: racing toward female forms like hogs toward mud, spoiling themselves through a desire like the overflow of a toilet or the corpse of a dog. And certainly it did women no good to be compared to the object of the lust of a dog in heat. But throughout this disquisition on the ill effects of desire, the Buddha took the position that lust is men's problem. In another place he might have analyzed women's problem and culpability, but here, advising the king, the accent was on what the king should root out of his own soul. If the evil queen could wrap him around his finger and twist his mind, the good queen had been the means of his obtaining the Buddha's instruction. Clearly, therefore, women could be either helps or hindrances, depending on both what they chose to be and how men chose to regard them.[28]

Philip Kapleau tells a traditional story in praise of Mahayana compassion. A beautiful geisha girl was already in debt to many of her admirers when she found that her mother required an expensive operation. Her usual creditors turned down her request for a further loan, so she was forced to approach a crude man she despised. He finally promised to give her the money, on the condition that she seduce a famous roshi, whom the crude man hated for his righteousness. The girl gained admission to the roshi's house by posing as a bedraggled traveler. She then tried to seduce him but failed utterly. Despairing of being able to help her mother, she broke down and poured out the whole story. The roshi then bid her spend the night with him, so that she could earn the money. Although the abbot of the monastery dismissed the roshi when he learned the women had spent the night, the other monks clamored for his reinstatement. He had taught them a great lesson in compassion, they claimed, and compassion was the heart of the Buddha's way.

Kapleau suggests that the problem with sex in Buddhist practice is one of balance. Neither being enslaved to lust nor despising sex and treating people of the other sex coldly hits the mark. The roshi judged that helping the woman was more important than keeping the letter of his celibacy. Apparently he was free of taboos about women, was able to show the understanding and kindness that Buddhist women, like any women, have always wanted and needed. When Buddhism treated women as both needy and strong, as fully human, it served them well.[29]

RECENT THEMES

We have treated themes rather constant in the Buddhist regard of women, often drawing from ancient, influential texts. Buddhism has not survived as well as it has without being very adaptable, however, and such adaptation continues today in its efforts to take root in new cultural situations, such as that of the United States. Various Buddhist groups have established monasteries, retreat houses, training centers, and schools in the United States and Canada. While Zen Buddhism has gotten special attention, Theravadin, Tibetan, Korean, and devotional Japanese sects have all also established foundations. In adapting to Western conditions, many of these groups have tinkered with such matters as the traditional posture for meditation, explaining its virtues but counseling beginners not to fixate on such an ideal—to use a chair if that works better. Similarly, they have tried to assimilate Western ideas about sexual equality, find their analogues if not equivalents in Buddhist tradition, and to open the Buddhist community to the fuller contribution of women's talents.

Shasta Abbey in California, an establishment in the Soto Zen tradition, where enlightenment is thought to come gradually, shows the extent of the Buddhist push for adaptation. The founder and roshi was an Englishwoman, Jiyu Kennett Roshi. Born of Buddhist parents, she entered a Theravada community at the age of sixteen and studied with various monks who were visiting London. At the same time, she pursued a career as a professional organist. In 1962 she was ordained a priest in the Rinzai Zen tradition (which tends to push for the dramatic experience of enlightenment called *satori*) in Malaysia, and shortly thereafter she went to Japan to become the personal disciple of the chief Abbot of the Sojiji Soto Zen temple in Yokahama. In two years she had received various degrees testifying to her progress and been named Abbess of her own temple in Mieken, Japan. In 1968 she was licensed as a full teacher, able to direct the meditation of disciples. At the wish of her teacher, she returned to the West to spread Zen. He was convinced that only Westerners could fully communicate Zen to the West. She founded Shasta Monastery, has written extensively, and has lectured at numerous colleges. One of her special themes has been that roshis should not allow themselves to be glorified by their students but should find ways of downplaying their own status.[30]

Half a world away from Shasta Monastery, Thai women are trying to establish women's status as *bhikkunis* (nuns) or full sharers in the Theravada monastic life. Theravada women have never had had this status in the seven hundred years of Thai Buddhism, although in other cultures, such as that of Sri Lanka, there have long been nuns. Thai Buddhism does admit women to a lesser ascetical status, in which they shave their heads, wear white, and observe some of the monastic precepts. Such women, though formally recognized through a religious ceremony, are finally accounted laywomen, since they do not have to observe the full rule of the traditional *bhikkunis*. Perhaps the Western parallel would be churches that admit women as deacons but forbid them full ordination as ministers or priests. The Thai religious women, known as *jis*, number perhaps 20,000 and have suffered from a lack of support. Generally they have not been well educated and have had to provide their own finances. In all ways, they have had much less status and prestige than Thai monks.

Since Thailand has never had *bhikkunis*, those considering starting a woman's monastic sangha in Thailand (by associating with a Theravada women's monastic sangha in Taiwan that presently counts about 4,200 nuns as members) have had to contend with a long-standing religious prejudice against women. Religion is considered a man's sphere, in which women are thought not competent, and as a result women have tended to be uninterested in most religious enterprises. Their main religious experience has been completely passive: listening to sermons by monks. The women interested in establishing a Thai women's monastic community have been somewhat heartened by the openness of some younger monks, but they realize that the clerical establishment in general is not likely to support their movement with much enthusiasm. The hopes of the movement therefore largely rest with the one Thai woman who has received ordination as a *bhikkuni*, Voramai Kabilsingh. She progressed from a concern for the poor, especially poor children, to a deepened interest in Buddhism. Finally in 1956 she became a *jis*. However, not satisfied with this lower-echelon status, she traveled to Taiwan and received full ordination as a *bhikkuni*. Now she works at a temple south of Bangkok called "Women Who Uphold Dhamma." For the Thai women who want to claim a share in their

Buddhist heritage equal to that available to Thai men, she has become a beacon of hope.[31]

A study of the position of nuns and wives of priests in the Soto Zen tradition of Japan suggests that feminism has been making some inroads there, too. Although traditionally women had only an inferior position in this sect, since World War II they have made such progress as gaining permission for nuns to become formal university students, allowing nuns to be appointed principals of nuns' schools, abolishing sexual discrimination in temple ceremonies, and establishing special convents for nuns who wish to practice Zen meditation. As well, nuns who historically had qualified as Zen masters have been more fully acknowledged and contemporary nuns have gained fuller freedom to conduct their own meditations and study with an eye to becoming priests. Nonetheless, even though some Japanese nuns have continued to push for progress toward equality, in the recent years they have still lagged far behind in rights within the Soto Zen community.

An interesting study in the sociology of Soto Zen Buddhism glimmers in the treatment of wives of Soto priests. Because of monastic traditions of celibacy, even though priests have long had the right to marry, their wives have had low status and often their marriages have not been registered. Instead of being fully acknowledged, their children often would be listed as students rather than blood offspring. In the 1950s wives began to receive new benefits, including the right to veto candidates to succeed their husbands as heads of temples after the husbands' death, the right to receive life insurance purchased for their husbands, and financial protection for themselves and their children should their husband die. Slowly the ritual possibilities for wives expanded, and they tended to take some training, so that they could assist their husbands in running the temples. However, this progress brought the wives into conflict with Soto Zen nuns, who had undergone a more rigorous training. As well, the nuns had fewer rights than priests and could not pass their temples on to their heirs. Despite this conflict between the nuns and the priests' wives, Soto women have made notable gains and now have much more visibility and power than they had even a generation ago.[32]

Presently both Buddhist women and feminist scholars of religion are devoting much energy to the study of how women have fared in Buddhist history. Sometimes the motive is simply the detached interest that propels scholarship. Other times the motive is trying to retrieve from the tradition indications of women's rights that might support fuller participation by present-day Buddhist women. Nancy Schuster Barnes concludes a study on women in Buddhism with the following estimate:

> The study of women in Buddhism is a new field. Modern scholars have only begun to seriously examine the manifold questions relating to women's place in Buddhist religion, and Buddhist women in Asia and the West have only begun to look hard at such questions. The next several years are certain to see

important advances in our understanding of this field, and new perspectives are bound to be opened as twentieth century Buddhist women become more aware of themselves within their religious tradition, and more public about their insights.[33]

One suggestion an outsider might make is that Buddhist thinkers be made more aware of the special liabilities women continue to suffer today and so include women as a special case when they discuss religious liberty and human rights. Presently males writing about human rights in Korea or in the Buddhist tradition generally seem blissfully unaware that women still constitute a bloc with special needs.[34]

DISCUSSION QUESTIONS

1. Is there anything nonfeminine about the Four Noble Truths or the five precepts of sila?

2. What is the significance of the link between the nun Lion-Yawn and the prostitute Vasumitra?

3. Why has traditional Buddhism considered monastic life superior to lay life?

4. How does a devotional figure such as Tara or Kannon tend to function in the life of ordinary Buddhist believers?

5. Why did Candrottara use emptiness as a basis for claiming that sex was irrelevant to the most profound dimensions of the Dharma?

6. What do you imagine was the great attraction meditation held for Ayu Khandro?

7. What could be the implications for Buddhist women of the Buddha's making men's addiction to sexual desire the root of men's problems with women?

8. What are the main obstacles standing in the way of Thai women who want to become bhikkunis?

NOTES

[1]See *1987 Brittanica Book of the Year* (Chicago: Encyclopaedia Brittanica, 1987), p. 338.

[2]See Ananda K. Coomaraswamy, *Buddha and the Gospel of Buddhism* (New York: Harper Torchbooks, 1964), p. 160.

[3]See Nancy E. Auer Falk, "Buddhist Puja," in *The Encyclopedia of Religion*, Vol. 12, ed. Mircea Eliade (New York: Macmillan, 1987), pp. 85–86.

[4]See Frank E. Reynolds and Charles Hallisey, "Buddhism: An Overview," in *The Encyclopedia of Religion*, Vol. 2, pp. 334–351.

[5]See Janice D. Willis, "Nuns and Benefactresses: The Role of Women in the Development of Buddhism," in *Women, Religion and Social Change*, ed. Yvonne Yazbeck Haddad and Ellison Findly Banks (Albany: State University of New York Press, 1985), pp. 62–63.

[6]See Edward Conze, *Buddhist Meditation* (New York: Harper Torchbooks, 1969), pp. 95–107.

[7]See Diana Y. Paul, *Women in Buddhism* (Berkeley, Calif.: Asian Humanities Press, 1979), pp. 94–105.

[8]See Nancy Schuster Barnes, "Buddhism," in *Women in World Religions*, ed. Arvind Sharma (Albany: State University of New York Press, 1987), p. 109.

[9]See Rita M. Gross, "The Householder and the World Renunciant: Two Modes of Sexual Expression in Buddhism," *Journal of Ecumenical Studies*, 22, no. 1 (Winter 1985), pp. 81–96; Nancy Auer Falk, "The Case of the Vanishing Nuns: The Fruits of Ambivalence in Ancient Indian Buddhism," in *Unspoken Worlds: Women's Lives in Non-Western Cultures*, ed. Nancy A. Falk and Rita M. Gross (San Francisco: Harper & Row, 1980), pp. 207–224.

[10]See J. D. Whitehead, "Vimalakirti," *Abingdon Dictionary of Living Religions*, ed. Keith Crim (Nashville: Abingdon, 1981), p. 795.

[11]Melford E. Spiro, *Buddhism and Society: A Great Tradition and Its Burmese Vicissitudes*, 2nd exp. ed. (Berkeley: University of California Press, 1982), p. 67.

[12]Ibid., p. 432.

[13]See Raoul Birnbaum, "Avalokitesvara," *The Encyclopedia of Religion*, Vol. 2, pp. 11–14.

[14]See John Bowker, *The Religious Imagination and the Sense of God* (Oxford: Clarendon, 1978).

[15]See Diana Paul, "Kuan-yin: Savior and Savioress in Pure Land Buddhism," in *The Book of the Goddess: Past and Present*, ed. Carl Olsen (New York: Crossroad, 1983), pp. 161–175.

[16]See Joanna Rogers Macy, "Perfection of Wisdom: Mother of All Buddhas," in *Beyond Androcentrism*, ed. Rita M. Gross (Missoula, Mont.: Scholars Press, 1977), pp. 315–333.

[17]See Edward Conze, *Buddhist Wisdom Books* (New York: Harper Torchbooks, 1972), pp. 77, 101–107.

[18]See Edward J. Thomas, *The History of Buddhist Thought*, 2nd ed. (New York: Barnes and Noble, 1951), p. 234. The *Lankavatara Sutra* is a key text.

[19]Stephan Beyer, *The Cult of Tara: Magic and Ritual in Tibet* (Berkeley: University of California Press, 1978), p. 3.

[20]Ibid., p. 55.

[21]See Paul, *Women in Buddhism*, pp. 289–302.

[22]See ibid., pp. 185–190.

[23]See ibid., pp. 190–199.

[24]See Anne C. Klein, "Primordial Purity and Everyday Life: Exalted Female Symbols and the Women of Tibet," in *Immaculate and Powerful: The Female in Sacred Image and Social Reality*, ed. C. Atkinson, C. Buchanan, and M. Miles (Boston: Beacon Press, 1985), pp. 115–118.

[25]Philip Kapleau, *The Three Pillars of Zen* (Boston: Beacon Press, 1965), p. 253.

[26]See Nancy Schuster, "Striking a Balance: Women and Images of Women in Early Chinese Buddhism," in *Women, Religion and Social Change*, p. 92.

[27]See ibid.

[28]See Paul, *Women in Buddhism*, pp. 27–59.

[29]See Philip Kapleau, *Zen: Dawn in the West* (Garden City, N.Y.: Anchor Press/Doubleday, 1980), pp. 82–83.

[30]See Charles S. Prebish, *American Buddhism* (North Sictuate, Mass.: Duxbury Press, 1979), pp. 159–161.

[31]See Chatsumarn Kabilsingh, "The Future of the Bhikkuni Sangha in Thailand," in *Speaking of Faith*, ed. Diana L. Eck and Devaki Jain (Philadelphia: New Society, 1987), pp. 148–158.

[32]See Kumiko Uchino, "The Status Elevation Process of Soto Sect Nuns in Modern Japan," in ibid., pp. 159–173.

[33]Barnes, "Buddhism," p. 133.

[34]See Yong-Bock Kim, "Religious Freedom and Human Rights in Korea," and Masao Abe, "Religious Tolerance and Human Rights: A Buddhist Perspective," in *Religious Liberty and Human Rights in Nations and Religions*, ed. Leonard Swidler (Philadelphia: Ecumenical Press, 1986), pp. 95–107 and 193–211.

CHAPTER FIVE

Chinese Women

INTRODUCTORY ORIENTATION

Today there are more than 1 billion Chinese within the People's Republic. Tens of millions more people of Chinese ancestry live in other nations. (For example, Singapore is about three-fourths Chinese, Malaysia is about one-third Chinese.)[1] While the influence of Communism makes the majority of citizens in the People's Republic officially nonreligious, both they and other Chinese are the cultural heirs of a complex religious background. Confucian, Taoist, Buddhist, and popular traditions have all shaped the thousands-year-old Chinese worldview. So Chinese women of today, to say nothing of their historical forebears, continue to be shaped by religious attitudes inseparable from their ethnic heritage. In China religion has been the usually subtle foundation for the general culture: Confucian mores, Taoist poetry, Buddhist meditation, and shamanistic concern with spirits both good and evil.

Prehistorians treat Chinese culture as well established by at least seven thousand years ago. Around 5000 B.C.E. a variety of tribes occupied most of the land we now consider China. Archeological indications suggest that these prehistoric peoples practiced a cult of the dead. Grave sites indicate purposeful burial, perhaps in hope of an afterlife, with the inclusion of valuable objects and animals. The traditional Chinese veneration of ancestors probably goes back to this earliest period. Dried shoulder bones of sheep and deer suggest that forms of **divination** (reading the cracks in bones) found in the historic period also had prehistoric beginnings.

The rituals one can infer from remains of the earliest historical period, the Shang, show no strong presence of a Great Goddess. The earliest Chinese divinity apparently was Shang-ti, the Lord on High, to whom the people probably sacrificed for good fortune. Whether a lady earth counterbalanced this heavenly lord is uncertain, but the concern for fertility that marks earliest Chinese religion, as well as the later interest in mother earth[2] and in balancing forces of yin (dark, wet, female) and yang (light, dry, male), suggests that she may. Patriarchal China has counted the family line through male ancestors, who predominate in the rites venerating forebears in the clan. On the other hand, female forebears have been acknowledged, and children have mourned the death of mothers (although, following Confucian orthodoxy, not so long or lavishly as the death of fathers).

Early Taoist thought, as we shall see, used more feminine associations for the Cosmic Way (Tao) than male. In popular religion both men and women have served as shamanic mediums, women tending to predominate as mouthpieces for the gods. The name used for female shamans, *wu*, has overtones of dancing. Although the major deities of popular religion have mainly been male, goddesses such as T'ien Sheng-mu, the patroness of seafarers, dot the pantheon. In coastal towns throughout China people long practiced the cult of T'ien Sheng-mu. After the impact of Buddhism Kuan-yin became a very popular deity, serving as a goddess of mercy and the help of women who wanted to conceive.[3]

The main sphere of women's religious influence has been the home, where they have tended to preside at the family cult. An altar in the central room typically would hold images of the family's patron deities and ancestors, who would both be honored several times each month. Women traditionally have instructed Chinese children in the native religious ways, explaining the significance of the family observances, telling stories about the gods and demons, and providing religious example. Domestic rituals have usually punctuated the life cycle, including observances of pregnancy and birth. The pregnant woman has been considered to carry a fetus spirit, whose whereabouts (in the bedroom today, on the roof tomorrow) could be charted. Family members would try hard not to offend this fetus spirit, for fear of harming the unborn child. In the popular mind, driving a nail into the wall of a room where the fetus spirit was staying could cause the child to be born with a harelip. Sewing or cutting in the presence of the fetus spirit could cause the child to be born with fingers or a limb missing. Both the blood of birth and menstrual blood traditionally were tabooed and thought offensive to the gods. For a month after birth the new mother has been treated as polluted and confined to the house, while the room in which birth took place would also be considered polluted and so be avoided.[4]

We shall see more of such popular religious conceptions later. To complete our introductory orientation, we should note that the vast majority of the Chinese population historically has been the peasantry and that the rural conditions in which most people have lived encouraged a popular religion close to the earth, full of spirits considered either helpful or harmful to fertility and prosperity. Through a combination of immemorial popular tradition and Confucian influence, the prevailing social hierarchy has placed women well below men. The official power in a household has rested with the father (who, in the extended Chinese family, often was the grandfather), although the actual influence of women, especially the mother (grandmother) often was greater. Boys have been preferred to girls, so much so that in many periods of Chinese history female infanticide was common, and elder brothers have had more official status than elder sisters. Once again, however, actual influence did not always coincide with official status. Because elder sisters usually had central roles in caring for younger children, they in fact have exercised great influence, both physical and psychological.

The patriarchal structure of Chinese family and political life meant that women tended to have little official independence and power. Monarchs and wealthy Chinese men usually had concubines, while a double standard of sexual morality held girls and wives to strict chastity. Women were valued in the measure they produced male children, who then became the focus of their efforts to achieve status and power. The more sons a woman had, and the more influence the sons had, the better off a woman would be. Regularly, therefore, husbands were caught in a tug-of-war between their mothers and their wives. The mothers prevailed more often than not, teaching the wives (the daughters-in-law) that they had best concentrate on manipulating their own sons. Until a young wife had produced children, especially sons, she was virtually the servant of her mother-in-law.

Other aspects of the informal power that Chinese women have tended to accumulate include a proverbially fiery temper and manipulation through gossip. Perhaps in tacit acknowledgment of the injustices in the relations between the sexes, many cultures grant women what amount to safety valves. Thus North African Islam has tended to indulge women's possession by spirits that render them sick unless favors (parties for the women and gifts) are forthcoming, while Chinese culture has tended to allow women temper tantrums. For the sake of peace, Chinese men often would let women have their way, just as for the sake of good reputation Chinese men often curtailed their physical abuse of women. A woman who had been abused by her husband, or whose husband was ruining the family by drinking or gambling, might show her bruises to the other women while they were washing clothes at the river or might let it slip that she was worried her family would soon have no money for essentials. The other women then would harass their husbands until their husbands put pressure on the offender to stop beating his wife or wasting the family income in gambling. Traditional Chinese society placed a high value on good reputation. Losing face or suffering **shame** was a powerful negative incentive. To avoid shaming parents and ancestors, men often would mend their ways and Chinese women were quick to capitalize on this possibility.

Apart from Buddhist monasticism, Chinese women have had little alternative to marriage and motherhood. The single life has been a rarity, with little honor. Chinese women have often worked hard—in the fields, at home, in shops, and later in industries—but seldom have had careers. Thus they have seldom produced high art, science, or religion. Usually they have served men and children.

CONFUCIAN VIEWS

Confucius (551–479 B.C.E.) became the most influential figure in imperial China. The classics associated with his authority have set the cultural ideals for social and political life in most eras during the nearly twenty-five hundred years since his death. In summarizing the attitudes toward women expressed in the five most important Confucian classics, Richard Guisso has written, "The female was inferior by nature, she was dark as the moon and changeable as water, jealous, narrow-minded, and insinuating. She was indiscreet, unintelligent, and dominated by emotion. Her beauty was a snare for the unwary male, the ruination of states."[5]

Dominating the lives of Chinese women was the Confucian conviction, expressed well by Mencius (ca. 371–ca. 289 B.C.E.), the leading proponent of the Master, that not to raise up offspring was the worst offense against their parents that children could commit (4A:26). This responsibility, as well as their positive sense of the potential for growth resident in marriage and family life, caused the Confucians to regard Buddhist monasticism as unnatural. From Confucian cosmology came the notion that the female yin force, essential for harmony, ought to be passive and docile, following the lead of the more important male yang force. Within Confucian social thought, Chinese women were like Indian women in ideally being obedient to men in all stages of their lives. As girls they were to obey their fathers, as mature women they were to obey their husbands, and as old women they were to obey their eldest sons. However, because China did not consider the female principle powerful like the Indian shakti, the overtones of the Chinese notion of obedience were less metaphysical and urgent.

In the Chinese ideogram for a wife occurs a broom, symbol of women's identification with the domestic sphere. Outside the domestic sphere, in politics or state religious ritual, a woman would be misplaced. This domestic destiny shaped women's education, which usually was restricted to such practical skills as sewing and good manners. One ideal was to celebrate a girl's coming of age at fifteen and her marriage at twenty. Marriage was a union of two family lines even more than the union of two individual people. If the individuals came to love one another, all the better, but their first obligation was to honor their parents and ancestors by raising up children to continue the line. The father of the groom would instruct him to take the initiative in family affairs, show his wife consideration, and consider her the image of his mother. Both the father and the mother of the bride would admonish her to obey the rules of the new household she was entering.

At marriage women passed out of their natal family and joined the family of their husbands. This eventually colored the popular preference for sons and generated such proverbs as "Raising a daughter is like weeding another man's field" and "The best daughter isn't worth a splay-footed son." The traditional Confucian wedding ceremony had such symbols of unity if not equality between bride and groom as their eating from the same piece of meat and drinking from cups made from the same melon. The reception of the bride into her husband's home stressed that she had replaced his mother as the prime childbearing female. A ceremony three months after the wedding established her place in the ancestral line of her new household. (Girls never had an official place in the ancestral lineage of their natal homes.) Within the household men and women tended to be segregated, except for sleeping, and many formalities defined their roles under the general Confucian rubric of *li*: proper protocol, fitting ritual. Both husband and wife ideally would make the comfort of the husband's parents their overriding concern.

Divorce was not easily come by, but women might be returned to their natal homes for such offenses as disobedience to the husband's parents, failure to bear a male child (an heir), promiscuity, jealousy, incurable sickness, talking too much, and stealing.[6] On the other hand, a husband was not to divorce a wife whose parents were dead, or who had carried out the mourning rites for one of his parents, or whom he had married before he came into riches. Women had no grounds for divorcing men, and widows ideally would not remarry, out of fidelity to their deceased husbands. Another reason widows were not to remarry was that they retained obligations to the ancestors of the family into which they had married.

Confucian manuals for prospective wives stressed proper reserve between the sexes, lest they lose respect for one another. Such loss of respect might lead to the husband striking the wife, after which the marriage would be in peril. Wives were exhorted to consider winning the love of their husbands their chief aim in life. The best way to win his love, they were counseled, was not flattery but utter devotion. In terms of virtues, wives would do best by concentrating on chastity, proper speech, personal cleanliness, and hard work. The manuals also suggested that a woman would get on best with her mother-in-law by acting as her shadow or echo and always obeying her. She would also best handle difficult sisters-in-law by being submissive. Despite such advice, Chinese brides often faced an unhappy early married life, for they were interlopers in a strange household and had little status until they had begotten a son. Indeed, as in India, significant numbers of new wives committed suicide. The benefit to women of gaining acceptance into their new homes was not just personal peace but a sense of fitting into the cosmic scheme of things, since for the Confucians women by nature were the inferior, submissive sex, and on their submission depended both the continuance of the race and harmonious households. The strength of the ideal Chinese woman would show in her selflessness.

In some sketches of the ideal wifely behavior women become the custodians of the morals of the household and of their husband's good name. So, for example, her devotion to his parents becomes a prop and if need be a model for his own. A wife is to treat her husband's concubines well, never demeaning them, just as she is to treat the animals of the household well. Other instructional literature went into details of carriage, household work, mourning dead in-laws, and child rearing. Models of excellent women included T'ai-jen, mother of one of the classical sages, who stressed the importance of prenatal behavior, that a mother might properly mold her child from conception, and the mother of the sage Mencius, who kept moving their household until she found a proper environment for her son. First they lived near a graveyard and the boy wanted to become an undertaker. Then they lived near a market and he wanted to become a businessman. Finally she found a house near a school, so he grew up to be a scholar.

Ideal women also tended to appear in the figure of wise queens, who were masters at indirectly reminding their husbands of their responsibilities to the people. One queen, observing that her husband spent more time making love to her than ruling the realm, publicly accused herself of stupidity and licentiousness, thereby bringing him to his senses. Often women were praised for heroic fidelity and sexual honor, such as the widow who refused to risk the compromises that going out of her house might entail and so perished in a fire. Another heroine was the young wife who refused to return to her natal home on learning her husband had leprosy. The examples of bad women tended to be either slovens who failed in their responsibilities or women who used their beauty manipulatively and so caused the downfall of rulers.

The Neo-Confucians, who attempted a new, more metaphysical synthesis after the advent of Buddhism, were if anything stricter in their ideals of wifely chastity. Perhaps because they had investigated the self quite deeply, they were more leery of relations between the sexes and sought even greater control of desire. So, for example, one Neo-Confucian held it better for a widow to starve than to remarry. Many Neo-Confucians assumed a woman would prefer suicide to rape.

TAOIST THEMES

The Confucian ideals we have just seen were bookish things, models worked out in the Confucian classics or in manuals inspired by Confucian principles. In practice many other aspects of Chinese culture—Taoist, Buddhist, and folk—impinged on how the average woman actually comported herself, treated her husband, raised her children, and interacted with her mother-in-law and neighbors. Nonetheless, Confucianism did furnish millennial China its basic social patterns, so Confucian ideals were not ineffective or innocuous. Insofar as idealistic women tried to live up to them, they certainly were a strong influence shaping Chinese women to docility.

Taoism has served Chinese culture as an alternative and complement to Confucianism. The slogan, "in office a Confucian, in retirement a Taoist," summarizes the main thrust of the two native schools. Confucianism served as the basic ideology for government, mores, and official matters. Taoism nourished the private spirit, the realms where people slipped the moorings of officialdom and thought thoughts more poetic, individual, and seditious. Both schools agreed that a Way come down from the past held the key to achieving good order in the present. But where the Confucians stressed the principles of *jen* (benevolence) and *li* (ritual) exemplified by the sages of the early historical period, the Taoists prized the impersonal, unpredictable ways of nature and the supposed simplicity of earliest times.

Taoism divides into two main parts, the philosophical school associated with such poetic thinkers as Lao Tzu and Chuang Tzu and the syncretistic religion built on both such philosophy and explorations into alchemy, meditation, and ritual. In the *Tao Te Ching*, the most honored Taoist text, femininity has a strong place in the Tao (and so approximates a philosophical Great Goddess, somewhat like the Buddhist Prajnaparamita). Thus Chapter 6 reads, "The Spirit of the Valley never dies. This is called the mysterious female. The gateway of the mysterious female is called the root of heaven and earth. Dimly visible, it seems as if it were there, yet use will never drain it."[7] The valley is a figure for the Tao, in contrast to the mountain. Where the valley lies low and is unpretentious, the mountain stands out. Lao Tzu, the legendary author of the *Tao Te Ching*, thinks that nature moves humbly, unpretentiously. To associate the spirit of the valley with the mysterious female is to put in play another set of images for the Tao. If pushed, Lao Tzu would say that the Tao of nature works more like a woman than a man. It works indirectly, subtly, as if trying to persuade rather than force. Two symbols for the Tao are a woman persuading a man to give her the fertility she seeks and an infant apparently helpless but in fact wrapping an entire household around its finger. Both employ *wu-wei*, creative not-doing or indirection. The gateway of the mysterious female is like the womb from which heaven and earth, the entire created realm, derive. The female principle, the source from which all creatures issue, seems inexhaustible. The Tao is the primordial reality, which mothers into being the ten thousand things of creation.

Many aspects of Taoist thought apparently predate both Lao Tzu and Confucius. Taoism shows affinities with Chinese shamanism, and religious Taoism frequently is virtually inseparable from popular religion: full of gods and demons. Ellen Marie Chen has speculated that the Tao had ancient ties to a mother goddess and that many of its operations are well seen as a motherly love.[8] In Chapter 62 of the *Tao Te Ching* the Way is said to embrace both good and bad, perhaps as a mother refuses to pass judgment on her children. The Taoists frequently criticized Confucian legalism as both untrue to the complexities of actual life and a decline from the simple vigor of earlier times. In this critique they seem to have found an ally in the rounder, less judgmental and legalistic intelligence attributed to women in many cultures.

In addition to the womb, the Taoists sometimes used the breast as a symbol of the influence of the Tao. The nurture of an infant at the breast became a figure for how the spirit could cling to the Tao and gain sustenance. The passivity associated with Chinese women also served Taoists well, because they felt people best flourished by seconding the initiatives of nature, by responding rather than intruding. The great trick, according to the Taoist sages, was to go with the grain, to retain the uncarved block that was basic human nature (before it had been shaped and limited by social conventions). Women generally seemed to have mastered this trick better than men, in that women were responders, discerners of the social flow, rather than aggressors or disrupters. The Taoists followed through on this real if stereotyped championing of women's ways by fighting female infanticide and arguing that the immortals (those who had gained the secrets of either the Tao or such alchemical marvels as the elixir of immortality) were not held to sexual boundaries. Chuang Tzu mentions a myth of an early matriarchy, but it is hard to know whether he intends anything historical (see *Chuang Tzu*, Chapter 29). When his own wife died he refused to mourn and exhibit the sad face prescribed by Confucian custom. She was simply returning to the Great Clod, as he called it, from which all creatures come and to which they return. For Chuang Tzu's brand of Taoism, such a cosmological bottom line relativized all pretentions, including implicitly the pretentions of men to superiority over women. On logical grounds as well, Chuang Tzu questioned many of the assumptions of the Confucians, and the entire upshot of his work was a call to put aside mental pigeonholes and see how the Tao actually worked. When one did this, one noticed that people who gained prominence seldom survived very long, while people who remained in obscurity lived long lives. It would have been completely in tune with Chuang Tzu's principles to make the further notations that women tended to live longer than men and that by social convention if not nature women chased after few of the man-made titles and honors. Women therefore frequently were good examples of Taoist wisdom.

Barbara E. Reed, studying the place of women in the history of Taoism, notes not only such themes of the early philosophers as those we have treated but also the significance of such later elements of the syntheses of the religious Taoists as yin-yang theory and shamanism. Insofar as feminine forces were accounted equiprimordial with masculine, the religious Taoists sought out the supposed feminine factor in many situations. Insofar as women traditionally had been shamanic mediums, serving the heavy Chinese traffic between the living and the dead or between the living and the gods, they were models of receptivity to divine inspiration. Religious Taoists allowed women a degree of organizational power remarkable in patriarchal China, perhaps from a sense that the ultimate powers being sought demanded strong feminine representation, as well as from a desire for male-female balance or androgyny. Individual women gained fame as Taoist masters and alchemists, which suggests that the openness to feminine participation went below official levels and actually penetrated the substance of religious practice. So, for example, Li Shao-yun, a widow in search of immortality, worked on cinnabar (mercuric sulfide), finally becoming nearly transparent from her use of this poison. Present-day shamanesses in Hong Kong, whom we might place under the general umbrella of religious Taoism, have tended to gain their facility as mediums only after they have "died" (spiritually) and so in a sense become immortals.[9]

Reed also notes that Chinese women profited from Taoist views of the body, which were sufficiently positive and feminist to dispute the widespread taboos against menstrual blood. In the blood Taoists saw power rather than **pollution**, so they made it the equivalent of male semen: the vital power whose nourishment would increase longevity. Indeed, Taoist myths of regeneration sometimes played on sexual transformation, usually in the direction of males becoming females. Women also could become Taoist adepts, supposedly capable of living on air.

BUDDHIST THEMES

Buddhism did not offer Chinese women the positive symbols of feminine nature that Taoism did, although it did bring to China such suggestive themes as the feminine character of the Prajnaparamita and the feminine persona of the goddess of mercy Kuan-yin. On the whole, however, Indian Buddhism transported to China both the second-rate status it had accorded women and its fears of the dangers women placed in the way of monks striving for enlightenment. In fact historical information about the impact of Buddhism on Chinese women is scanty, virtually nothing existing until the fourth century c.e., by which time Buddhism certainly had become a significant presence in China.

A biography of the Kashmiri monk Dharmayasas mentions a Cantonese laywoman who became his disciple around 400. Royal patronage of Buddhism in Nanjing in the fourth and fifth centuries led to mention of upper-class women who supported the new religion. Thus Empress He founded a nunnery in 354 while Empress Chu founded both nunneries and monasteries. She also kept close contact with several nuns, apparently viewing them as friends and helpful advisors. In 424 Empress Yuan invited a Kashmiri monk, Dharmamitra, to celebrate Buddhist rituals at the imperial palace. A royal concubine, Pan, used her influence to arrange the enlargement of the convent of a nun she greatly admired. And so it went: insofar as Buddhism was making inroads with the royal and upper classes, it tended to gain support for its monastic establishments, those for women as well as those for men. It appears that in the general bedazzlement with Buddhist philosophy and rituals, Chinese women who wished to pursue the religious life full time found patrons in high places.

Precisely what this impact of Buddhism meant for ordinary, lay Chinese women is hard to say. We find evidence that many Chinese men, true to Confucian sentiments, regarded the Buddhist nuns as threats to Chinese family life. Insofar as Buddhism offered women an option other than marriage, and insofar as it proffered views potentially at variance with Confucian convictions, Buddhism loomed as a disruptive force. Nonetheless, the Buddhist sangha built a firm foundation in China, so firm that nuns have existed from the middle of the fourth century down to the present day. A document detailing the lives of eminent nuns who flourished from the fourth to the sixth century furnishes a series of somewhat stylized portraits that suggest the range of activity the early Buddhist nuns achieved.

The main virtues for which the nuns were singled out were learning and prowess in meditation. Most of those eulogized came from the south of China, around the capital of Nanjing, which was probably the most cultured city of its day. The impression the portraits leave is that, far from living in retirement and solitary accomplishment, the leading nuns were influential in both politics and culture. As noted, nunneries often received royal patronage. The biographies of the eminent nuns stress their personal friendship with leading figures in the realm and the influence they wielded as advisors. In addition to offering religious instruction, usually to women but sometimes to men, they gave counsel on political matters. So, for example, Miao-yin, whom we mentioned in the chapter on Buddhism, became a close friend of the emperor and was esteemed for her learning. In the middle of the fifth-century Fa-jing, a director of the nuns' religious routines, attracted Chinese women in droves. Bao-xian, another superintendent of nuns' activities, awed many by her learning and austerity and received many gifts from fifth-century emperors.[10]

In estimating this influence, one has to realize that Buddhism could appeal to Chinese people on several levels. For educated people, it offered a philosophy more profound than what either Confucianism or Taoism had elaborated and meditation techniques much more thoroughly tested. As well, it carried the clout of a philosophy for which people were willing to give up family life and undertake impressive austerities. For the common people, Mahayana Buddhism offered a plan to improve one's state in life by improving one's karma. As well, it offered numerous rituals and devotional figures—buddhas, bodhisattvas—that held out emotional help. And to all members of Chinese society Buddhism represented especially impressive funerary rites and explanations of death. Until the great persecution of Buddhism in 845, these factors combined to make the new religion more than competitive with Confucianism and Taoism, often earning it considerable hostility.

The Chinese usually have not felt compelled to make clear-cut, either/or choices among their different religious options. Not only could one be a Confucian in office and a Taoist in retirement, one could meditate according to Buddhist principles and be buried with a Buddhist funeral. The nuns who represented the feminine side of the Sangha and Buddhist religious life therefore had a lot going for them. To Chinese women, especially, but also to Chinese men, they could bring the compassion and wisdom of the Buddha in feminine accents of sensitivity, gentleness, peace, and learning.

The ideal that Buddhism held out to the Chinese people was summarized in the bodhisattva. On the whole, the bodhisattva—the saint who was on the verge of becoming a buddha but postponed entry into nirvana to labor for the salvation of all living beings—was a figure who had transcended sex. We have seen that Buddhist texts dealing with women such as the Naga princess and Candrottara make their transformation into men the price of their entering upon buddhahood. One remarkable exception to this trend was the transformation of the bodhisattva Avalokiteshvara, who in India was male, into the goddess of mercy Kuan-yin. The bodhisattva is featured in the Lotus Sutra, where he is a powerful figure who can extinguish fires, still rivers, calm winds, free those facing execution, blind demons, free the enslaved, and disarm the enemies of his devotees.

When the *Lotus Sutra* was translated into Chinese, these attributes of Avalokiteshvara were transferred to Kuan-yin, a more motherly figure. Like him she was an assistant of Amitabha, the buddha of light who ruled the Western paradise. Known as Amida in China and Japan, this buddha became greatly beloved in several influential devotional sects. In the same way, Kuan-yin became a leading focus for East Asian devotional Buddhism. During the T'ang dynasty (seventh through tenth centuries C.E.), devotional Buddhism flourished and with it the significance of Kuan-yin. She was credited with reminding people to call on Amida, especially at the hour of death. She would convey the dead to the Western paradise. Increasingly she became associated with mercy and salvation, in contrast to the stress on wisdom and enlightenment placed by earlier Buddhism. As though people thought the times too difficult to allow them to gain enlightenment and wanted a figure willing to take them with all their warts and wrinkles, they went to Kuan-yin as to an approachable, tender-hearted mother who was bound not to refuse them.[11]

Kuan-yin continued to play a strong, even a predominant role in popular Chinese religion well into the modern era. In the nineteenth century, women of rural Canton, somewhat anticipating their urban, educated sisters who would agitate for an improvement in women's condition just before the rise of the Republic in 1912, refused to marry in numbers significant to gain widespread attention. They either never went through marriage ceremonies or extended the traditional postceremonial visit to their natal homes indefinitely, never consummating the marriage. Some formed religious sisterhoods and dedicated themselves to celibacy. Kuan-yin served them as patroness, and they developed stories that the goddess herself had been a princess who opposed her parents' wishes and became a nun. The model of Kuan-yin told the women dedicated to her that one could exist, indeed wield great power, without having to contend with a husband, a mother-in-law, and children. This Cantonese movement lasted well over a century, raising fierce opposition from Confucians.

FOLK THEMES

Long before the rise of Confucian and Taoist philosophies, the religion of the common Chinese people centered on fertility and warding off malign influences. Astrology, geomancy (*feng-shui*: the influence of wind and water), exorcism, divination, communication with the dead, and numerous ways of trying to gain good fortune all wove their way through popular religion. When Buddhism became a strong factor, Buddhist notions of karma, ghosts, bodhisattvas, heavens, and hells all enriched the prior mixture. Venerating their ancestors, trying to gain a diet in which yin and yang balanced, wearing amulets to ward off evil spirits, praying to the god of their guild or area, peasants and working-class people lived within a rich mythology. Women's special share in this common mythology was the stories, symbols, and rites that pertained to domestic matters. Pressured to become fertile mothers of children, they naturally petitioned Kuan-yin or other forces thought helpful for conception and easy childbirth. Stigmatized by menstrual blood, they naturally sought the charms and seclusions that would minimize their pollution. To safeguard their children, they erected the traditional protections against the evil eye. To help their husbands get safe passage on the sea or prosper in business, they naturally petitioned the gods thought responsible for such matters.

The Taoist contribution to this popular religious amalgamation included tales such as one about Lady Mei-ku, a third-century B.C.E. adept who was thought capable of walking on water. She drowned when her husband was enraged at her violation of a Taoist law and threw her into a lake. A shaman placed her corpse in a shrine by the lake, and twice-monthly Lady Mei-ku would appear walking on the water. In deference to her aversion to seeing animals suffer, the people banned hunting and fishing in the area.

Taoist priests generally were the prime Chinese exorcists, and in their fights against demons they would call on various military spirits for help, among them General Hsiao-lieh, a beautiful woman. She was judged to be eight feet tall, with a clear complexion and delicate eyes. Another military spirit employed in exorcisms was General Kang-Hsien, a woman far less lovely to behold. She was accounted ten feet tall, with an ugly face, yellow hair, and large, protruding teeth.

Taoist yoga sometimes sponsored intercourse along the lines of Indian tantra, urging men to draw from women the vital power associated with menstrual blood. The object of the ritual intercourse was to prolong life, and by uniting with women Taoist men thought they could increase their power beyond what semen alone could give them.[12]

The force of spirits and taboos in ordinary people's lives comes through in a story narrated by Maxine Hong Kingston. On coming of age as a girl in San Francisco, she was admonished by her mother to avoid the example of her aunt and preserve her chastity. Kingston hadn't known she had that aunt. The mother explained that the aunt had been stricken from the family line because of the shame she had brought on the family in China. The aunt's husband had been working away from home for more than a year when it became apparent the aunt was pregnant. The night after the baby was born the villagers came to her family house hooting, presenting themselves as angry spirits, and trashing the premises. The next day the aunt and the baby were found dead at the bottom of the family well. The only way the aunt could conceive of atoning for her breech of the local mores and her violation of cosmic order was to commit suicide.

Kingston's mother was a remarkable woman, able to tell such stories with full conviction yet also full of stories about her own triumph over superstition. The mother had trained as a doctor in China, at a time when Western medicine existed alongside traditional folk beliefs. She was the oldest of the trainees, so it fell to her to debunk the rumors going through the students' dormitory that several rooms were haunted by ghosts. The mother stayed up to confront the ghosts and persevered by her strength of will. Still, even in San Francisco she continued to live in a world populated by powerful spiritual foes. A brief excerpt from one of the mother's speeches that Kingston has recreated suggests both this folk mentality and the pathos of many immigrant Chinese women:

> "I didn't need muscles in China. I was small in China." She was. The silk dresses she gave me are tiny. You would not think the same person wore them. This mother can carry a hundred pounds of Texas rice up and downstairs. She could work at the laundry from 6:30 A.M. until midnight, shifting a baby from the ironing table to a shelf between packages, to the display window, where the ghosts tapped on the glass. "I put you babies in the clean places at the laundry, as far away from the germs that fumed out of the ghosts' clothes as I could. Aa, their socks and handkerchiefs choked me. I cough now because of those seventeen years of breathing dust. Tubercular handkerchiefs. Lepers' socks." I thought she had wanted to show off my baby sister in the display window.[13]

In fairy tales one catches other glimpses of the images that Chinese women, past and recent, have borne. One story tells of a young student who was reciting his lessons when a girl appeared outside his window. She praised his diligence and wafted into the room. She was extremely graceful, dainty, dressed in a green blouse and a long gown. He began to suspect she was not human. When he asked her where she came from, she put him off. They slept together that night, he marveling at the tininess of her waist. When the drums announced the end of night she fluttered away.

This became the regular nightly pattern, until an evening when he asked her to sing. She resisted, thinking that someone might overhear, but finally agreed. After she sang, melting his heart, she looked around anxiously, fearing someone had overheard. She complained of heart palpitations but the student calmed her anxieties. In the morning her anxieties returned and she begged him to see her out safely. He did, but as he returned to his room he heard an anguished cry. In the eves he found a small green bee trapped in a spider's web and on the verge of death. He rescued it and kept it on his desk for many days. When it had recovered, it dived into his inkwell, drew itself out, and walked back and forth forming the word, "thanks." It then flew out the window, and the student never saw his lover again.[14]

In folk religion lovely maidens can turn into bees and students longing for fair damsels can have their hearts broken if what they desire should come near and then disappear. The story is not profound, but it adds more shadings to the picture of feminine grace one might compose from more orthodox sources. The girl who appeared was tiny, graceful, and self-effacing, Indeed, she feared being revealed in a place she was not supposed to be, and her fear proved well founded. The message, one might say, was that women who sang out when they ought to have been quiet risked heavy losses. Even to please their men, women were not to violate prudence or seem presumptuous. Whether by the laws of karma or the instincts of peasant fear, Chinese culture implied that those who wanted too much would soon be brought low.

Last, our picture of Chinese folk religion should include a panel for the women who served their local communities as diviners and mediums. The assumption behind their work was that the dead remained close to the living for some time, before they entered their final repose. It was especially important to placate them during that time. Even later, however, they could be frustrated and want their children to do things for them (for example, send them money or food, by burning replicas). The children might sense this, have a dream that implied it, or think that the unhappiness of their deceased parents was the reason for the children's bad luck. Any of these reasons could bring them to the medium, who represented their link with the dead. Similarly, female diviners offered people a way to discern whether a choice was likely to prove lucky and so guarded them against fate.

EVERYDAY LIFE

As contemporary historians have plotted strategies for gaining a better feel for how ordinary people experienced a given epoch, they have come to scour records with an anthropologist's eye. Even prior to this recent trend, however, what we might call classical scholars of Chinese civilization often so immersed themselves in the details of a particular era that they came away able to communicate many of the concrete aspects that bring a period alive. So, for example, the French sinologist Jacques Gernet wrote about Chinese life in the mid-thirteenth century c.e., on the eve of the Mongol invasions, treating of the capital city of Hangchow; of the social stratifications; of housing, clothing, and cooking; of the life cycle; of the seasonal celebrations; and of leisure pursuits. His most extended treatment of women occurs in his discussion of the life cycle, for the Chinese of that period, as of most periods, largely associated women with marriage and family life.

There were exceptions to such a domestic definition of women, however, and we can profitably note two that Gernet mentions. Although literature ordinarily did not feature prominently in women's education, occasionally a woman would become recognized as a leading poet. For example, in the period prior to that Gernet was studying, Li Ch'ing-chao (1081–1140) had established herself as one of the greatest poets of the Sung dynasty. Long before her, a little girl of seven, famous locally as a prodigy, had been summoned to the court of the Empress Wu Tse-t'ien (685–704), commanded to improvise a poem on the theme of saying good-bye to her brothers, and produced the following little gem: "In the pavilion of separation, the leaves suddenly blew away. On the road of farewell, the clouds lifted all of a sudden. Ah! How I regret that men are not like the wild geese, who go on their way together."[15] Gernet goes on to suggest that this child prodigy was the exception that proved the rule. Generally women received only a very practical education in spinning and domestic crafts. Only lower-class women had anything like professions, and they tended to be menial.

Most of what we have sketched as the Confucian pattern for marriage and family life continued to obtain in the thirteenth century. Marriage was a liaison between two families, often arranged as much for the benefit of the families as for the good of the bride and groom. Indeed, in some regions of north China in the twelfth century children who had died young would be "married" at the time they would have come of age, to allow the families to gain the closer relationship marriage afforded them. Another story illustrating the manipulation by families tells of a young scholar who emerged from the official examinations at the top of the list and immediately was kidnapped. His captors took him to the house of a wealthy family, where a large gathering of people watched a beautifully clad young woman approach him, say that she wished to become his wife, and ask for his consent. He replied that he considered this a great honor, but perhaps she would grant him permission to consult with the wife he already had, to see how they should regard the proposition. Obviously, in planning to get a desirable young man for their daughter, the wealthy family had skimped on their homework.

To arrange a marriage, people called upon women who acted as matchmakers. One of the first parts of the negotiation was to take the date of birth of the prospective bride to a soothsayer, who would decide whether her marriage to the prospective groom would be auspicious. To marry a person whose birth date was in astrological conflict with one's own was to court disaster. Similarly, one had to marry on an auspicious day, when the planets and other forces were aligned in one's favor. As negotiations progressed, the matchmakers ferried back and forth such information as the posts the men of the families had held during the past three generations, where the prospective bridegroom stood among his siblings, and what property he would receive on the occasion of his wedding. For the prospective bride the relevant information included her place among the family's children, the dowry she would bring, and her personal property. A ceremony of cups was the decisive factor in sealing the agreement. The family of the bride would visit the family of the groom. The prospective groom would drink four cups of rice wine and the prospective bride would drink two, showing that he would bring to the marriage the strong constitution and she the weak (or the temperate). Sometimes the decision whether the prospective bride was acceptable was left to the prospective groom, who signaled his agreement by sticking two hairpins in her chignon. Other times the man's family employed a physiognomist, who examined the woman's face and judged whether the marriage was likely to prove favored.

Although official morals in the capital city in the thirteenth century continued to be as strict about the chastity of wives as the Confucian ideals we have previously sketched, then contemporary sources suggest that in fact things often were considerably looser. So, for example, Gernet cites an author who claimed that wives in the capital sometimes were so flirtatious and greedy that poor husbands, unable to satisfy their wives' demands for ornamentation, would close their eyes to the wives' having numerous lovers. The same source claimed that when such women lived near Buddhist monasteries, they might take several monks as lovers.[16] Gernet adds, however, that such behavior would not have been tolerated in the upper classes. In other words, social level often had a lot to do with behavioral standards.

Upper-class wives of the period lived leisurely, spending much time on their toilet, on supervising the servants, and on parlor games. Wives of merchants often took an active part in running the business and waiting on customers. Occasionally middle- or lower-class women managed restaurants on their own. The other principal professions for women were to be midwives, nurses, matchmakers, or domestic servants.

We get a sense of relations between the sexes in the love poetry handed down from the T'an and Sung dynasties. One popular theme was love at first sight, and two stock female types were the femme fatale and the coquette. Both usually were portrayed as leading men, and even kingdoms, to perdition. Still, the tone of such affairs remained impersonal, and they seldom threatened the clearly superior love of faithful spouses. So strong was the sense of duty inculcated by Confucian mores, and so influential were the considerations of shaming one's family, that raw passion had relatively little space in which to cavort. In both the T'ang and the Sung dynasties the ideal of feminine beauty hymned in such poetry, and so bruited about as most desirable, was quite elaborate. The typical T'ang beauty was adorned with fine clothing and was stately, her hair piled high on her head. Under the Sung this ideal shifted toward the slender, petite wisp of a woman we have seen in Maxine Hong Kingston's mother's memories and the fairy tale about the student and the bee-sprite.

A last feature of everyday life in medieval China was footbinding. Gernet suggests that it did not appear in China before the tenth century and probably was not much practiced in thirteenth-century Hangchow.

The purpose was to produce tiny feet and a mincing gait, both of which fit the ideal of daintiness developed in Sung times. He also suggests that women destined for the "gay life" (not homosexuality but entertainment, hospitality, and sometimes prostitution) where men took recreation would have their feet bound. Mary Daly, powered by a fierce anger at the ways men have deformed women, takes a much grimmer view. She lists Chinese footbinding alongside Indian suttee, African clitoridectomy, and Christian witch burning as a major abuse of women. When one considers what actually happened to the feet that were bound—they tended to become extremely painful rotten stumps—one is inclined to agree. Even if only a small percentage of Chinese women suffered that fate, it was outrageous evidence of the inhumanity of Chinese men.[17]

RECENT DEVELOPMENTS

The constriction of women's lives that Confucian ideals produced continued in force until the Communist takeover of 1949. Indeed, it seems clear that even today many aspects of traditional Chinese family life remain much what they were hundreds of years ago. Religiously, the blend of folk, Buddhist, and Taoist elements that we have seen also continued until the victory of Mao Tse-tung, as did the ritualistic aspects of Confucianism (veneration of the ancestors, sacrifices at government occasions, reverence for Confucius and other great scholars, living as well as dead), C. K. Yang's sociological study of Chinese religion suggests the main patterns that have obtained through the centuries, and an anecdote he offers exemplifies how the advent of new laws and practices under the Communists by no means overthrew the millennial traditions:

> When a widow in Shanghai tried to remarry in 1951 under the Communist new Marriage Law, her mother-in-law told her: "Widowhood is your fate and the best thing for you is to observe the moral rules of widowhood . . . and be pious to the spirits and gods so that you will be reborn into a beautiful life in your next existence."[18]

This advice blends Confucian instincts about widowhood with Buddhist ideas about karma (fate) and rebirth in the way that had shaped most Chinese lives for at least a dozen centuries.

The Communist movement that came to full power in 1949 was part of a broader modernization that had stirred China, keeping it in an ongoing state of revolution from 1895. Western ideas had penetrated the intelligentsia, and with those ideas came a growing demand for reforms in education, politics, and social structures. Chinese aware of movements in the rest of the world felt humiliated at what they considered China's backwardness. Thus the motives of a Mao Tse-tung included a strong desire to enable China again to hold its head up in the world community.

As Jonathan D. Spence's study of this period shows, many women played leading roles in the modernization of China, and many of the men who spearheaded the new thinking took women's equality with men as a key plank in the new social platform China needed. Thus Kang Youwei, influenced by the example of his widowed mother struggling to care for their family, and by the dismal fate of his three sisters, two of whom became widowed while young and suffered miserably, considered women's equality of paramount importance. He fought to end footbinding and refused to let his own daughters be bound.[19]

The problem with opposing footbinding was that it could reduce a girl's marital prospects. Yet Qui Jin, a leading feminist essayist, felt strongly that abolishing footbinding was a key to women's liberation. Apparently her feet had been bound when she was a child and she had unbound them herself. She thought that as long as women hobbled around on three inch feet, they would never contribute to the revolution she was promoting, seize their own freedom, or live up to the models of heroic Chinese women of the past, whose memory she tried to resurrect. She also opposed arranged marriages, supported the increased educational opportunities for women that were developing, and finally left the no-good husband who had been arranged for her. In the early twentieth century she was the animating force behind a women's journal published in Shanghai, and her poems capture the welter of emotions—literary and political, feminist and revolutionary—that jostled intellectual women of her day.

This ferment among intellectuals soon worked its way down into the ranks of ordinary women. For example, in August 1922 women in Shanghai created the first strike by industrial women in Chinese history. They were silk workers protesting their working conditions: standing over vats of boiling water in the summer heat and receiving only forty cents for their thirteen-hour workdays. Several thousand of them responded to organizing initiatives of Chinese Communists and refused to work until they got better conditions. The Communists were active in other industries, organizing seamen, dockworkers, miners, and other laboring men into unions. By this inclusion of female workers, they gave their slogans about women's equality flesh and nerve.

On the other side of the political spectrum, women such as the Soong Sisters, Mayling and Chingling, participated in the ferment of the years 1911 through 1936 as wives of the two revolutionary leaders Sun Yat-sen and Chiang Kai-shek. The sisters were the daughters of a Chinese Christian educated in the United States for work as a Methodist missionary. He sent them to Wesleyan College in Georgia, and throughout their careers in China they drew on their facility in English and their American contacts. One sister became quite enamored of Communist ideas, much to the irritation of her brother-in-law Chiang Kai-shek, who was fighting the Communists for control of postimperial China. But both were formidable women, moving with a freedom and exerting an influence rarely possible before their time.[20]

When the Communists gained power they moved quickly to put their ideas into effect. Among the first reforms targeted by new laws were those concerning land and marriages. Thus the comprehensive Marriage Law of 1950 freed women from arranged marriages, allowed women to take the initiative in obtaining divorce, and protected children from both infanticide and being sold. Within a year of its enactment, more than one million Chinese women had obtained divorces. Women also played an important role in land reform, all the more so in areas where men were away fighting the war in Korea.

The Communist regime did not, of course, create a utopia for women. The story of Fu Yueha can indicate the problems that remained and the reasons why Chinese feminists charged that the Party was not advancing the cause of women as it had originally promised to do. In 1971 Fu Yueha was separated from her husband because of job assignments meted out to the two by the state. In 1972 the head of her unit in the construction company where she was working made sexual advances and when she refused threatened to accuse her of being a counterrevolutionary. Subsequently he raped her. She left her job, was unable to get the references necessary to obtain a new job, and suffered both mental breakdown and severe poverty. When she brought charges of rape against her former superior, they were thrown out of court. By 1979 she had been sufficiently radicalized to have become a liaison worker organizing peasants around Beijing who were protesting their low standard of living. She was arrested in a demonstration, and after a year of investigations and trials was sentenced to a year in prison for libeling her former boss and disrupting the public order. The judge passing sentence referred to her as morally degenerate.[21]

Thus women who wanted the equality, and the protection from abuses such as rape, held out by the Communist revolutionaries often found themselves of several minds. Thirty years after the Communist takeover all was far from well, and the throes of the cultural revolution Mao had inspired to try to restore the original Communist fervor, as well as the struggles that followed the death of Mao in 1976, had tossed women to and fro.[22] Mao's widow, Jiang Qing, was arrested as one of the Gang of Four responsible for the mistaken cultural revolution and convicted of treason in 1981. A new Party constitution in 1982 broke with Maoist radicalism, but student demonstrations have continued in recent years, as China has struggled to develop a new generation of leaders capable of dealing with both their own country and the world in definitely post-Maoist terms. Women seem to have participated willingly in the campaigns to limit the birth rate (by 1986 China had reached the replacement rate of 2.1 children per woman and Chinese women had the highest use of contraceptives in the world)[23] and in China's industrial, economic, and technological advances. Precisely what conflicts they have suffered from shifts away from their traditional roles is hard to say. Perhaps often they have simply updated old skills, as they did when the Communist era first began.[24]

DISCUSSION QUESTIONS

1.   What are some of the indirect sources of power that Chinese women traditionally have tapped?

2.   What was the significance for most women of the Confucian notion that reverence for parents was a child's first obligation?

3.   Why did the classical Taoists associate the Way of Nature with femininity?

4.   How has Kuan-yin functioned as a source of Chinese women's comfort and strength?

5.   How did the bee-spirit of the fairy tale exemplify Chinese notions of feminity?

6.   What does the range of professions open to medieval Chinese women suggest about the average woman's everyday life?

7.   How did footbinding epitomize the status of women that feminist revolutionaries wanted to change?

NOTES

[1]See *1987 Britannica Book of the Year* (Chicago: Encyclopaedia Britannica, 1987), pp. 622, 697, 744.

[2]See Marcel Granet, *The Religion of the Chinese People* (New York: Harper Torchbooks, 1977), pp. 50 ff.; and Mircea Eliade, *A History of Religious Ideas*, Vol. 2 (Chicago: University of Chicago Press, 1982), pp. 11–12.

[3]See Daniel L. Overmyer, "Chinese Religion: An Overview," and Alvin P. Cohen, "Chinese Religion: Popular Religion," in *The Encyclopedia of Religion*, Vol. 3, ed. Mircea Eliade (New York: Macmillan, 1987), pp. 257–289 and 289–296.

[4]See Stevan Harrell, "Domestic Observances: Chinese Practices," in *The Encyclopedia of Religion*, Vol. 4, pp. 410–414.

[5]Richard Guisso, "Thunder over the Lake: The Five Classics and the Perception of Women in Early China," in *Women in China*, ed. Guisso and Johannesen (New York: Philo, 1981), p. 59.

[6]See Theresa Kelliher, "Confucianism," in *Women in World Religions*, ed. Arvind Sharma (Albany: State University of New York Press, 1987), p. 143. I have found this chapter a fine summary of the Confucian themes.

[7]D. C. Lau, trans., *Lao Tzu: Tao Te Ching* (New York: Penguin, 1963), p. 62.

[8]See Ellen Marie Chen, "Nothingness and the Mother Principle in Early Chinese Taoism," *International Philosophical Quarterly*, 9 (1969), pp. 391–405, and "Tao as the Great Mother and the Influence of Motherly Love in the Shaping of Chinese Philosophy," *History of Religions*, 14 no. 1 (August 1974), pp. 51–64.

[9]See Barbara E. Reed, "Taoism," in *Women in World Religions*, p. 170.

[10]See Nancy Schuster, "Striking a Balance: Women and Images of Women in Early Chinese Buddhism," in *Women, Religion and Social Change*, ed. Yvonne Yazbeck Haddad and Ellison Findly Banks (Albany: State University of New York Press, 1985), pp. 87–112.

[11]See Diana Paul, "Kuan-yin: Savior and Savioress in Chinese Pure Land Buddhism," in *The Book of the Goddess Past and Present*, ed. Carl Olson (New York: Crossroad, 1983), pp. 161–175.

[12]See Reed, "Taoism," p. 175.

[13]Maxine Hong Kingston, *The Woman Warrior: Memoirs of a Girlhood Among Ghosts* (New York: Alfred A. Knopf, 1977), pp. 104–105.

[14]See Moss Roberts, trans. and ed., *Chinese Fairy Tales and Fantasies* (New York: Pantheon, 1979), pp. 17–18.

[15]Jacques Gernet, *Daily Life in China on the Eve of the Mongol Invasion 1250–1276* (Stanford, Calif.: Stanford University Press, 1970), p. 157.

[16]Ibid., p. 164.

[17]In addition to Mary Daly, *Gynecology* (Boston: Beacon, 1978), see Maxine Hong Kingston, *China Men* (New York: Alfred A. Knopf, 1980), pp. 3–5.

[18]C. K. Yang, *Religion in Chinese Society* (Berkeley: University of California Press, 1970), p. 56.

[19]See Jonathan D. Spence, *The Gate of Heavenly Peace: The Chinese and Their Revolution 1895–1980* (New York: Viking, 1981), p. 39.

[20]See Michael E. Lestz, "The Soong Sisters and China's Revolutions 1911–1936," in *Women, Religion and Social Change*, pp. 377–394.

[21]See Jonathan D. Spence, *The Gate of Heavenly Peace*, pp. 366–368.

[22]For a literary interpretation, see Chen Jo-hsi, *The Execution of Mayor Yin and Other Stories from the Great Proletarian Cultural Revolution* (Bloomington: Indiana University Press, 1978).

[23]See *1987 Britannica Book of the Year*, p. 319.

[24]See Margery Wolf, "Chinese Women: Old Skills in a New Context," in *Women, Culture and Society*, ed. M. Z. Rosaldo and L. Lamphere (Stanford, Calif: Stanford University Press, 1974), pp. 157–172.

CHAPTER SIX

Japanese Women

TRADITIONAL BACKGROUND

Since the third century C.E., Japanese religion has been strongly influenced by Chinese culture, which exported Confucian, Taoist, and Buddhist ideas. Thus Japanese women have long lived in family structures where males predominated and the care of one's elders was one's first responsibility. As well, their religious culture has had symbols for ultimate reality (the Tao, the buddhanature) which carried feminine overtones. Nonetheless, the native Japanese culture, which on the occasion of contact with Chinese notions became articulated as Shinto, shifted all the ideas received from China and brought them into a distinctively Japanese framework.

The origins of Shinto lie in the paleolithic era, between ten and thirty thousand years ago, when there were land passages from the continent to the Japanese islands. In the earliest period people lived by hunting and gathering, so the likelihood is that women worked as gatherers, herbalists, and the prime custodians of children. Remains from the oldest archeological period, the Jomon, which lasted from about 4000 B.C.E. to 250 B.C.E., suggest a primary concern for fertility. Figurines of women with swollen breasts, extended abdomens, and ghostlike heads may relate to ancient folk beliefs about the function of mountains in human birth or rebirth, because traditionally such figurines have been called *yamagata* (mountainlike). Folktales tell of a divine mother of the mountain who would guide travelers, assist hunters, and appear in the guise of a poor maiden. Once she appeared with a newborn child to two brothers who were hunting. One rejected her plea for food, because he feared becoming polluted by contact with blood (birth). The other gave her his lunch and received a handsome reward. In much later times, ascetics sometimes would retire to the mountains for shamanistic trials and a ritual rebirth that entailed entering a great womb—a hall hung with red and white cloths representing the blood vessels of the Great Mother. At the end of the ritual they would race down the mountain emitting loud cries like an infant's first screams.

During the Yayoi period, from about 250 B.C.E. to 250 C.E., more than one hundred states arose in Japan, most acknowledging an hereditary ruler located in Yamatai. In Chinese records dealing with the second half of the second century C.E., an unmarried shamaness named Pimiko or Himiko became queen and settled the prior political turmoil. She was renowned for her magical skills, lived in seclusion, was attended by more than a thousand female servants, and would transmit her instructions to the people through a single male servant. At her death the people built a great grave mound and dispatched more than one hundred servants to follow her to the next world. The king who succeeded Pimiko was unable to keep order, so Iyo, a girl of thirteen, became queen and restored the peace.

The aunt of an early emperor gained great influence because she was possessed by a kami who revealed the cause of the epidemic that was killing half the population. She prophesied an uprising, as well, by interpreting the strange songs of a female ecstatic. The legends about her culminate in the somewhat archetypal story of the curious wife and her divine spouse. Ordinarily her spouse (*kami*) would only visit at night, but one time she persuaded him to stay until dawn, so that she might finally see him. When she discovered that he was a small golden snake, she was filled with remorse, stabbed herself in the pudenda with a chopstick, and died. He slunk back to his mountain throne, accusing her of having shamed him by her lack of restraint. Other queens, such as Empress Jingu, whose reign was a turning point in the economic and cultural development of ancient Japan, were more than curious ecstatics (or grist for a Freudian mill). They were strong and effective, if undeniably charismatic rulers, and some Shinto priests to this day count them among their semidivine ancestors.

The early shamanesses played an important cultural role, too, because, like women still found in remote villages today, they expressed their seizures by the kami in poetry. Many of the early Japanese poems were written by women, and their quality suggests that these women must have been well educated. Also, the themes of this poetry—lamenting the death of a brother or husband, praising the beauty of nature, or the ecstasy of love—suggest that the authors had a good range of human experience on which to draw. This changed, following the first serious contacts with China, for the Japanese were so impressed by Chinese culture that they took to Confucian ethics wholeheartedly. This, in turn, led to a depreciation of women, and by the second half of the eighth century, it was thought unseemly for women to rule. From that time, only severe crises opened political influence to women for brief periods, and by the fifteenth century, women had largely lost all their civil rights.

Much of this change in women's status is reflected in literature depicting two medieval views—that of the court lady, and that of the ideal female *samurai* (warrior-knight). Court ladies of the Heian era, Japan's golden age, epitomized elegance and romance. In addition, many of them were gifted writers, for the sophisticated literature of this period (tenth and eleventh centuries) was almost entirely the work of women. The reason for this, ironically, is that men largely limited themselves to clumsy imitations of Chinese models (women were thought incapable of mastering Chinese). From the court ladies' voluminous diaries there emerges a picture of the aristocratic beauty—face powdered white, thick artificial eyebrows painted high on her forehead, teeth blackened, and thick glossy black hair reaching to the floor. Supposedly, court women were kept in seclusion, but the diaries are replete with intrigue and nighttime trysts. In *The Tale of Genji* by Lady Murasaki, which may be the world's first novel, the picture is much the same—ladies were at the center of the mannered, erotic court life.

There is more complexity in the upper-class woman of classical times than we may have indicated so far, however, because her wine parties, poetry readings, and seemingly endless round of flirtations are offset, or perhaps framed in quite a different context, by the insights the diaries afford into the transitoriness of life. No doubt Buddhist teachings had left a mark there, but, whatever the source, it is clear that many of the court ladies knew that their *dolce vita* had more than a few hollow spots.

Upper-class life, then, tended to push Japanese women to channel their creative energies into art. Cut off from political power, and too leisured to find motherhood all-absorbing, they contributed strongly to Japanese aesthetics. It is perhaps strange that the official histories of the Japanese line (chronicles assembling the traditional mythology, in order to enhance the ruling family and prove that Japanese culture was as venerable as Chinese) should have given women stronger, or at least more political, role models. Written in the early eighth century, these accounts begin with creation myths in which a divine primal couple give birth to the Japanese islands, and to Amaterasu, the sun goddess. She, in turn, becomes the divine ancestress of the imperial family, which makes Japan singular, if not unique—a land thinking itself directly descended from a goddess. The early queens clearly reflected Amaterasu's aura, and the Shinto emblems of royal power related later kings to her patronage. It is true that the myths display seeds of later sexism (when the first couple produces a defective offspring, it is because she violated proper protocol: "It is not proper for the woman to speak first"), but they more powerfully reveal that women's circumscription in classical times was a fall from their early proximity to divinity and power.

By the twelfth century, the Heian golden age had degenerated into internecine warfare, giving prominence to local lords and the samurai who lived and died for those lords' glory. For close to seven hundred years, such militaristic feudalism dominated Japanese culture. The samurai mentality was fertile soil for Confucian obsession with hierarchy, rank, and protocol, and from this interaction there evolved the unwritten code known as *Bushido* or "the way of the warrior." Significantly, the Japanese liege-warriors who followed bushido did not, like their medieval European counterparts, link chivalry with an ideal glorification of women, often quite unpracticed. The samurai were too single-minded for that, tunneling in at terrorizing the enemy with shouts of their own exploits and those of their famous ancestors. In addition, the samurai were annealed to absolute loyalty to their lords and brother warriors, which rendered them largely unable to relate to women.

The curious result was that the bushido ideal for women made them a blend of amazon and domestic slave. First, they were urged to overcome female frailty and match males' fortitude. Many young girls were trained to repress their emotions and steel themselves for the possibility of using the dagger each was given when she acceded to womanhood. The occasions for such suicide seem to have abounded. Chief among them were threats to chastity. Indeed, the manuals dryly discourse on teaching girls the proper point at the throat for inserting the sword, and then on how, after insertion, to tie one's lower limbs together so as to be modest even in death. Another occasion for suicide was finding that a samurai warrior's love for her was threatening his loyalty to his lord. In one cautionary tale, the young maiden disfigures herself (an intermediate step, we might say), so as to bring her young man to his senses. In another, a young wife, having heard that affection for their spouses had kept some warriors from fighting unto death, wrote to her husband that she was freeing him to give his all for his lord in an upcoming battle, by killing herself right now. A third story indicates another occasion when honor might demand suicide by samurai women. Compromised by a powerful noble, one Lady Kesa promised to submit to his advances if he killed her samurai husband. He agreed, and she told him to steal into her bedchamber and kill the sleeper who had wet hair. Then she made sure that her husband drank enough to sleep soundly, washed her hair, and lay calmly awaiting her fate.

Second, the bushido woman's fortitude largely went into serving her lord. She annihilated herself for her husband, as he annihilated himself for his lord. On the battlefield women were worthless, but in the home their martial discipline was glorious. Lady Kumano, for instance, left alone with two young sons while her husband was away at war, went to the extreme of killing them (after due explanation) in order to preserve the household from the stain of her being violated by the approaching enemy. The sons understood, said goodbye to their absent father and deceased ancestors, and were dispatched by her motherly sword. Then, assisted by a faithful retainer, she herself fell upon the suicide sword.

Bushido stoicism has shaped the Japanese well into the twentieth century, being a part of the explanation of *kami-kaze* (gods' wind) pilots in World War II. Suicides by such prominent writers as Kawabata and Mishima also depend on a bushido background for their explanation. While Confucianism underlay bushido ideals, Zen Buddhism often furnished the self-control to live them out. Zen masters, from the thirteenth century on, taught Japanese that enlightenment comes through *zazen*, the meditation or mind-body discipline that brings a person into total oneness. As this discipline and oneness influenced the tea ceremony and flower arrangement, so too it influenced the martial arts. Understandably, discipline for women related them more to aesthetics than to warfare, but behind the selfless, effaced Japanese wife and mother of even the present, lies the code and religious philosophy that also gave rise to swordsmanship and archery.

Religiously, rural Japan has never lost the presence and impact of shamanesses. Working with a blend of folk beliefs, Shinto, and Buddhism, these women have continued to function as mediums and diviners—for instance, in the Buddhist exorcism rites. Traditionally, the shamanesses tended to travel in bands of five or six, walking a regular round of villages. They would tell fortunes, pray for the sick, contact the dead, purify homes, and so on. The bands no longer travel, in part because the authorities, who always resented them, and often defamed them as prostitutes, finally tended to prevail, but many remote areas still have their practicing shamaness. In the Tohoku area of Honshu, for instance, blind girls are still regularly apprenticed to shamanesses for three to five years training, to learn the arts of trance, divination, and contacting the spirit world, as well as to learn traditional ballads and folklore. After an initiatory rite which has a marked death-resurrection motif, they will graduate and begin their practice. In fact, they may even become not general practitioners, but specialists—experts at contacting the newly dead, and thus consoling the mourning, for instance.

Over the centuries, this shamanistic tradition, which is largely a rural phenomenon now, has had great cultural impact, for the wandering bands seem to have created or developed such arts as ballad singing, poetry recitation, and even religious painting. These arts were originally for the purpose of teaching the people their folk traditions, but they have been linked to such institutions as the Kabuki theater and the Bunraku and Joruri puppet shows. There is more than a little irony here, for classical Japanese theater barred women from the stage.

Female shamanism lingers on, if transformed, in the women who have functioned importantly in the rise of several of Japan's "new religions." These religions have blossomed since World War II, although they have roots in the first contacts with modernity, and they pivot on charismatic leaders with messianic claims. Usually the leaders—many of them women—have suffered great physical or emotional trauma that has been healed by a religious vision. Their new groups are organizations designed to help others share in such vision, healing, and peace. After the war, the situation was so depressed, psychologically, that millions took to the new religions' messages. Some of the prominent women have been credible holy people, a few have been social reformers, others have been charlatans, but all have owed not a little of their effectiveness to the tradition that women often have special access to the kami.

Overall and summarily, however, Japanese women have been expected not to upset male predominance. During the U.S. occupation, a man who had an assertive wife might well hear, "Poor fellow. He married a MacArthur." I do not know what the equivalent would be today, but it is clear that the shamaness's powerful, respected sister is hard to find on the streets of contemporary Tokyo.[1]

Females also played important roles in Japanese mythology, which formed the minds and religious practices of the common people. Among the deities figuring in Japanese folk religion were Ugatama, the *kami* (divine force or spirit) caring for food and clothing, and Ame no Uzume, a goddess who regularly brought the sun back to the darkened world by exposing her genitals in an ecstatic dance. The imperial Shinto shrine at Ise, which dates to the year 5 C.E., was dedicated to the sun goddess Amaterasu. In one story about her conflicts with the wind god, Susanoo, we read that he broke the irrigation ditches she had set up in the imperial rice field, flayed a piebald colt and threw it into the imperial hall, and completed his little brotherly antics by stealing into the hall and excreting on the goddess's imperial throne. Unaware, she went straight to the throne and sat down. Then, as the text respectfully puts it, "the Sun Goddess drew herself up and was sickened."[2]

SHINTO MYTHOLOGY

In the Shinto chronicles that collected the native Japanese myths, we find tales of a food goddess, ritually slain so that the vegetative cycles might go forward, which may go back to the earliest period of cultivation, the Yayoi. During the Nara period (710–794), the emperor became considered the incarnation of Amaterasu, whose myths were contained in the chronicles composed in that period. The primal human couple, Izanagi and Izanami, also appear in the chronicles, after seven generations of male and female deities. The story of their interaction is amusing. First, they agree that it would be good to join the "excess" of Izanagi to the "deficiency" of Izanami. Then they walk around the cosmic pillar (the connection between earth and heaven) but because Izanami speaks first, Izanagi is upset and their first child is defective. Women are not to take the initiative. The couple are responsible for the production of the earth (they stir the ocean waters with a jeweled spear). When they get themselves rightly ordered, their intercourse produces the Japanese islands as their offspring, as well as the various nature deities. In giving birth to the god of fire, Izanami is burned to death and Izanagi must follower her to the underworld and beg her to return. When he disobeys the conditions she sets and sees her putrified and full of worms, she chases him up to the door separating the underworld and the upper world, where they swear a divorce. Thereafter he rules the land of the living and she rules the land of the dead. According to one chronicle such deities as Amaterasu then were born from Izanagi. According to another, Izanagi and Izanami had begotten them together. Several myths concerning Amaterasu and other female deities repeat the theme of male deities breaking injunctions not to look at females (for example, at the daughter of the dragon king in childbirth, when she would turn into a dragon).

The Shinto mythology suggests some of the subterranean features of the Japanese psyche that influenced the perception of women throughout the millennia. Women were associated with blood, and so were tabooed during menstruation and childbirth. In the figure of Izanami, they could be associated with death, another major source of pollution. On the other hand, the shamanic capacities of women tended to present them in a positive religious light. When it came to serving as mediums for contact with the dead (Japan venerated ancestors much as China did), or as healers, women were the main recourse, especially in rural villages. The shamanesses who were most esteemed had undergone severe training, including techniques for going into trance.[3]

In later sections we shall deal more fully with relations between the sexes, the images of women in Japanese culture, and such phenomena as the geisha. Here it remains to summarize by suggesting that Japanese women, like women in most other cultures, have tended to concentrate on the domestic sphere. Japan developed codes for women's chastity much like those developed in Confucian and Neo-Confucian China. Such arts as the tea ceremony and floral arrangement placed women in the role of embodying refinement and grace. Indeed, the strong aesthetic component in Japanese religion has meant a place for feminine delicacy as well as male starkness and discipline. Still, the ideal Japanese woman has been a model of devotion to her husband and her children. She had entered a marriage arranged by her parents and thought homemaking her prime function. Traditionally, only peasant and trading-class women worked alongside men.[4]

STATUS AND IMAGE

In her helpful study of Japanese society, Chie Nakane stresses that the key ingredient in traditional Japanese social relations has been status:

> Age and sex are superseded by status. For example, the head of a household, regardless of age, occupies the highest seat. Age will become a deciding factor only among persons of similar status. Status also precedes sex. It is well known that Japanese women are nearly always ranked as inferiors; this is not because their sex is considered inferior, but because women seldom hold higher social status. Difference of sex will never be so pronounced in Japanese thinking as in America, where classification (though not for purposes of establishing rank) is primarily by sex. I am convinced that in American society sex-consciousness predominates over status-consciousness, the exact opposite of Japan.[5]

Further questions remain, of course, including why Japanese women seldom hold high social status. If sex is not the basis for entry into the positions that give high status, why do so few women hold them? Is it not likely that being female has usually meant not being eligible for high-status positions?

In Japanese society, rank functions everywhere. One who is the superior at work is also the superior when met in private life. Even at ordinary meals at home the mistress of the household is expected to serve the bowls of rice to people in the order of their rank, from highest to lowest: head of the household, his successor (son or son-in-law), other sons, and then daughters in order of seniority. Last come the mistress of the household and the wife of the successor of the head of the household. Wives and daughters-in-law who have come into a family system (*ie*) from outside through marriage are more important than sisters and daughters who have married and moved away. Generally, kinship has only limited importance. Thus siblings living in different family systems have few obligations toward one another: seasonal greetings and gifts, attendance at weddings and funerals. Only if financial need is great would one sibling expect aid from another. It is not uncommon for siblings to differ greatly in rank: a brother a prosperous lawyer and a sister a poor domestic servant. Neighbors tend to be considered more important than relatives outside the immediate family system and living apart.

New brides join the family system of their husbands and, like Hindu and Chinese brides, often have to cope with formidable mothers-in-law.

The Japanese ideal of marriage has the husband leading and the wife obeying. The two should be one flesh, which mainly means wives are not to disagree with their husbands publicly. Similarly, the head of the family system expects all members to share his opinions and so produce a united front. Employers in Japanese firms have tended to extend this pattern to their employees, expecting to have a say in their personal lives and to receive complete support. Loyalty like that a wife gives her husband is the ideal. Rank also shapes women's interactions, because they tend to treat one another according to the status of their husbands or the heads of their households. Nakane notes that Japan has had no story of love between a man and a woman comparable to the tale of the Forty-seven Ronin (samuri warriors), a group famous for their loyalty to their leader:

> In traditional morals the ideal man should not be involved with a woman. I think that if he were involved to such an extent in this kind of man-to-man relation [the Forty-seven] there would seem to be no necessity for a love affair with a woman. His emotion would be completely expended in his devotion to his master. I suspect this was the real nature of Samurai [warrior] mentality, and to a certain extent the same may be true of the modern Japanese man.[6]

An extension of this traditional male bonding occurs when modern Japanese men recreate in bars. Their main release comes from drinking with trusted friends, with whom they can let off steam. They may also talk out their troubles with bar madams and bar girls, a large part of whose function is to listen patiently and supportively. Wives are excluded from these sessions, and while wives may have friendships with neighbors, these rarely develop into family-to-family friendships. Consequently, wives tend to be isolated and to concentrate on their children. Despite some pressures on husbands to return home directly from work at night and spend Sunday with their families, the family usually consists of the mother and children, to whom the husband is an attachment. Even though many modern Japanese live in nuclear families, the old concept of the family system (the extended *ie*) means a tendency among husbands to think of the whole household rather than the personal qualities of their wives and children. The more men advance in their careers, the less time they spend at home. Japanese women therefore function more as mothers than as wives. Family relations now tend to be stronger with relatives on the wife's side of the family than the husband's, no doubt because she cultivates that side.

Lest this sketch of the sociological structures in which Japanese women find themselves imply that interactions between husbands and wives are only functional, let us consider the following exchange between a husband, Oki, and his wife Fumiko, who figure in a novel by the Nobel laureate Yasunari Kawabata. Oki is a novelist who has written about his extramarital love affair with a sixteen-year-old girl. Admittedly the conversation he and Fumiko, to whom he has revealed the illicit relationship by having her type the manuscript of the novel, have is private—not the sort of thing that need disrupt the faces they show the outside world. Still, it suggests what one expects: at some level Japanese men and women do contend with one another as distinct individuals of different sexes. Fumiko begins:

> "Thanks to your novel I've come to understand Otoko [the sixteen-year-old girl] very well. As much as I've suffered from it, I can see that meeting her was a good thing for you." "Didn't I tell you she's idealized?" "I know. There aren't any lovely girls exactly like that. But I wish you'd written more about me! I wouldn't care if I'd come out a horrible, jealous shrew." Oki found it hard to reply. "You were never that." "You didn't know what was in my heart." "I wasn't willing to expose all our family secrets." "No, you were so wrapped up in that little Otoko you only wanted to write about her! I suppose you thought I would soil her beauty and dirty up your novel. But does a novel have to be so pretty?" Even his reluctance to describe his wife's jealous rage had invited a new outburst of jealousy. Not that he had omitted it altogether. Indeed, to have written so concisely of it might have strengthened the effect. But Fumiko seemed to feel frustrated he had not gone into detail. He was baffled by his wife's psychology. How could she feel ignored? Since the novel was about his tragic love affair it was centered on Otoko. He had included without change a great many facts hitherto concealed from his wife. That was what had worried him most, but she seemed more hurt that he had written so little about her. "I didn't like to use your jealousy that way," Oki said. "Because you can't write about someone you don't love [Fumiko said], someone you don't even hate? All the time I'm typing I keep wondering why I didn't let you go."[7]

The creator of Oki and Fumiko, Yasunari Kawabata, won the Nobel Prize for Literature in 1968. Many of his novels deal with the conflicts between traditional, pre–World War II, Japanese sensibilities and the new patterns created after the war. On the whole, the female characters he creates are both subordinate to males and the victims of males. Both Otoko and Fumiko, for example, suffer from Oki. He is not a bad man, but his confusions hurt both women. For Kawabata, men seem cast adrift when they don't have the clear structures of the vertical rankings of traditional Japanese society. The two places where his male characters most come into crisis are where recent democratic changes have muddied traditional patterns and where they must deal intimately with women. Perhaps recent dealings between the sexes have been more confused and potentially hurtful than was true before the war, but one suspects conversations like that between Oki and Fumiko historically have long occurred much more frequently than the sociologists would imply. Romantic love overturns many rankings.

The aesthetic ideals raised by authors such as Kawabata remind us that Shinto has influenced many Japanese to fuse a certain sense of beauty with their conceptions of social order and cultural identity. Shinto has been the aboriginal, native tradition responsible for the Japanese tendency to locate divinity in a nature populated with 800,000 kami and to equate ethics with acting so as to honor one's family and clan. Shinto has molded women to think of their beauty as something harmonious with the grace and simplicity of traditional floral arrangements, tea ceremonies, and naturalistic shrines. It has supported a woman's sense that her sexual life reflects on her family, for weal or woe, and that men naturally will distinguish between the women who give them agreeable companionship and the women suitable for running their household and raising their children.

"Shinto," in other words, is the religious tradition closest to the Japanese sense of what is fitting, what best imitates the nature replete with the kami, what is compatible with the ancient sense of clan loyalty. Certainly Confucian social patterns and Buddhist ideas about ultimate reality also were influential, but Shinto seems the strongest influence on the Japanese aesthetic sensibility. One cannot separate this aesthetic sensibility from the Japanese religious instinct. They are not identical, but they certainly are fused. The religious instinct comes to the fore when one asks what the Japanese have considered holy (in contrast to fitting). The best answer seems to be, "the power of nature that makes the world fertile, arresting, and unpredictable." Insofar as women could symbolize natural fertility, beauty, and spontaneity, Shinto sponsored a culture intrigued with the feminine. Insofar as men better symbolized the disciplined, astringent, hard aspects of divine nature, women could find Shinto another force for their subordination.

In practice, of course, individual men and women have varied these general Japanese attitudes considerably. Spouses have come to various accommodations in their own households and many strong women have wielded at least half the domestic power. But in the national culture—business, education, warfare—Japan has been extremely patriarchal. Japanese business and government remain male preserves. There is no significant Japanese movement for women's liberation.

Looked at from afar, Japanese women seem, rather poignantly, citizens of a beautiful land that loves their beauty but doesn't know how either to pursue them through romantic love or integrate them as full partners in the productive side of national life. Something in the cool, nature-dominated foundations of Shinto keeps Japanese women from easily gaining the status of lovers who can be friends, of equals who can generate half the cultural creativity and claim half the cultural rewards. The theoretical agreement that the kami inhabit feminine natural shapes as well as masculine does not carry over into the practical realm of giving both sexes equal influence in formal, official, normative culture. One therefore suspects that patriarchal biases lay close to the foundations of the traditional Japanese worldview—that from the beginning of the articulation of Shinto male views predominated.

THE GEISHA

No portrait of Japanese women would be complete without reference to the geisha, those romantic players in men's recreational life. For many Japanese they represent something quintessentially Japanese—the "flower and willow world" in which Japanese notions of beauty and culture come to perhaps their most exquisite blend. By their identification with this world, the geisha stand out in the popular mind as more Japanese than virtually any other sector of the population.

The first thing to be said about the geisha is that they and wives fall into two categories not only different but mutually exclusive. When a geisha marries, she stops being a geisha. Men think of wives and geisha as complementary. One cares for the home, making it a place of refuge from his work, mothering him as well as the children. The other provides lovely companionship, graceful entertainment. As Liza Dalby puts it,

> In contrast to Americans, Japanese married couples do very little entertaining as a couple. Further, romance is not necessarily a concomitant of marriage, even as an ideal. Geisha are supposed to be sexy where wives are sober, artistic where wives are humdrum, and witty where wives are serious—keeping in mind that any of these contrasts is culturally construed, and that "sexy" for a Japanese does not necessarily mean what it might to an American.
>
> Foreign women are frequently outraged by the idea of the geisha. "Playthings for men!" they say, decrying the very existence of such a profession. Certainly from an outside perspective, which by almost any lights shows Japan as an egregiously male-dominated society, this split nature of femininity seems unfair to women. Why can't wives go out with their husbands? Why can't geisha marry and work too? Why are there geisha at all? But Japanese wives and geisha themselves often have a different view of these institutions, one that we cannot simply dismiss as distorted or false consciousness.[8]

Curiously, geisha are among the few women in Japanese society who can attain economic independence and positions of influence on their own merits. They have freedoms not allowed wives, and they need not fear being dropped from the company payroll when they are thirty-five, as women working in offices have to. Such women, called "office flowers," are hired as much for adornment as productivity. Seen from the inside, as Dalby (the first Westerner to train as a geisha) saw it, the flower and willow world can seem more liberated.

How do geisha function? If one were in Kyoto, the ancient capital that was spared bombing during World War II and so perhaps best represents Japanese cultural traditions, during April, when the cherry blossoms bloom and the geisha put on a dance festival, one would find teahouses and restaurants jammed with visitors from all over Japan. The blossoms, the river, and the geisha all contribute to a mood of romance and spring awakening. Inside many of the teahouses, a geisha family life unfolds. The woman who manages the house is called "mother," while a geisha senior in virtue of an earlier debut is called "older sister." There are also ceremonies uniting particular geisha in more particular sisterly bonds. The path to the highest status as a geisha begins with an apprenticeship. A typical apprentice might be the daughter of a former geisha—there are six recognized geisha communities around Kyoto; in some of them women cross the line between the geisha and the prostitute. The apprentice is instructed in etiquette, speech, deportment, dance, and music, usually by the household mother, who tends to be a former geisha, as well as by older geisha. Many geisha acquire a patron, an older man who offers financial support and sometimes also the option of retiring from active geisha work to be his mistress. One of the teahouse mothers whom Dalby met began managing her house because her patron died, leaving her with a young son and limited financial resources. That mother slowly built up a good clientele and then started training geisha. Her son lived in the house with her, although he was not much in evidence.

The business hours of a typical geisha house run from about 6 P.M. to early morning. The teahouses of Pontocho, one well-known area in Kyoto, are interspersed between gaudier bars. The image of the area is of a quarter dedicated to men's relaxation and pleasure, but in fact it is also a quarter where women run things and establish an intensely female world. The teahouse mothers are business women, entrepreneurs. Apart from the male customers, few men—perhaps accountants or wig stylists—are needed or find employment. Children born to geisha are all illegitimate, but whereas female children usually fit in well, male children uniformly are troubled by the all-female surroundings and turn out badly. Thus the geisha world is probably the only place in Japan where the birth of a girl is more welcome than the birth of a boy.

Geisha must master a variety of traditional Japanese arts to some degree, but usually they specialize in one, for example, classical dance. If they can distinguish themselves for such art, they have a better chance of becoming desirable companions and eventually owners of their own houses. In May and October the geisha of Pontocho give public performances in a recital hall built in that area. Some are dancers, appearing in the limelight. Others are musicians providing instrumental accompaniment or contributing songs. The apprentices get much notice, because traditionally they have the most distinctive outfits and the fullest bloom of youth. The more demanding roles go to experienced geisha able to interpret classical characters from the ancient dances. The whole geisha family gets involved in such productions, the mothers coaching and supporting and the children being fascinated by the elaborate makeup and preparation. When the geisha perform numbers from the Kabuki repertoire, they reverse the trend of the Kabuki stage itself. In Kabuki theater all the roles, male and female, are played by men, while in geisha productions all the roles are played by women. The two professions, geisha and Kabuki, go back several hundred years and have many connections. Frequently, therefore, actors know geisha and vice versa. Both groups might be called entertainers, and both have developed from poor, even ill-regarded beginnings to their present status of cultivated arts patronized by the refined and wealthy. Because both groups concentrate on dance, they often have the same teachers, cultivate the same sensibilities, and so get involved in love affairs and marriages.

Usually geisha sleep until late morning, because they work until early morning. During the months for public performances, however, they rehearse from midmorning and then return home for their regular night's work. The geisha who had been Dalby's older sister and guide died in a fire during the performance season, apparently because she was worn out from the combination of rehearsing and carrying on her regular work and so did not hear the cries of alarm.

There are many other aspects of the geisha life that offer fascinating tidbits for reflection. For our purposes, however, the main point seems to be the influence the geisha have had on Japanese views of women. As noted earlier, they have helped to split femininity into two distinct parts: a maternal role and influence, exerted by wives in the home, and a lover-companion role, where women entertain men and beautify their recreation. Central to both roles, however, is women's subservience. Both wife and geisha wait upon men, massage their egos, and smooth away their cares. The male preserve is business and public affairs. Both wives and geisha are seen as freeing or equipping men for optimal performance there. Men don't want to hear about domestic troubles, so in fact Japanese wives have more control over such matters as spending the household money than wives in other countries usually do. Geisha represent feminine adornment with no responsibility, only the man's ability to pay. Occasionally emotional ties develop, but they are not the rule.

RECENT TRENDS AND BUDDHIST THEMES

Officially, Japanese women have an opportunity equal to men's in such areas as work and education:

> Article Fourteen of the Japanese Constitution stipulates that no one shall be discriminated against on the basis of sex, as well as of race and creed, and throughout the lengthy educational process, which for 95 percent of the young population lasts for twelve or more school years, girls are given basically the same education as boys. Their performances are judged only on the basis of individual achievement. And many college professors acknowledge, sometimes reluctantly, that girls usually perform better.[9]

However, when girls graduate from school and seek employment, they find that they are far from equal with men. Many companies will not

let them take the entrance examination for employment, and most companies prefer high school girls to college graduates, because the former will
be easier to dismiss. Even when women get jobs with companies, they find
their work subsidiary to men's. Japan simply does not have a place for
career-oriented, experienced female workers. So while more than 50 percent of married women work at some time, very few develop careers. Most,
in fact, retire to the domestic sphere once they bear their first child.

Japanese women themselves more accept this state of affairs than
challenge it. Thus in an opinion survey sponsored by the government in
1982, 72 percent of Japanese women agreed that women should be more
concerned about their families than themselves. Comparable figures for
other countries—Sweden, 6.1 percent; Britain, 9.9 percent; United States,
17.6 percent; West Germany, 41.4 percent, and Philippines, 57.5 percent—
suggested that Japanese women were among the most family conscious in
the world.[10] This tendency to associate women with the home and sharply
distinguish their roles from men's carried through on such other matters as
whether boys and girls should be disciplined differently (62.6 percent yes),
whether women quit their jobs when they married (66.6 percent yes), and
whether the wife had the final say about how the family income should be
spent (79.4 percent of Japanese wives did). In all these matters, Japanese
women showed themselves more family oriented or more identified with
their household role than Swedish, Britain, American, West German, or
Philippine women.[11]

The traditional beliefs lying behind these figures include the notion
that the two sexes have different roles determined by heaven. Men work,
usually outside the home, to gain income. Women keep house and raise
children. In the home, or in her role as wife and mother, a woman has
more power and status than she could ever hope to gain in the world of
work. Men do not learn domestic skills and depend on their wives as completely as they depended on their mothers when they were children. The
author of the study from which the figures just given came associates this
predominance of the female in the home with Japan's not having developed the notion of a creator god. Traditionally life and death were in the
hands of an impersonal **heaven** or fate. Consequently, in general Japanese
culture (which has been shaped by Shinto and Buddhism but does not always reflect their orthodox theologies) creativity is associated with women,
mothers. The author does not mention Kannon, the mother goddess, but
the profile of Japanese mothers she sketches fits well with the idealization
one sees in Kannon. Women are most prized for the fact that it is through
their fertility that the family line continues.

If Japanese women are to gain liberation on the Western model, they
probably will have to give up the status they have as rulers in the domestic
realm. Relatedly, they probably will have to develop a concept of individual
personhood hitherto not well developed in Japan. Presently most of their

identity comes through the relationships they have, especially those with their children. As Japan becomes more industrialized and families become more isolated from traditional communities, many Japanese women feel their functions diminishing:

> In addition, many women, full of energy and time, do not feel fulfilled by simply taking care of the family, with all the mechanical and institutional help now available. For better or worse, many Japanese women have already begun to walk in a new direction. We do not know where the path leads us, but somehow we have to find new meaning and self-respect in our rapidly changing situation.[12]

One of the ways that Buddhism supported traditional Japanese social patterns was by urging a selflessness that easily led people to accept the situations in which they found themselves. Thinking that self-concern was a major reason people remained trapped by karma and suffering, Japanese Buddhists urged taking life as it came, moment by moment, with neither worry nor regret. A contemporary Soto Zen master, Shunryu Suzuki, put it this way:

> When you are practicing zazen [meditation], you may hear the rain dropping from the roof in the dark. Later, the wonderful mist will be coming through the big trees, and still later when people start to work, they will see the beautiful mountains. But some people will by annoyed if they hear the rain when they are lying in their beds in the morning, because they do not know that later they will see the beautiful sun rising from the east. If our mind is concentrated on ourselves we will have this kind of worry. But if we accept ourselves as the embodiment of the truth, of Buddha nature, we will have no worry. We will think, "Now it is raining, but we don't know what will happen in the next moment. By the time we go out it may be a beautiful day, or a stormy day. Since we don't know, let's appreciate the sound of the rain right now." This kind of attitude is the right attitude. If you understand yourself as a temporary embodiment of the truth, you will have no difficulty whatsoever. You will appreciate your surroundings, and you will appreciate yourself as a wonderful part of Buddha's great activity, even in the midst of difficulties. This is our way of life.[13]

People do not have to have such notions clearly predominant in their minds to be considerably influenced by them. Women who were not Zen practitioners easily could have accepted their traditional role because it fit their sense of fate. By not kicking against the goad of their fate, by accepting where and what they were, they could feel they were going with the grain of the existence meted out to them. This kind of surrender need not have displaced the sort of shrewd calculation Japanese women might have made that keeping to the domestic sphere offered them their best chance for status. All people need both active and passive strategies, ways to get themselves to take initiative and ways to cope with things they cannot change. Buddhism offered Japanese women the comforts of icons (of

Kannon, other bodhisattvas, and buddhas), of religious ceremonies, and of doctrines such as karma and the intrinsic goodness of each being's buddhanature. Women who were looking for reasons to accept their traditional roles probably found it easier to develop a Buddhist rationale than did women looking for reasons to enter the worlds of geisha or business, but the Buddhist stress on living day by day, on being present to where one actually was, could serve any woman well.

The special fascination of Japanese women probably stems from the subtlety and complexity of the social world they have inhabited. The ethnic solidarity of Japanese is well known and much commented upon. In the networks of social relations they have woven through the centuries, the ranks and roles of women naturally have had a prominent place. The recent development of Japan as an industrial and financial power has only heightened the distinctiveness and force of its traditional sociology. Religion has more sanctioned this traditional sociology than challenged it. Apart from marginal figures such as Buddhist nuns and female ecstatics (leaders of new religions who have updated the role of the shamaness), the religion of Japanese women has helped them to specialize in raising children and supporting men to do the nation's business.

DISCUSSION QUESTIONS

1. How did Japanese shamanesses serve their communities?
2. How does romantic love threaten to overturn rank and status?
3. How do geisha and wives divide Japanese femininity?
4. How do Japanese women rule the domestic sphere?

NOTES

[1]See Kyoto Motomochi Nakamura, "No Women's Liberation: The Heritage of a Woman Prophet in Modern Japan," in *Unspoken World's*, ed. Nancy A. Falk and Rita M. Gross (San Francisco: Harper & Row, 1980), pp. 174–190.

[2]G. Bonas, "Shinto," in *The Concise Encyclopedia of Living Faiths*, ed. R. C. Zaehner (Boston: Beacon, 1967), p. 357.

[3]See Ichiro Hori, *Folk Religion in Japan* (Chicago: University of Chicago Press, 1968); also Carmen Blacker, *The Catalpa Bow* (London: Allen & Unwin, 1975).

[4]See Joseph M. Kitagawa, "Japanese Religion: An Overview," Allen L. Miller, "Japanese Religion: Popular Religion," and Matsumae Takeshi, "Japanese Religion: Mythic Themes," in *The Encyclopedia of Religion*, Vol. 7, ed. Mircea Eliade (New York: Macmillan, 1987), pp. 520–538, 538–545, and 545–552.

[5]Chie Nakane, *Japanese Society* (Berkeley: University of California Press, 1972), p. 32, note.

[6]Ibid., p. 71, note.

[7]Yasunari Kawabata, *Beauty and Sadness* (Tokyo: Charles Tuttle, 1975), pp. 38–39.

[8]Liza Crihfield Dalby, *Geisha* (Berkeley: University of California Press, 1983), pp. xii–xiv.

[9]Masako Tanaka, "The Myth of Perfect Motherhood: Japanese Women's Dilemma," in *Speaking of Faith: Global Perspectives on Women, Religion and Social Change*, ed. Diana L. Eck and Devaki Jain (Philadelphia: New Society, 1987), p. 75.

[10]See ibid., pp. 76–77.

[11]See ibid., pp. 77–78.

[12]Ibid., p. 83.

[13]Shunryu Suzuki, *Zen Mind, Beginner's Mind* (New York: Weatherhill, 1970), pp. 117–118.

CHAPTER SEVEN

Jewish Women

OVERVIEW

The full story of Jewish women covers close to four millennia. If we date Abraham and Sarah to about 1800 B.C.E., for nearly thirty-seven hundred years women covenanted to the God of Abraham and Sarah, Isaac and Rebekah, Jacob and Rachel have contributed to a culture of world-historic proportions. Through most of this long period, Jewish women have lived in patriarchal situations. Biblical, talmudic, medieval, and modern Judaism all assumed that men were to lead, teach, and legislate while women were to follow. To be sure, there were exceptions to this pattern, and present-day Jewish feminists have been happy to retrieve them. Deborah, for example, was a judge and prophet in Israel—a charismatic leader credited with a military victory over Canaanite enemies (see Judges 4–5). Judith and Esther were similar heroines, whose courageous actions liberated their people. In medieval times Beruriah, wife of Rabbi Meir, was celebrated for learning and Oudil, daughter of the Baal Shem Tov, for charismatic piety. Modern Judaism has numbered such outstanding women as Henrietta Szold, founder of the Hadassah Medical Organization, and Golda Meir, prime minister of Israel. Nonetheless, the vast majority of women throughout

Jewish history have made their mark as wives and mothers—mistresses of the domestic rather than the public sphere.

In any encyclopedic treatment of Judaism, several aspects predominate.[1] The first is the historical development from biblical times, through a medieval period dominated by the rabbis and the **Talmud**, to the Jewish encounter with European modernity. The second is the geographic and so cultural spread of Judaism, which calls for treatments of how Jews lived in the Middle East, in North Africa, in Asia, in Europe, and in the Western Hemisphere. The combination of historical development and geographic diversity suggests that all generalizations about the experience of Jewish women have to be taken with several grains of salt. Here, as in our treatments of women in other long-standing religious traditions, the advice of Alfred North Whitehead should apply: seek simplicity and distrust it. The stories and examples we treat certainly illumine common trends, but Jewish women have lived in so many different circumstances that what **Torah** (divine guidance), patriarchy, concentrating on raising children and the other apparently common factors have meant in specific situations are bound to remain inexact, unique, and reasons for surveyors to remain quite humble.

At present there are about 18 million Jews worldwide. About 275,000 live in Africa, 2,000 in East Asia, 1.5 million in Europe, 975,000 in Latin America, 8 million in North America, 85,000 in Oceania, 4.4 million in Israel, and 3 million in the Soviet Union. Eighty-four percent qualify as Ashkenazis or are from Northern and Eastern European stock. Ten percent qualify as Orientals, and 4 percent qualify as Sephardim, people from Iberian stock.[2]

Among the main ideas and events that have structured the experience of Jewish women, the following stand out. First, there was the Exodus from Egypt, under the leadership of Moses, and the consequent reception of the Torah, the guidance or law, associated with the **covenant** mediated by Moses. The Exodus came to function as the great symbol of God's concern for Israel, of God's redemptive or liberating character. The covenant was a unique (although rather patriarchal) bond between God and the people who looked back to Abraham and Moses as their founding fathers. One might say that it formalized the predilection and concern God had revealed in the Exodus, obliging the people to make God the foremost treasure in their lives. Receiving a land of their own was part of the covenant, while obeying the laws attributed to God's disclosures to Moses on Mount Sinai became the concrete way the people were to manifest their fidelity. One can consider the teachings and laws developed by the rabbis an extension of the Mosaic Torah, as the people strove to interpret what the covenant meant in new circumstances.

Second, later biblical history provided a series of events associated with the Israelite monarchy that also became prime symbols Jews used when they reflected on the meaning of their history. The sovereign rule and prosperity achieved by David and Solomon in the ninth century B.C.E. came to shade the covenantal bond with God slightly differently from what we find in the Mosaic covenant. Where the Mosaic covenant, as interpreted by the "Deuteronomistic history" (found in the biblical books Deuteronomy through 2 Kings), taught that fidelity to God would bring prosperity and infidelity would bring ruin, the Davidic covenant was less conditional: God had sworn (to stand by the people) and would not repent. Both interpretations of the covenant came into play when the great prophets Isaiah, Jeremiah, and Ezekiel interpreted the destruction of the monarchy—the fall of the northern portion of the kingdom to Assyria in 721 B.C.E. and the fall of the southern portion to Babylon in 586 B.C.E. From 538 B.C.E., when leaders of the people returned from exile in Babylon, Jews nearly always were subject to foreign powers. However, their theologians continued to think about the Torah as the law of a people whose worship and daily life ideally occurred in a sovereign **theocracy**—a state where the sacred and the secular blended under the rule of the God of the covenant (whom the biblical kings had represented).

A third major event was the destruction of Jerusalem in 70 C.E. and the dispersion of most Jews from the holy city that had been the center of their lives. In dispersion (**diaspora**), the leading rabbis of the first and second centuries C.E. both settled the shape of the Hebrew Bible and collected the traditions of the teachers who had recently flourished. In making this collection they created the **Mishnah**, the first building block of the Talmud. By 500 C.E. the Talmud (the Mishnah enlarged by the Gemara—commentaries on the Mishnah) was relatively complete and functioning as the operative guide for Jewish life. If the Hebrew Bible is our best source about the religious experience of Jewish women before the Common Era, the Talmud is the most important document about the official status of women in Judaism of the Common Era.

Throughout the Common Era, the vast majority of Jews have lived in cultures dominated by either Christians or Muslims. Perhaps the most dramatic line in the story of this second portion of Jewish history therefore has been how the people kept their Jewish identity. This dramatic line was prefigured in the Bible, insofar as the prophets inveighed against accommodating to the practices of Israel's neighbors and the postexilic reformers Ezra and Nehemiah argued for separation from those neighbors. But the psychology of the Jewish home where women came into their own during the Common Era regularly was dominated by interpretations of the Bible and the Talmud geared to assisting survival against persecution and assimilation.

Only in modernity, which came late to European Jewry (for the majority, only in the nineteenth century), did concepts such as democracy and pluralism arise to suggest Jews might become equal participants in national cultures that supposedly made religion and ethnic identity secondary. Even then, the history of standing on the margins and being subject to the whims of non-Jewish majorities made most Jews suspicious. In the twentieth century, Nazi Germany proved this suspicion all too well founded. The creation of the contemporary state of Israel in 1948 consummated a centuries-old longing to return to the land of David and certainly has greatly influenced the lives of recent Jews. Even in Israel, however, the meaning of modernity is subject for fierce controversy, and with it the rights and roles of Jewish women. Such controversy greatly affects Jewish feminists, who usually have great affection for their cultural tradition as a whole but are troubled, if not deeply angered, by those who resist accommodating it so that the rights of women, religious as well as civil, might equal the rights of men. Thus patriarchal tradition is much on the minds of Jewish feminists.

TEXTS OF TERROR

The foundations of Jewish culture have lain in the Hebrew Bible, and even when Talmudic interests shaped the interpretation of biblical stories to make them serve much later circumstances, the bare power of the stories kept drawing people back to the original texts. Recently Phyllis Trible has commented intensively on four biblical texts suggesting the terror into which women could be plunged. These four texts are neither the whole of the Bible's stimuli to consider the perils of powerlessness nor the whole of the Bible's estimate of relations between the sexes. As we shall see in the next sections, many positive tales and insights offset these scenarios of brutality. But it is useful to confront the worst of what biblical religion did to Israelite women, all the more so if we are accustomed to taking the Bible as divine wisdom pure and simple. Certainly there are many reasons for taking the Bible as divine wisdom, but after studying texts such as Trible's four, little seems pure or simple.

First is the story of Hagar that one may piece together from Genesis 16:1–16 and 21:9–21. In the first phase of the story, Sarai (who later becomes Sarah), wife of Abram (who later becomes Abraham), is barren—the greatest affliction a biblical wife could suffer. Desperate for children, she conceives a plan: let Abram go in to Hagar, Sarai's Egyptian maid. This Abram does, making Hagar pregnant, but the result turns back on Sarai. Instead of getting the child for which she had hoped, she gets the contempt of Hagar. In Trible's interpretation, this turn of events expresses a certain justice. Hagar, a slave with few rights, forced to place even her sex and fertility in the service of her mistress and master, finally gains a perspective that redresses some of the imbalance. Sarai becomes "slight" in the eyes of Hagar because Hagar realizes power can be of different sorts.[3] Washing his hands of the conflict between the two women, Abram tells Sarai to handle Hagar as Sarai wishes. So Sarai deals harshly with her and she flees.

In the wilderness an angel of God visits Hagar, commands her to return to Sarai and submit and promises that her child will be the start of a great multitude of descendants. This promise, which is quite like the promise given to the patriarchs, singles Hagar out. So does her sense of having seen God. But when Sarah later conceives her own son, Hagar suffers still further. Sarah sees her son Isaac playing with Ishmael, the son of Hagar, takes offense, and pressures Abraham to cast out both Hagar and Ishmael. Although Abraham is reluctant, God tells him to do as Sarah wishes, and so God seems to sanction the cruelty about to be visited on Hagar. When the bread and water that Abraham gave them run out, Hagar places the child under a bush and takes herself some distance from him, so she will not have to watch him die. What occurs at this point is a matter of interpretational dispute. As Trible puts it,

> Hagar wept. Pointedly, the Hebrew text says, "She lifted up her voice and wept" (21:16c). From ancient times, however, translators have robbed this woman of her grief by changing the unambiguous verb forms to masculine constructions. Such alterations make the child lift up his voice and weep. But masculine emendations cannot silence Hagar. A host of feminine verb forms throughout this section witness unmistakably to her tears: she departed and she wandered in the wilderness; she found a place for the child to die; she kept a vigil; and she uttered the dread phrase, "the death of the child." Now, as she sits at a distance from death, *she* lifts up her voice and *she* weeps. Her grief, like her speech, is sufficient unto itself. She does not cry out to another; she does not beseech God. A madonna alone with her dying child, Hagar weeps.[4]

Eventually an angel does save the two, but Trible reads the text as the awful trial of a fugitive. Hagar has little if any voice throughout the whole story, and for obscure divine purposes she has to suffer not only abuse but the desolation of terrible rejection: slavery, being cast out by Abraham, and feeling utterly abandoned.

The terror of this text is perhaps the mildest of the four Trible treats. In the story of Tamar (II Samuel 13: 1–22), we see a princess raped by her brother, the prince Amnon, and disregarded by her father, King David. Like the story of David's adultery with Bathsheba and murder of her husband Uriah, this story shows the dark side of the Israelite monarchy and the defenselessness of even high-class women. Amnon schemes to get Tamar into a position where he can satisfy his lust for her. She tries to reason with him and points out that if he merely asks the king, he can have her lawfully. As Trible underscores, the text plays the folly of Amnon off against the wisdom of Tamar: hers is the voice of reason and decency. But Amnon will have none of it, and after he has violated her, he hates her and sends her away. This rejection is even worse than the rape, for it means Tamar is shamed and condemned to lifelong desolation. Eventually Tamar's brother Absalom has Amnon killed and turns against King David.

Absalom takes Tamar's part, but throughout she is simply a pawn, moved back and forth by the lust and hatred of the men in the royal household. Amnon will not hear reason, David pays his daughter little mind (his sending her to minister to a supposedly sick Amnon first put her in Amnon's clutches, and although David was angry when he learned of the rape, he did not punish Amnon. Worse, there is no indication he said anything to Tamar or did anything for her), and although Absalom treats her well, he urges her to stay silent and only two years later works revenge, perhaps more from other motives than to gain justice for Tamar. So even a princess weeps from abuse.

In Judges 19:1–30 we witness both rape and murder. This story is one of the most brutal in the Bible. An unnamed concubine flees from the Levite (member of the tribe of Levi) with whom she is living and returns to the house of her father. The Levite pursues her there and is entertained by the father, the concubine slipping away from the narrator's interest. After back and forth between the two men, Levite and concubine set out to return to their home. They pause half way to spend the night and encounter naked evil. Men of the town want to violate the Levite. The host and Levite respond as follows:

> "No, my brethren, do not act so wickedly; seeing that this man has come into my house, do not do this vile thing. Behold, here are my virgin daughter and his concubine; let me bring them out now. Ravish them and do with them what seems good to you; but against this man do not do so vile a thing." But the men would not listen to him. So the man [Levite] seized his concubine, and put her out to them; and they knew her, and abused her all night until the morning. And as the dawn began to break, they let her go. And as morning appeared, the woman came and fell down at the door of the man's house where her master was, till it was light. And her master rose up in the morning, and when he opened the doors of the house and went out to go on his way, behold, there was his concubine lying at the door of the house, with her hands on the threshold. He said to her, "Get up, let us be going." But there was no answer. (Judges 19:23–28)

The Levite puts the concubine on his ass, and when they are home he hacks her body into twelve pieces to distribute to the twelve tribes and make the infamy known. The result of this is war with Benjamin, the offending tribe—a war in which women are the greatest losers. But the scene of the host and the Levite offering to abandon the women to the rapists has to be the nadir: one can do anything to virgin daughters and concubines, but let nothing threaten one's male guest.

The fourth of Trible's texts of terror, the human sacrifice of the daughter of Jephthah (Judges 11:29–40), completes the mosaic of degradation. The daughter is sacrificed in fulfillment of her father's foolish and faithless vow. The only redemptive note comes in verse 40: "And it became a custom in Israel that the daughters of Israel went year by year to lament the daughter of Jephthah the Gileadite four days of the year." Her sisters remember the virgin victim and so give her a sort of posterity.

THE PLACE OF WOMEN IN BIBLICAL SOCIETY

Speaking of history in general, Gerda Lerner has distinguished two senses of the word. One is simply what happened in the past. The other is how the past got recorded—written down, made available to later "historians." Concerning what simply happened in the past, we have to grant women a full 50 percent of the agency. They contributed just as much as men to the daily reality of their people. Concerning how the past has gotten recorded, we have to realize that almost always only men did the recording and interpreting. History in the second, more formal and academic sense therefore is shot through with sexism. Again and again events featuring men and of interest to men framed the narratives, while events featuring women and of interest to women were shunted to the sidelines, if not ignored altogether.[5]

In studying her four texts of terror, Phyllis Trible is sensitive not only to what the text says about the experience of the women in question, but also to what it does not say. For even when a sense of outrage clearly forms the narrative, and it is plain that rape and murder are being condemned, one does not find the feminist focus that a full historical or scriptural (revelational) narrative would entail. Because the Hebrew Bible was composed by men (for instance, by members of an all-male priesthood), it is nowhere near being an adequate record or interpretation of what all of Israel, female and male, experienced, suffered, or thought.

This is completely true of the legislation that framed relations between the sexes and family life. A bride was expected to come to her husband as a virgin (so that her husband could think of her as unused and be confident any early child was his), but the husband was not so constrained. If he could prove she had not been virginal at marriage, he could have her stoned (Deuteronomy 22:13–21). Biblical legislation did provide safeguards against false testimony, but in matters such as these its basic assumption was that the female was property. What outraged the legislators was that damaged goods had passed hands. This shamed the father, from whom the bride was going, and it offended the husband, who was not getting what had been pledged.

Similarly, adultery was a matter of abusing something that belonged to a husband. By violating another man's possession, the adulterous male risked death (Leviticus 20:10–11). So did the wife who strayed. Her body was not her own. She belonged to her husband. No similar understanding of the body of the husband made adultery a two-way street. For a husband to cheat on his wife did not constitute an abuse of her property, a violation of her rights, that merited harsh punishment.

If a man violated an unmarried woman, he offended her father. He did not incur harsh punishment, however, only the obligation to marry the woman, pay her father a bride price, and not divorce her (Deuteronomy 22:28–29). Women had no rights to initiate divorce, and the only protection they had against being divorced arbitrarily was that a husband was supposed to provide substantial reasons and a formal decree (Deuteronomy 24:1–4).

This is not to say that the Hebrew Bible viewed marriage only in terms of adultery and divorce. From Genesis (2:24) through the prophets (especially Hosea), marriage was treated as natural, beautiful, and a figure for the covenant between God and Israel. Ideally husbands would love their wives, finding in them the complement and delight that Adam found when first contemplating Eve. It was more assumed than expressed that wives would find in their husbands both complement and delight. The main reason for marriage, in fact, was not delight but procreation. Without downplaying erotic love, the Bible is more interested in fertility. Thus women regularly are reduced to their wombs, and it is assumed that a woman's greatest longing and need is to have children.

One finds this in Hannah, the mother of the prophet Samuel, whose story can stand duty for myriad unnamed biblical women:

> There was a certain man of Ramathaim-zophim of the hill country of Ephraim, whose name was Elkanah the son of Jeroham, son of Elihu, son of Tohu, son of Zuph, an Ephraimite. He had two wives; the name of one was Hannah, and the name of the other Peninnah. And Peninnah had children, but Hannah had no children. Now this man used to go up year by year from his city to worship and to sacrifice to the Lord of hosts at Shiloh, where the two sons of Eli, Hophni and Phinehas, were priests of the Lord. On the day when Elkanah sacrificed, he would give portions to Peninnah and to all her sons and daughters; and, although he loved Hannah, he would give Hannah only one portion, because the Lord had closed her womb. And her rival used to provoke her sorely, to irritate her, because the Lord had closed her womb. And so it went on year by year; as often as she went up to the house of the Lord, she used to provoke her. Therefore Hannah wept and would not eat. And Elkanah, her husband, said to her, "Hannah, why do you weep? And why do you not eat? And why is your heart sad? Am I not more to you than ten sons?"
>
> After they had eaten and drunk in Shiloh, Hannah rose. Now Eli the priest was sitting on the seat beside the doorpost of the temple of the Lord. She was deeply distressed and prayed to the Lord, and wept bitterly. And she vowed a vow and said, "O Lord of hosts, if thou wilt indeed look on the affliction of thy maidservant, and remember me, and not forget thy maidservant, but wilt give to thy maidservant a son, then I will give him to the Lord all the days of his life, and no razor shall touch his head." (I Samuel 1: 1–11)

Several features of this text deserve comment. First, notice how the introduction of Elkanah stresses genealogical line and so fertility. One can assume that Elkanah married Hannah and Peninnah precisely to further his genealogical line through their fertility. Second, notice the rivalry between the two women, reminiscent of the rivalry between Sarai and Hagar. Because they have been acquired for their fertility, the women are pressured to compete in childbearing—a sort of uterine warfare. Third, although Elkanah may be sincere enough in his affection for Hannah, he seems a dolt not to appreciate how his distribution of the sacrifice was bound to affect her. Fourth, the distress and bitter weeping of Hannah before she makes her vow seem the telltale emotions. She feels useless, worthless, because she has not begotten a son (daughters don't count for much). If ever a woman was defined by her womb, pressured to neglect her brains and spiritual creativity, it was Hannah. Last, the promise that no razor would touch the head of the child marks the child as a **Nazarene**—one dedicated to God for holy purposes, as the great prophet Samuel proves to be. Eventually Hannah has her prayer answered, and the paean of joy she expresses in 1 Samuel 2 served as the basis for the Magnificat that Luke has Mary, the mother of Jesus, utter in thanksgiving for her conception (Luke 1: 46–55). One can rejoice with Hannah and Mary without admiring how their culture made their physical fertility their be-all.

One further aspect of biblical women's status that begs attention at this point is the blood taboos under which they labored. Although the main job of women was producing children, the authors of the biblical law codes weren't happy with the way women's productive mechanisms worked. As we see in Exodus 35:22–29, menstruation was considered incompatible with the ritual sacrifices made to God. So a woman was considered unclean from the onset of her bleeding until seven days had passed. Even when she had fulfilled her mission and begotten a child, blood made a woman unclean—for forty days if the child were male, eighty days if it were female (double pollution—see Leviticus 12:1–8).

These ritual considerations, along with the Israelite convictions about the uniqueness (monotheism) of their (male) God, combined in an ongoing attack on the different view of divinity and femaleness prevalent among Israel's neighbors. The Canaanite goddesses suggested that female fertility was a central part of the divine order, something capable of symbolizing ultimate holiness. Therefore, the Bible had to denounce them.[6]

FURTHER BIBLICAL IMAGES

Thus far what we have seen of the lot of biblical women has been fairly negative. At best they have been second-rate citizens, subordinated to male control. At worst they have been raped, slain, made to focus on their wombs, and castigated for the uncleanness of how their wombs functioned.

A major directive symbolism for the sexes' relations occurs in the Genesis accounts of how woman and man were created and first behaved.

Both accounts make the same claims: (1) man and woman have been willed into being by the direct action of God as the high point of creation; (2) they complement one another and *together* constitute humankind. This is all put dramatically by having woman created from man's rib and so to be a helper fit for him. Written from a male viewpoint, it makes primal man in effect say, "She is just what I need, an identical match for me, bone of my bone." In creation, then, Genesis intuits a basic equality for the sexes.

Further, dealing with the Fall (the divided human condition), Genesis depicts the sexes as types of early Israelite male and female behavior. So Eve, intelligent and practical, decides that the fruit is good to eat, delightful to behold, and a possible source of wisdom—a bargain. Adam simply eats what his wife has prepared. Both sin, both are punished. "Thenceforth," men have to sweat laboriously, women have to bear children in pain. Later biblical tradition (Ecclesiastes 25:24) misogynistically makes Eve the cause of sin, but the original story simply relates both sexes to the mystery of a life that is much less than our intuition says it should be.

The other women of the Bible support this Genesis interpretation of Eve, proto-woman, as intelligent and decent. Bathsheba is a clever woman, as is the woman from Tekoa, whom Samuel used to reunite David and Absalom (I Kings 1:11–31; II Samuel 14:1–20). Deborah is a mighty prophetess, Ruth is a noble daughter-in-law, Esther was able to save her people. Proverbs 31, cited earlier, shows the sort of model laid before Israelite women, and it suggests that all woman's fruitfulness, not just her sexuality, was prized.

In the Book of Ruth, however, we find the fully positive story of two women developing a mature friendship and loyalty. Naomi, the mother-in-law, bids her widowed daughter-in-law Ruth leave her to find a new husband. But even though Ruth is not an Israelite, she stays with Naomi, and together they succeed, first in surviving and then in carrying on the family line, as Ruth produces a child who becomes an ancestor of King David. The lines that Ruth speaks after Naomi has urged her to leave are a landmark in love between women:

> But Ruth said, "Entreat me not to leave you or to return from following you; for where you go I will go, and where you lodge I will lodge; your people shall be my people, and your God my God; where you die I will die, and there will I be buried. May the Lord do so to me and more also if even death parts me from you." (Ruth 1:16–18)[7]

This fusion of fates is especially precious to the biblical author because it is sealed in Ruth's acceptance of Naomi's God. Yet the same intensity of love, to the point of death, occurs in the Song of Songs without particular reference to God. There the love in question is heterosexual, so much so that the rabbis found the Song an allegory of Israel's bond with her God. The Song probably first appeared as secular love poetry, but even in that case it was remarkable, because the lovers give and receive quite equally.[8] For once the woman is not simply the underling, subject to the whim of the man. And certainly she is not simply a brood mare, valued mainly for her offspring. The Song pays procreation little mind. It is interested in eros, the love of beauty that compels maid and lad to rush toward union. Toward the end of the Song, like an editorial insert, occurs the poetic appreciation of love that links it with death as utterly primordial. When Israel listened to these verses, it knew that men and women were supposed to be to one another as flesh of flesh and bone of bone:

> Set me as a seal upon your heart, as a seal upon your arm; for love is strong as death, jealousy is cruel as the grave. Its flashes are flashes of fire, a most vehement flame. Many waters cannot quench love, neither can floods drown it. If a man offered for love all the wealth of his house, it would be utterly scorned. (Song of Songs, 8:6–7)

Aware of some of this potential, great prophets such as Jeremiah, Hosea, and Ezekiel pursued the intense union between Israel and God through marital symbolism. In good times, which for the prophets meant times of religious fidelity and material blessing, Israel was to God as a beautiful young bride. Unfortunately, however, bad times of infidelity and hardship brought the prophets to lay greater stress on Israel's wantonness. In not offering God a pure (monotheistic) cult and not offering one another social justice, Israelites had played the harlot, loved wantonly, exposed themselves shamefully. The problem with this imagery was its sexual bias. Insofar as God was masculine and Israel feminine, Israelite deficiencies became cast in terms of feminine infidelity. Hosea, for example, used the example of the infidelity of his wife Gomer to illumine the defections of his people from God. Since he loved Gomer despite her failings, this gave him profound insight into the long-suffering character of the divine love. On the other hand, because there was little if any theology from female prophets, drawing on experiences of male infidelity and intuitions of a feminine divine persona, the Bible seems to consider women the unfaithful, unreliable, wanton sex.

This prophetic tendency reached a low point in Ezekiel, who tried to explain the exile to Babylon as due to the harlotry of God's bride:

> But you trusted in your beauty and played the harlot because of your renown, and lavished your harlotries on any passer-by. You took some of your garments, and made for yourself gaily decked shrines [to false gods], and on them played the harlot; the like has never been, nor ever shall be. You also took your fair jewels of my gold and of my silver, which I had given you, and made for yourself images of men, with them played the harlot; and you took your embroidered garments to cover them, and set my oil and incense before them. Also my bread which I gave you—I fed you with fine flour and oil and honey—you set before them for a pleasing odor, says the Lord God. And you took your sons and your daughters, whom you had borne to me, and these

you sacrificed to them to be devoured. Were your harlotries so small a matter that you slaughtered my children and delivered them up as an offering by fire to them? And in all your abominations and your harlotries you did not remember the days of your youth, when you were naked and bare, weltering in your blood. (Ezekiel 16: 15–22)

Countless generations of both Jews and Christians read the prophets devotedly, thereby taking in such negative stereotypes of women. Because the basic symbolism for God was masculine and the basic symbolism for Israel (and later the Christian Church, which claimed to be the New Israel) was feminine, all right and perfection fell on the masculine side of the equation, all sin and failing on the female side. Nonetheless, there were cracks in this wholly masculine theology, places where care and nurture brought biblical poets to speak of God as though the deity were female.

So, for example, in Jeremiah 31:20 the root metaphor used to express the divine compassion is being moved to one's womb. Standard translations blur this root metaphor, but Phyllis Trible has both commented upon it insightfully and translated it faithfully:

> And the conclusion makes explicit the maternal metaphor for God. As Rachel mourns the loss of the fruit of her womb, so Yahweh, from the divine womb, mourns the same child. Yet there is a difference. The human mother refuses consolation; the divine mother changes grief into grace. As a result, the poem has moved from the desolate lamentation of Rachel to the redemptive compassion of God. Female imagery surrounds Ephraim; words of a mother embrace her son [note that Israel/Ephraim for once is considered masculine, in counter-point to a feminine God]. My translation is the following: Is Ephraim my dear son? my darling child? For the more I speak of him, the more do I remember him. Therefore, my womb trembles for him; I will truly show motherly-compassion upon him.[9]

Another positive feminine imagery concerns wisdom, an attribute of God that became extremely important at the end of the biblical period and is highly significant in both the Writings (the third portion of the Hebrew Bible) and the New Testament. Proverbs 8 speaks of wisdom as a maiden with God at the beginning and delightful to him. In Proverbs 9 wisdom is like a gracious hostess, anxious to nourish those starving by foolishness (the "simple"):

> The Lord created me at the beginning of his work, the first of his acts of old. Ages ago I was set up, at the first, before the beginning of the earth . . . when he marked out the foundations of the earth, then I was beside him, like a masterworkman; and I was daily his delight, rejoicing before him always, rejoicing in his inhabited world and delighting in the sons of men. . . . Wisdom has built up her house, she has set up her seven pillars. She has slaughtered her beasts, she has mixed her wine, she has also set her table. She has sent out her maids to call from the highest places in the town, "Whoever is simple, let him turn in here!" To him who is without sense she says, "Come, eat of my

bread and drink of the wine I have mixed. Leave simpleness, and live, and walk in the way of insight." (Proverbs 8:22–23, 29–31, 9:1–6)

These positive appreciations of female nature, which put it either within the divinity as an apt symbolism or alongside the divinity as a wise companion, did not outweigh all the negatives, but surely they were heartening.

TALMUDIC VIEWS OF WOMEN

The antecedents of the rabbis who fashioned the Talmud were the Pharisees. In contrast to their portrait in the New Testament, the **Pharisees** were concerned about both the letter and the spirit of the Torah. Nonetheless, the pre-Talmudic literature influenced by the Pharisees regularly was misogynistic. Thus Leonard Swidler has judged that "the Pharisees thought of women as 'in all things inferior to the man,' and 'evil,' as 'overcome by the spirit of fornication more than men,' as ones who 'in their heart plot against men,' and that every man should 'guard [his] senses from every woman.'"[10] Writings from the first century B.C.E. such as *The Book of Jubilees* and *The Testaments of the Twelve Patriarchs* are similarly negative, as are the writings of the Jewish historian Flavius Josephus. The authors have a special animus against foreign women, but any woman carries the danger of fornication and so should be held suspect.

The Mishnah, which arose in the first centuries of the Common Era, deals with women as one of its six principal divisions. The special interest it exhibits focuses on when a woman is in transit, entering or leaving marital union to a man. When united to a man by marriage, or functioning as the ward of her father, a woman is holy: in her proper place. She becomes dangerous when she is unplaced—on the loose, moving. So marriage functions as a way of sanctifying women by placing them (putting them in their God-given place). In marriage God and the man involved are the active agents, while the woman is passive. The relations of women to one another fall outside the Mishnaic pale. Indeed, the Mishnah isn't much interested in women as wives and mothers. It is only when women are marrying and divorcing that they become problematic and so matters of legal concern. Behind this concern is a distrust of female sexuality like that of the Pharisaic literature. Women on the loose, unplaced, are likely to be loose women. But even women who are placed and so holy are not as human as men. In the interpretation of Jacob Neusner, the Mishnah verifies Simone de Beauvoir's analysis of women's abnormality. Since the rabbis considered male humanity the norm, female humanity was bound to seem deficient or anomalous. That seems the principal reason they forbade women access to the priesthood and so to performing the religious cult. When study of Torah replaced the cult as the supreme act of Jewish religion, the rabbis were only logical in extending their prohibition to study: women were not to have access to Talmudic learning.[11]

Despite this basic bias, we find passages in the Talmudic literature that praise the good wife and mother almost lavishly. To be sure, a "good" wife and mother submitted to the Talmudic scheme of things. For example, one text says that women acquire merit before God by sending their children to study Torah in the schools and their husbands to study with the rabbis (Ber. 17a). In other words, women are to be the enablers of men's study. Within the family, women had primary care for cooking, cleaning, and raising the children, while a man was supposed to study Torah as much as circumstances allowed. Frequently this meant that women carried a large share of the burden of making a livelihood, working in the shop or contributing to the trade that brought the family their bread. Since marriage was considered the normal estate and the unmarried person, male or female, was considered incomplete, arranging marriages was an important business. One rabbinic story asked what God had been doing since he finished the six days of creation. The answer was that he had been busy arranging marriages.

The ordinary Talmudic term for marriage is "sanctification" (*kiddushian*). The husband consecrates his wife, setting her aside as something dedicated to the sanctuary (Kid. 2b). Blessings come to a man because of his wife, so he should honor her (B.M. 59a). Although the Talmud counsels frugality concerning food and drink, when it came to his wife and children, a man was supposed to spend beyond his means (Chul. 84b). Thus wives had solid rights: to financial support, medical care, money in case of the husband's death or a divorce, and sexual satisfaction. Were a wife kidnapped, a husband was obliged to spend all that he had to ransom her. Although all inheritance went to sons, a man was also supposed to provide for the welfare of his daughters after his death.

The obligations of a wife to her husband included providing him sexual satisfaction, physical comfort (food and rest), and leisure in which to study Torah. Thus the wife of Rabbi Eleazear cooked sixty different kinds of food for him when he was sick. Good wives knew that the best way to guard their husbands from temptation was to give them sexual pleasure at home. Indeed, this Talmudic view of marital relations led to lengthy discussions of just when menstrual prohibitions of intercourse were and were not in force.

The wife's great fear was sterility, for to be childless was to be as one dead (Gen. R 71:6). On the other hand, fruitfulness was such a blessing that one text said that in the next life women would bear children daily (Shab. 30b). The rabbis permitted contraception if more children were likely to harm the mother (Jeb. 12b), but to have many children was a great blessing, because each was a gift from God. Thus when Rabbi Meir was weeping at the death of his two sons, his wife reminded him that they had only been on loan from God. So they prayed: "The Lord gave and the Lord hath taken away, blessed be the name of the Lord."

If all children were gifts from God, male children were special gifts. Sometimes the Talmudists expressed this thought quite negatively: "Happy is he whose children are sons and woe to him whose children are daughters" (B.B. 16b). A father must worry about a girl, lest she be seduced. When she comes of marrying age he must worry that she not find a husband. While she is married he must worry that she might prove barren. And when she is older (after menopause) he must worry that she might become a witch. Thus in commenting on Numbers 6:24 ("The Lord bless thee and keep thee") the Talmud adds, "bless thee with sons, and keep thee from daughters because they need careful guarding" (Num. R. 11:5).

In the Talmudic period, divorce continued to be the prerogative of men. On the other hand, the Talmudists strove to protect women from arbitrary divorce. Also, rabbis would pressure men to grant their wives' petition and give them a divorce, if the marriage seemed broken irreparably. Only the woman who had committed adultery had to be divorced. In other cases, as long as the marriage showed a chance of being saved, the rabbis would drag their feet in allowing a divorce. Divorce involved preparing a bill that formalized the abolition of the marriage and working out the finances of the marriage settlement. However, if women gave scandal they could be divorced without giving them a settlement. In lax interpretation, "scandal" could include appearing in public with an uncovered head or speaking too loudly, so women always had to fear they might be divorced without a penny.

Still, rabbis would favor the pleas of a woman who sought divorce (sought to get her husband to divorce her, since she could not actually divorce him) on such grounds as impotence (male barrenness), his refusing her sexual relations, and his staying away from home longer than his job required. (Scholars were especially free to travel.) If a man had boils, goiter, or leprosy, or if he worked as a collector of dog-dung, a coppersmith, or a tanner—smelly occupations—a wife might find it too much and petition to get free of him. As one Talmudic text put it, even though she knew what his occupation was before she married him, she might claim, "I thought I could endure it, but now I find that I cannot" (Ket. 7:10). Desertion, however, was not a valid basis for granting a divorce, and only when a woman could bring forward two male witnesses that her husband was dead (female witnesses did not count) could she gain the right to remarry. Thus widows of men lost in war often were not free to remarry.

TRADITIONAL VALUES

Feminist scholars such as Judith Hauptmann and Judith Baskin have made solid contributions to the work of assessing not only what the Talmud says about women but how it formed the consciousness of both sexes.[12] In Baskin's view,

> Women did not play an active part in the development of rabbinic Judaism, nor were they granted a significant role in that tradition's religious life. By examining the way the rabbis divided the world between men and women, however, particularly in light of insights derived from anthropological and structuralist approaches to social life and religious traditions, the general separation of the sexes can be seen as part of a larger system of dichotomies and oppositions. In fact, rabbinic Judaism's definition of women shares many characteristics with that of other conservative societies. Here, as elsewhere, women do not emerge as beings inferior to men, but are instead a creation completely and necessarily different from the unblemished male who alone can serve God fully. In rabbinic Judaism, no woman is deemed capable of any direct experience of the divine.[13]

Baskin goes on to enumerate some of the consequences of this rabbinic view, which shaped the lives of most Jews throughout the Common Era. Concerning witness in court, for example, women were unacceptable, as were slaves and children. Concerning religious obligations, which weighed heavily on men, women were exempt, in part lest prayer and study take them from their domestic obligations, but probably more profoundly because the rabbis thought little of women's religious capacities. Indeed, the pious Jewish man would thank God each day for three blessings: not having been made a Gentile, not having been made a slave, and not having been made a woman.

In not having been made a woman, a man avoided such supposedly typical female vices as greed, curiosity, sloth, envy, and talkativeness ("God gave the world ten measures of speech and women took nine of them"). The only woman traditionally credited with learning was Beruriah, wife of Rabbi Meir, and she supposedly fell into adultery. Like the deaf-mute, the imbecile, the child, and the androgyne, women were not commanded to appear at the temple for worship. The common denominator in this catalogue seems to be incompleteness, lack of human wholeness. (As a Gentile equivalent, one thinks of Aristotle's view that a woman was a misbegotten man.) Of the 613 precepts or obligations taught by the rabbis, only 3 held for women, and in Baskin's view the rabbis did not consider these three *mitzvot* (divine commands that enhance religious life). The three precepts applying to women were

> the lighting of candles to signal the advent of the Sabbath; the breaking off and burning of a bit of dough used in forming the Sabbath loaf (*challah*); and the observance of the laws of *niddah* (legislation pertaining to the menstruating woman) which strictly limit a woman's contact with any man during and for a week following her menstrual period. It is a crucial fact that rabbinic tradition does not regard these ordinances as *mitzvot*, that is, as divine commandments whose observance enhances the religious life of the observer and assures divine favor. Rather these precepts are described as eternal punish-

ments brought upon woman to remind her of Eve's responsibility in the death of Adam, and therefore in all human mortality.[14]

On the other hand, the traditional separation of women from men and official religion did not mean no appreciation for women's gifts. Perhaps the best epitome of the traditional appreciation was the passage from Proverbs 31 frequently read before the Sabbath meal:

> A good wife who can find? She is far more precious than jewels. The heart of her husband trusts in her, and he will have no lack of gain. She does him good, and not harm, all the days of her life. She seeks wool and flax, and works with willing hands. She is like the ships of the merchant, she brings her food from afar. She rises while it is yet night and provides food for her household and tasks for her maidens. She considers a field and buys it; with the fruit of her hands she plants a vineyard. She girds her loins with strength and makes her arms strong. She perceives that her merchandise is profitable. Her lamp does not go out at night. She puts her hands to the distaff, and her hands hold the spindle. She opens her hand to the poor, and reaches out her hands to the needy. She is not afraid of snow for her household, for all her household are clothed in scarlet. She makes herself coverings; her clothing is fine linen and purple. Her husband is known in the gates, when he sits among the elders of the land. She makes linen garments and sells them; she delivers girdles to the merchant. Strength and dignity are her clothing, and she laughs at the time to come. She opens her mouth with wisdom, and the teaching of kindness is on her tongue. She looks well to the ways of her household, and does not eat the bread of idleness. Her children rise up and call her blessed; her husband also, and he praises her: "Many women have done excellently, but you surpass them all." Charm is deceitful, and beauty is vain, but a woman who fears the Lord is to be praised. Give her of the fruit of her hands, and let her works praise her in the gates. (Proverbs 31: 10–31)

Feminists looking for positive images of women on which to build have stressed the competence and activity laid out in this portrait. Even though the woman is an enhancement of the man and the penultimate verses fearful of charm and beauty have a sour ring, the overall picture is energetic and positive.

Both the positive and the negative views of women wove through the fabric of the small village (*shtetl*) life of Eastern Europe, where traditional Jewish values had centuries in which to take root. In the shtetl women were active and busy, running the home, caring for the children, helping with any business, and looking out for community members in need. Regularly they faced the practical problems of life much more directly than men, who received many exemptions to study. In commenting on the relations between the sexes in the shtetl, Mark Zborowski and Elizabeth Herzog have stressed how the traditional mores reached into each individual's life:

> The invariable involvement of the family and the community in the behavior of the individual is nowhere more evident than in the explanations offered and the attitudes expressed with regard to the rules for behavior between

men and women. One of the "fences" erected to protect both the mitsva [precept] of learning and the sanctity of the home is that which separates the sexes during the daily round of activities. Extreme avoidance of women by men is the prescribed pattern of the shtetl. Usage with regard to this pattern varies from fanatic observance to nonchalant semi-conformity, and demonstrates the ease with which behavior spans the distance between the spirit and the letter of the Law.

The people of the shtetl give a number of reasons for the avoidance rule, all of them bearing on the need to insure fulfillment of the two leading mitsvos. A woman too freely contemplated would fill a man's thoughts with sex when he should be concentrating on study. It is striking that, despite the emphatic avoidance rule, sexual enjoyment is considered healthy and good—at the proper time and place, and in the proper context. To bring children into the world is the duty of every Jew and it is right for man and wife to enjoy intercourse as a means to procreation. Such enjoyment is not only permitted, it is prescribed. God does nothing without a purpose and since He made man with sex organs and appetite, the exercise of them must be good.

Excess in anything is bad, however, and not only bad but un-Jewish. The ideal Jew is moderate in all things. It is good for him to enjoy intercourse with his wife under correct circumstances. But it is wrong for him to entertain sexual thoughts or impulses toward her or any woman outside of actual intercourse.[15]

HASIDISM AND REFORM

The Eastern European shtetl was home to Hasidism, the devotional movement begun by Israel Baal Shem Tov (1700–1760). The Hasidim took the rabbinic law (*halakah*) seriously, but they were more interested in religious ardor: feeling the love of God. The leading Hasidic rabbis were mystics, rapt in the splendors of the divine beauty yet wondering why their people had to suffer so much persecution.

Elie Wiesel has spoken of the leading feminine figure in Hasidism, the Baal Shem Tov's daughter Oudil, as follows:

> The Besht [Baal Shem Tov] had two children: Reb [Rabbi] Tzvi-Hersh and his sister Oudil. They were totally different in character and temperament. Reb Tzvi-Hersh was shy, forlorn, unassuming, withdrawn—unable and unwilling to assure his father's succession at the head of the rapidly expanding movement. His sister, on the other hand, was an extrovert. No woman is as romanticized, as admired in Hasidism, as she was. She brought to the movement an added dimension of youth and charm. Oudil—the name is probably taken from Adele, Adella—was honored by Hasidim as though she were a Rebbe herself. And, in a way, she was. At her father's side—always. Full of life, ideas, projects; forever in the middle of events, forever generating excitement, enthusiasm; forever in the middle of a story. Hasidim believe that the Shekina [divine presence, conceived as feminine] rested on her face.[16]

Hasidic teaching usually proceeded by way of stories. The story of how Oudil became the mother of Rebbe Baruk is typical of the tales told of the Besht and of the Hasidic sense of divine providence:

One evening she [Oudil] was present at a celebration. Her father's disciples sang and danced for hours on end, aiming to achieve communion with God, trying to let their souls enter His. They chanted with fervor, they danced with exuberance—until they left behind all links with things earthly. They forgot their own senses; shoulder against shoulder, hand in hand, their eyes closed, they formed a circle of friendship, a circle around God and His people.

Oudil was looking at them, finding it breathtakingly beautiful, when suddenly she noticed that one disciple was losing his balance. His shoes had disintegrated, and sad, distressed, he had to leave his friends.

"Poor young man," Oudil said to her father.

The Besht smiled: "Promise him a pair of new shoes, if he promises you another son." [Oudil must have already had one son; perhaps she was widowed.]

Both did. And thus, for the price of a pair of shoes, Oudil got her second son, Barukh.[17]

Hasidism continues in small enclaves, where pious Jewish families have striven to keep as many of the traditions and laws as contemporary life allows. In Lis Harris's wonderful description of a Hasidic community in Brooklyn, one senses how the people have humanized all the rituals concerning food and purity, making them ways of enhancing both their religion and their interpersonal relations. For example, Harris's informants explain to her that the laws prohibiting sexual contact during menstruation function as a break that makes the renewal of relations after menstruation like a honeymoon. When Harris visits the **mikvah**, the ritual bath, she experiences the sense of cleansing and renewal that the Hasidic women have told her they enjoy each month:

I tell Brachah [the attendant] that I've never taken a *mikvah* before. She folds her hands over her stomach and beams. "Well, then, we'll treat you like a *kallah* [a bride]" and proceeds to explain some of the basics of the ritual to me. Then she asks, enumerating the various items on the checklist one by one, if I have remembered to do all of them. I have not. I have forgotten to comb my wet hair and I have forgotten my nose, which I proceed to blow, rather showily. Then, after blotting my eyes with a linen cloth to make sure no mascara lingers on my lashes, Brachah leads me over to the *mikvah*. I take off the robe and stand expectantly in the chest-deep warm green water. Brachah tells me to keep my eyes and lips closed but not too tightly and to keep my feet and arms apart, so that the water will touch my whole body. When I go underwater I instantly curl into the fetal position because of the position of my body. When I come up, Brachah places a linen cloth over my head and I repeat the *mikvah* blessing after her. Then, the cloth removed, I go down two more times. The second time down, I see a little speeded-up movie of all the religious people I know, performing this ritual. I think of all the generations of people I have not known who have considered the impurities of the world dissolvable. My grandmother floats by, curled up, like me, like a little pink shrimp. I see her as she was in her very old age, senile and mute, curled up in this same position on her bed. The third time down, I think of my boys suspended inside me, waiting to join the world. I look up and see Brachah's smiling face through the water. I feel good. As I am climbing out, Brachah tells me that some people prefer to immerse themselves with their bodies in a horizontal position, and asks me if I'd like to try it that way. I try it, but find it less satisfactory. It's too much like going for a swim.[18]

The advent of modernity brought many changes to Judaism. As a result, very few Jews now follow a Hasidic way of life, keep the laws for diet and the Sabbath as strictly as the medieval rabbis expected, and visit the ritual bath. From the time of the European Enlightenment, traditional Judaism came under question, if not attack, from Jews interested in correlating their faith and culture with the modern stress on reason and ethics. For those with such an interest, many of the laws and traditional stories seemed myths that modern times made laughable. Reform Judaism was the effort to rethink Jewish faith in modern terms. By contrast to it, traditional faith came to be called Orthodoxy. Where Orthodoxy claimed those reluctant to give up the old ways, Reform attracted Jews who wanted to mingle with Gentiles and enter the cultural mainstream. Conservative and Reconstructionist Jews attempted other reworkings of tradition and accommodations, Conservatives standing between Orthodox and Reformed and Reconstructionists taking the most radical position, to the left of Reform.

The Breslau Conference called by the Reform Movement in 1846 called for sexual equality in all areas of religion and so seemed to promise Jewish women considerable liberation. However, this call was little heeded. One woman who took advantage of the beginnings of change, though, was Henrietta Szold. She lobbied for equality for Jewish women in the 1890s, studied at the Jewish Theological Seminary in New York, and spent the last decades of her life in Palestine, building the remarkable health care network that became the Hadassah Medical Organization of present-day Israel. Not surprisingly, she drew her share of male detractors, but she had more than enough wit to keep them at bay. For example, regularly she would refer to such men as "our more awkward fellow creatures."

Rabbi Isaac Mayer Wise, who founded Hebrew Union College in Cincinnati as a Reform Seminary, championed women's rights. In 1846 he admitted women into the choir of his congregation in Albany, New York, and during his presidency of Hebrew Union College, he encouraged women to attend. In 1921 the issue of ordaining women as rabbis arose, and after some debate the faculty of Hebrew Union College went on record as in favor of opening this option to women. However, the Board of Governors would not approve the change, and only in 1956 did the College promise that it would ordain any woman passing the required courses. Another sixteen years later, Sally Priesand became the first woman actually ordained, and since 1972 more than sixty-one women have followed her. Slowly they are gaining better acceptance. The case seems similar within Reconstructionist Judaism (a branch stressing humanistic values and downplaying revelation): "At present, fourteen women (almost 20% of all Reconstructionist rabbis since the movement's Reconstructionist Rabbinical

College opened in 1968) have received ordination."[19] Of the students ordained by 1983, almost half were women (23 of 47).

In terms of Jewish civil law, too, women still need relief in several
areas, for this is often commingled with halakah (religious law). Like the
deaf-mute and the idiot, women are still "protected"—prohibited from appearing in court, for instance. They do not yet have equal inheritance, marriage, and divorce rights. The deserted wife still cannot obtain a divorce
and permission to remarry, unless she can prove her husband's death. In
Israel, this civil statute has resulted in the widows produced by three recent
wars often being doubly afflicted. They have lost husbands to combat and,
because no bodies were recovered, also have lost the legal right to remarry.
If men were anchored by such legislation, it is said by more than just the
cynical, things would have changed long ago. That things have not
changed in the civil code is for many a continuing testimony to Jewish
males' chauvinism and traditional religion's misogynism.

To combat this, feminists not only have called for women's access to
religious studies, they also have devised new rituals, so that the image of the
Jewish woman, in both her own eyes and that of the whole community,
might change from that of an underling to that of a mature and equal par-
ticipant. In the traditional marriage ceremony, for instance, the bride is totally silent, which has tended to enforce an image of effacement or
nonpersonhood. The new rituals try to make it clear that woman and man
are strictly copersons—that humanity is, as Genesis teaches, created male
and female. Similarly, rituals are being devised for the female life cycle, so
that key moments in girls' lives will be solemnized, as they have always been
for boys. This means celebrating a daughter's birth with a special blessing,
paralleling the gift giving for a boy's "redemption" with one for a girl's,
working out *bas-mitzvah* rituals in which girls read Torah on their coming to
maturity, and so on. It is simply a matter of social justice, the feminists say,
and increasingly their view is gaining converts.

In Israel one can see the conflict of ancient traditions and new claims
for social justice especially clearly. The Declaration of Independence as-
sures complete equality of social and political rights, without regard to religion, race, or sex. The Women's Equal Rights Law of 1951 gives married
women equality in ownership of property and guardianship of children. It
also makes unilateral divorce, against the wife's will, a criminal offense.
The Equal Pay for Equal Work Law of 1964 applies to both private and
government employment. However, many of these civil rights, especially
those surrounding marriage, have been diluted or vitiated by the religious
courts, which will not cede their old, Talmudic ways. Because of their
influence, a determined husband can still keep his wife from obtaining a
divorce, no matter how impossible the relation has become for her. The
Orthodox are not beyond playing hard politics with such issues, either, for
they defend the old religious prerogatives with appeals to "national secu-
rity," arguing that religion is Israel's chief unifying force. The result is that

if a woman remarries without Orthodox sanction, a large percentage of the population will consider her children bastards, unable to marry legitimate offspring. In the field of labor, women are protected as "women." This means that night work and heavy labor are forbidden and also that women have earlier retirement than men. Postnatal care and child raising almost completely devolve to women, as well, so the labor legislation, overall, has not broken with sexual stereotyping.

Finally, the vaunted equality of the *kibbutz* (agrarian commune) has turned out in practice to be less than full. Today fewer than 10 percent of the women work in the valued areas of production, and since this is tied to leadership roles and committee work, the kibbutzim are now largely run by men alone, women having become the staff of the nurseries, laundries, and kitchens. Moreover, this lower status has become self-perpetuating. In 1972, for instance, only 14 of the 220 university students from kibbutzim were women. With such a return to segregated roles, observers record, kibbutz women have again begun to worry about their sex appeal and concern themselves with beauty aids. On the other side, industrialization and the women's movement appear to be challenging these trends, and baby production may soon become less of a national imperative. Nonetheless, for Israeli women, as for Jewish women generally, the ethnicoreligious identity that they so passionately affirm or seek is still shadowed by the traditional Talmudist's daily prayer: "I thank Thee, God, for not having made me a woman."

Recently some humanistic Jewish women have added their voices to those opposing not only the stranglehold the Orthodox have had on official religious influence in Israel but also hawkish, militaristic trends. For example, Shulamith Koenig has eloquently explained the depression that comes over humanistic Jews when they have seen the freedom and ethical sensitivity of the prophets ignored in the name of a restrictive *halakah* and a vindictive need to punish Palestinian enemies. To her mind this depression represents a natural reaction to the default on the promise held out when Zionists like her parents emigrated to Israel more than fifty years ago. Women, Jews who are religious but not Orthodox, nonreligious Jews, and non-Jews have all suffered because of this default. Due to Orthodox intransigence, the lovely freedoms enshrined in the 1948 Bill of Rights associated with Independence have never been officially promulgated as the law of the land.

Moreover, in Koenig's view Zionists of all persuasions have indulged a fatal blind spot. In their exultation at coming back to their ancestral land, they have overlooked the fact that for centuries that land had been the possession of others, who were bound to resist Jews' return. So she thinks only a deepened commitment to the equality of all the inhabitants of Israel and a spirituality free of religious dogmatism are likely to redeem the original ideals of the Zionist movement. As long as patriarchal religion prevails over the conception that Judaism is a freeing way of life, and retribution prevails over the generosity of spirit necessary to make peace, it will be hard for any Jews who want equality between the sexes and peace throughout the land to be fully happy with Israel.[20]

CURRENT JEWISH FEMINISM

All the major branches of Judaism now house feminists interested in making the tradition more acceptable to present-day women. Among the Orthodox, for example, considerable work has been done on trying to change the religious laws that have pushed women to the margins of religious participation and have put them at a disadvantage in marriage and divorce.[21] As we have seen, Reform and Reconstructionist Jews have admitted women to the rabbinate. Conservative Jewry has witnessed similar trends, beginning to ordain women as rabbis and cantors. On the other hand, many of the women in the kibbutzim of Israel have reasserted traditional women's roles.

The leading Jewish participants in the feminist critique of patriarchal cultures have applauded the liberalizing trends without thinking that they are likely to do the needed job. In the minds of Jewish feminists such as Judith Plaskow and Naomi Goldenberg, tinkering with the traditional laws is but a halfway house. Until the assumptions of rabbinic Judaism are challenged and replaced, the laws will still be dealing with women who are not men's equals in religious dignity or capacity. Indeed, as we saw when dealing with the Mishnah and have postulated concerning recorded history as a whole, men's cultural creations regularly have ignored women's interests and needs, so that even when women were not being penalized by sexist laws they were being ignored—rendered invisible.

Judith Plaskow has summarized the pass to which this has brought more radical Jewish feminists:

> Third—and for me, this is the most important point—the invisibility of women cannot be remedied within the legal structure. In fact, the Jewish feminist movement of the last ten years has focused largely on *halachah* and the rectification of certain problems it raises for women. For example, according to Jewish law, women are not required to put on a prayer shawl or phylacteries or say the *she'ma* (Deuteronomy 6:4–5) three times daily. But since in Jewish law one who is not obligated to perform a commandment has a lower status in its performance than one who is obligated, Orthodox women cannot form part of the minyan, or quorum of prayer, made up of those obligated to pray. (In other branches of Judaism women can be part of the minyan.) Divorce is another important feminist issue. According to Jewish law, only a man can write and deliver the *get*, or divorce decree, which ends a Jewish marriage. This means that in a case in which a man cannot or will not give his wife a *get*, she is forever prevented from remarrying.

These concerns can and have been addressed within a halachic [legal] framework, and adjustments have been made. In fact, the tradition has been trying for hundreds of years to remedy the inequity of the divorce laws by finding ways to get a recalcitrant husband to give his wife a *get*. But these only partially successful efforts reveal very clearly that the desire to render justice to women is secondary to the preservation of the halachic system. For really the only way to solve the problem of divorce is to give women equal agency, to allow them to write a *get*. But this is precisely what has not been and cannot be done within the traditional framework, because it would entail a recognition of women's situation as women, which goes beyond the system. It is to just such a recognition, however, that we as feminists are committed. Once we begin to see women as a class, and gender as a central category for the analysis of any culture or tradition, we are bound to break out of a system which renders women's status invisible. At this stage, in any case, a feminist Judaism must insist on the importance of women's experience and, thus, on shaking up the categories and processes of Jewish life and thought.[22]

Plaskow is aware that even within the old patterns Jewish women forged bonds among themselves and found ways of ignoring the official repressions. She speaks with appreciation, even with nostalgia, of the sisterhood that traditional Jewish women experienced through the laws that prescribed sexual segregation. In the marketplace, at the *mikvah*, or on the women's side of the synagogue, women shared gossip, ideas, common frustrations. Because of the commitment of Jewish men to study, Jewish women often carried the main economic responsibilities and so were active in crafts, trade, and even business travel. Much of how one regards the oppression of traditional Jewish women therefore depends on where one is looking, what one is choosing to stress. Nonetheless, the official structures of the past strike most present-day Jewish feminists as deeply sexist, so most present-day Jewish feminists are asking for a thorough reconception of how "Jewish" and "woman" should be put together.

In a recent symposium published in the *Journal of Feminist Studies in Religion*, five Jewish feminists discuss the question of separation and union in Jewish religion, with special reference to the implications for women. The discussions suggest the ways that feminist theory is making Jewish women rethink the most basic assumptions of past Jewish theology. As well, the discussions frequently spotlight the importance of ritual and community life. Several of these concerns come together in a contribution by T. Drorah Setel:

What it means to develop a Jewish *practice* based on relational values is a more difficult question. It is far easier to discuss and redefine theological perspectives than it is to challenge the holiness of practices such as keeping kosher, observing the Sabbath or performing male circumcision. It may be easier to transform specific rituals less concerned with contemporary identity, such as *havdalah* (lit.: "separation"), the ceremony separating the Sabbath from the rest of the week. *Havdalah* concludes with a paradigmatic statement of hierarchical dualism: "You are praiseworthy, Lord our God, Power-over the whole world, The-One-Who-Separates: holy from common; light from darkness; Israel from the other peoples; the seventh day from the six days of common labor. You are praiseworthy Lord, The-One-Who-Separates holy from common."

The ritual of *havdalah* then closes with a dramatic act: the extinguishing of the candle used in the ceremony, thus *making* separation and not merely describing it. At first glance, *havdalah* appears impossible to incorporate into Jewish feminist practice but it contains at least one action which forces us to confront the issue of diversity within unity: the smelling of fragrant spices, which traditionally represent a sense of the sweetness of *shabbat* that may remain throughout the week—in other words, an acknowledgment that the Sabbath cannot and even should not be wholly separate from the other days. In fact, the tradition describes *shabbat* as "a taste of the world to come," thus envisioning a time when the separation becomes obsolete.

I believe that that time has begun. I think feminism has clearly shown that separational modes of thought have run whatever course they may have had as empowering constructs. As a Jewish feminist I think my present task is to speak no longer in that obsolete language. At the same time I must acknowledge that we are still far from the realization of a repaired, unified world, and ask what distinctions still remain useful and significant. I may still wish and need to preserve the observance of *shabbat* as a model for the rest of the week, a time focused on the task of unification. I may wish to maintain a kosher home as a means of relationship to my people and/or a process of awareness concerning the lives that have brought food to my table. To be honest, I cannot see any way that Jewish feminists can *intellectually* justify the practice of male circumcision but I think feminists, of all people, understand that such decisions are not necessarily theoretical ones.[23]

One sees, therefore, that feminist instincts of wholeness, unity, and relationship are entering into the theology of current Jewish women. As they insist on the importance of honoring women's experience, they find themselves drawn into the complexity and richness of the tradition they are reviewing. The result is a proper sophistication, a proper awareness that bad forms (of both thought and practice) have sometimes been used to good ends and that good forms do not necessarily guarantee justice, piety, and love. We need both good forms and good use.

DISCUSSION QUESTIONS

1. What was the significance of the Mosaic covenant?
2. What was your reaction to the story of the nameless concubine who was raped, murdered, and dismembered?
3. What made biblical women valuable property?
4. Explain the positive implications in the story of Ruth and the Song of Songs.
5. Why did the Mishnah's interest in women focus on their transitions?

6. What were the three obligations to which traditional Jewish women were held and what were their negative overtones?

7. Write a brief endorsement of the mikvah, stressing the positive religious ends it could serve.

8. Lay out the pros and cons of keeping the traditional kosher laws.

NOTES

[1]See Eugene B. Borowitz et al., "Judaism," in *The Encyclopedia of Religion*, Vol. 8, ed. Mircea Eliade (New York: Macmillan, 1987), pp. 127–205.

[2]See *1987 Britannica Book of the Year* (Chicago: Encyclopaedia Britannica, 1987), p. 338.

[3]Phyllis Trible, *Texts of Terror* (Philadelphia: Fortress, 1984), p. 12.

[4]Ibid., pp. 24–25.

[5]See Gerda Lerner, *The Creation of Patriarchy* (New York: Oxford University Press, 1986), pp. 4–14; and Jo Ann Hackett, "In the Days of Jael: Reclaiming the History of Women in Ancient Israel," in *Immaculate and Powerful: The Female in Sacred Image and Social Reality*, eds. C. Atkinson, C. Buchanan, and M. Miles (Boston: Beacon, 1985), pp. 15–38.

[6]See Steve Davies, "The Canaanite-Hebrew Goddess," in *The Book of the Goddess: Past and Present*, ed. Carl Olson (New York: Crossroad, 1983), pp. 68–79.

[7]See Phyllis Trible, *God and the Rhetoric of Sexuality* (Philadelphia: Fortress, 1978), pp. 166–200; and Karen Doob Sakenfeld, *Faithfulness in Action: Loyalty in Biblical Perspective* (Philadelphia: Fortress, 1985), pp. 32–38.

[8]See Trible, *God and the Rhetoric of Sexuality*, pp. 144–165; and Samuel Terrien, *Till the Heart Sings* (Philadelphia: Fortress, 1985), pp. 29–49.

[9]Trible, *God and the Rhetoric of Sexuality*, p. 45.

[10]Leonard Swidler, *Women in Judaism* (Metuchen, N.J.: Scarecrow, 1976), p. 56.

[11]See Jacob Neusner, "Thematic or Systematic Description: The Case of the Mishnah's Division of Women," in his *Method and Meaning in Ancient Judaism* (Missoula, Mont.: Scholars Press, 1979).

[12]See Judith Hauptmann, "Images of Women in the Talmud," in *Religion and Sexism*, ed. Rosemary Radford Ruether (New York: Simon & Schuster, 1974), pp. 184–212; and Judith Baskin, "The Separation of Women in Rabbinic Judaism," in *Women, Religion and Social Change*, ed. Y. Z. Haddad and E. B. Findly (Albany: State University of New York Press, 1985), pp. 3–18.

[13]Baskin, "The Separation of Women in Rabbinic Judaism," p. 3.

[14]Ibid., p. 7, drawing on P. Shabbat 2, 5b, 34; Gen R. 17:7.

[15]Mark Zborowski and Elizabeth Herzog, *Life Is with People: The Culture of the Shtetl* (New York: Schocken, 1962), pp. 134–135.

[16]Elie Wiesel, *Four Hasidic Masters* (Notre Dame, Ind.: University of Notre Dame Press, 1978), p. 33–34.

[17]Ibid, p. 34.

[18]Lis Harris, *Holy Days: The World of a Hasidic Family* (New York: Summit, 1985), pp. 147–148.

[19]Ellen M. Umansky, "Feminism and the Reevaluation of Women's Roles Within American Jewish Life," in *Women, Religion and Social Change*, p. 484.

[20]Lee Shulamith Koenig, "A Jewish Perspective from Israel," in *Speaking of Faith*, ed. Diana L. Eck and Devaki Jain (Philadelphia: New Society, 1987), pp. 61–69.

[21]See Blu Greenberg, "Marriage in the Jewish Tradition," *Journal of Ecumenical Studies*, 22, no. 1 (Winter 1985), pp. 3–20.

[22]Judith Plaskow, "The Wife/Sister Stories: Dilemmas of the Jewish Feminist," in *Speaking of Faith*, pp. 125–126.

[23]T. Drorah Setel, "Roundtable Discussion: Feminist Reflections on Separation and Unity in Jewish Theology," *Journal of Feminist Studies in Religion*, 2, no. 1 (Spring 1986), pp. 117–118.

CHAPTER EIGHT

Christian Women

OVERVIEW

Christianity began after the death of Jesus of Nazareth, when disciples claimed he was still alive as a spiritual force. In the beginning it had the character of a dissident Jewish sect. Thus, it inherited the Hebrew Bible (usually in its Greek—Septuagint—form) as its Scripture. From the first century, **Hellenistic**—Greek cultural—influences were significant (as they had been in the last centuries before the Common Era, when the Writings of the Hebrew Bible arose). Memories of the person, message, and work of Jesus of Nazareth started accumulating soon after his death about 30 C.E. Eventually the memories of different Christian communities were arranged into four generally accepted gospels. At the same time, the writings of the Apostle Paul circulated among the communities he had founded or visited. The combination of these two sets of writings, gospels plus Pauline epistles, gave the core of what became the New Testament. With the addition of miscellaneous letters and the Book of Revelation, by about 100 C.E. Christians had a second portion of Scripture. Ever since, their Bible has had an Old and a New Testament.

By the end of the first century the Christian Church had broken irreparably with the Jewish synagogue. For the next two hundred years it successfully competed with Judaism and the Hellenistic religions, gradually become a mainly Gentile church. From time to time it suffered persecution by Roman authorities, who saw the new religion as potentially seditious and a threat to the unity of the Roman Empire. However, early in the fourth century Christians gained imperial favor. From that time the followers of Jesus were the leading force in the Empire, destined to become the shapers of Western history.

Women were members of the Christian community from the outset. Jewish women had followed Jesus during his ministry, standing by him as he died on the cross. The New Testament has the risen Christ appear first to Mary Magdalene, and the community that formed around Peter and the other eyewitnesses of Jesus included both men and women. We shall deal with the way Jesus treated women and how women fare in the New Testament. Right now we need only note that the early Church's attitudes toward women came from several sources: Jewish traditions, as determined by both the Old Testament and the beginnings of rabbinic theology; Hellenistic traditions—Greek and Roman attitudes and mores; and growing experience of Christian faith, which included reflection on what the Christian life meant for relations between the sexes.

By the midfourth century, when Christianity had a favored position in the Empire, a Christian patriarchalism was well established. The **patristic age** that mediated between the end of the New Testament era and the early Middle Ages was dominated by bishop-theologians who uniformly were men. Eastern Christianity turned the patristic theology and the work of the first seven ecumenical councils into a patrimony that has determined Orthodox faith and practice to this day.

During the Middle Ages both religious and secular power was in the hands of men—popes, bishops, and priests; princes; lower nobility; and soldiers. Women shaped family life, and Christian women had the option of entering monasteries for women. Individual women commanded respect for their sanctity and social services. But on the whole medieval Christianity was a man's world, structured very hierarchially and not much interested in relational, democratic arrangements that would have better incorporated women. The great paradigm of Christian femininity throughout the medieval period was the Virgin Mary, the Mother of God who offered believers the comforts of love, understanding, and intercession with an often forbidding Christ and God the Father.

By the end of the thirteenth century the Catholic medieval synthesis was starting to come apart. The fourteenth and fifteenth centuries witnessed increasing disarray, and the waves of reform that rocked the Church in the first half of the sixteenth century received a good welcome. Women had suffered as much as men from the disorders of church life and the plagues of the pre-Reformation centuries. With the Protestant reforms, marriage gained in esteem, but the Reformers' return to the Bible often implied a renewal of biblical views about patriarchy. In left-wing Protestant churches, which tended toward egalitarian forms of government and pacifism, women had some opportunities for leadership. Otherwise, the Reformations, Protestant and Catholic, did little for women's liberation.

Modernity took the Protestant Reformers' stress on individual conscience and removed its reference to the Spirit of God. From Reformed and Renaissance sources came a new humanism. During the Enlightenment human reason became the great treasure, but few Western cultures considered women sufficiently possessed of this treasure to welcome them into the ranks of the philosophers and scientists who were shaping history. Within the Church, missionaries followed the explorers who had opened up both the Orient and the New World. After the missionaries came expatriate settlers, families as well as individual adventurers. In the New World women often worked alongside men and so shared both economic importance and significant status. Most Christian religious assemblies still counted women as second-class citizens, however, not admitting them to the ranks of ministers and powerholders.

The feminist movements of the recent centuries frequently have brought women into conflict with their Christian roots, as people who sought the equalization of relations between the sexes ran into Christian patriarchal traditions. The Protestant church groups who directly relied on the Bible found the subordination of women to men encoded in the Christian foundations, while the Roman Catholic and Eastern Orthodox churches insisted that an all-male clergy was part of Christ's original plan for the Church. Pious Christian women therefore found it hard to be feminists, while feminists found it hard to be mainstream Christians. Only very recently has this situation begun to change.[1]

Nowadays most feminist theoreticians are not committed Christians, and regularly one finds secular feminist theory treating religion as mainly a source of women's oppression. Even when such theory admits the significance of religious symbols in past history, it assumes that the feminist future it is trying to build will either oust religion altogether or have a new religion of women's making (which often turns out to be the old religion of the prehistoric Goddess).

Among the questions most troubling to those contemporary feminists who do retain a Christian allegiance are the sexism of the present-day churches and their connivance in women's oppression. The churches that do not admit female candidates for the priesthood or ministry usually are judged obtuse if not hypocritical when they claim to be servants of women's deepest aspirations. Similarly, the churches that oppose birth control, sex education, and women's right to abortion more often than not are listed among the oppressors. More positively, a corps of feminist Christian theologians has been working through such questions as how to overcome the sexism of traditional religious language and the traditional symbolism for

God, how to fashion a spirituality that will answer women's distinctive religious needs, and how to join justice for women to the general agenda of political work to combat racism, war making, and the destruction of the natural environment.

Presently Christians number about 1.6 billion worldwide—nearly a third of the global population. Roman Catholics are about 900 million, Protestants about 325 million, and Eastern Orthodox about 160 million. Another 235 million (70 million Anglicans and 165 million from various churches) fall outside these three categories, although most of them are related to mainstream Protestantism. Only in East Asia are Christians not a highly visible presence (75 million). In all other areas their fraction of the population runs into double digits.[2]

JESUS AND WOMEN

A recent study of how women functioned in the ministry of Jesus comes to the following conclusions: First, Jesus's teaching on divorce—that both sexes were bound to marriage since in marrying they had become a new whole, "one flesh"—would have offended most of his contemporaries, who considered divorce a legitimate option. The main beneficiaries of this new, more stringent teaching were women, because the prevailing view placed the right to divorce nearly exclusively in the hands of men. Second, Jesus's legitimizing a single state also went against the trends prevailing in both Palestine and most other parts of the Roman Empire. The prevailing view was that people had the duty to procreate. By teaching that service of the gospel could legitimate an unmarried life, Jesus freed both men and women from absolutist interpretations of that duty. For women, Jesus's view had the practical effect of allowing them to assume roles in the Christian community other than those of wife and mother.

Third, Jesus rejected the double standard of sexual morality that obtained in his day and held both men and women to an internal as well as an external fidelity. The drift of this teaching was to free women of special responsibility for sexual misdeeds—to whittle down their image of temptress (daughters of Eve) and lessen their use as scapegoats. Fourth, unlike many authors contemporary to him, Jesus was not derogatory about women's nature, ability, and religious capacities. No doubt this was an important reason women found his teaching attractive and joined his movement. Fifth, in teaching that the family of faith was more important than the physical family, Jesus opened the door to women's leaving their natal families and rejecting marriage in favor of a life of religious service. In germ, he legitimated the monastic life for both sexes.

On the other hand, Jesus did not radically reject the patriarchal family structure that obtained in his day. In addressing divorce, responsibilities toward parents, and the value of children, he supported the ideals of his Jewish contemporaries. Further, he stressed the responsibility of husbands and male leaders to give moral example, and as leaders of his new religious community he chose twelve men (perhaps as symbols of a new twelve tribes of Israel).

Sixth, Jesus dealt with women more freely than probably was customary for rabbis in his day (our written records only come from some decades after Jesus, so how unique he was is not certain). He interpreted the laws of uncleanness leniently, was willing to heal a woman on the Sabbath (and so risk criticism for working on a day of rest), and on occasion conversed with unknown women in public. As well, he dealt with whores and tax-gatherers: two categories of public "sinners" that a rabbi concerned about his reputation would have avoided. Seventh, that Jesus admitted women as disciples ran contrary to rabbinical trends: rabbis did not accept women as students.

In these and other matters, Jesus displayed a remarkable creativity. He drew from Jewish tradition what fitted his sense that a new time, the Kingdom of God, was at hand, and what did not fit his sense he rejected or bracketed. Before him rabbis had used women as examples of faith and told stories that redounded to women's praise, but his positive stance remains distinctive. In the wake of his example, the gospels of Luke and John take pains to present women as models of faith. In comparison to both contemporary Judaism and some of the Hellenistic cults, the Jesus movement would have seemed more welcoming of women. As Ben Witherington, the source I have been following, puts this point,

> The necessary and sufficient explanation of why Christianity differed from its religious mother, Judaism, in these matters is that Jesus broke with both biblical and rabbinic traditions that restricted women's roles in religious practices, and that He rejected attempts to devalue the worth of a woman, or her word of witness. Thus, the community of Jesus, both before and after Easter, granted women *together* with men (not segregated from men as in some pagan cults) an equal right to participate fully in the family of faith. This was a right that women did not have in contemporary Judaism or in many pagan cults.[3]

In presenting the women whom Jesus befriended and accepted as disciples, the gospels seem to go out of their way to show a reorientation that gives traditional female roles a new context and significance. Thus Mary, the mother of Jesus, is depicted as learning to be a mother as a disciple, while Martha is shown learning to be a hostess as a disciple. By the time one comes to the communities described in Acts, this trend has matured to the point where women might be teachers of men (Acts 18:14–26). For the gospel of John women have become signal witnesses to Jesus, especially valued for their testimony about his death, burial, empty tomb, and appearances as the risen Lord.

My own reading of the gospels leads me to stress the warm relations

Jesus had with women such as Martha and Mary, the sisters of the man Jesus brought back from the dead. John 11:5 says it plainly: "Now Jesus loved Martha and her sister and Lazarus." Later in the narrative of the raising of Lazarus we read,

> Then Mary, when she came where Jesus was and saw him, fell at his feet, saying to him, "Lord, if you had been here, my brother would not have died." When Jesus saw her weeping, and the Jews who came with her also weeping, he was deeply moved in spirit and troubled; and he said, "Where have you laid him?" They said to him, "Lord, come and see." Jesus wept. (John 11:32–35).

For the author of John, Mary is the woman who had anointed the feet of Jesus and wiped them with her hair. The story in Luke 7 displays both Jesus's willingness to deal with a woman of ill repute and his discernment of the emotions boiling in her heart:

> And behold, a woman of the city, who was a sinner, when she learned that he was at table in the Pharisee's house, brought an alabaster flask of ointment, and standing behind him at his feet, weeping, she began to wet his feet with her tears, and wiped them with the hair of her head, and kissed his feet, and anointed them with the ointment. Now when the Pharisee who had invited him saw it, he said to himself, "If this man were a prophet, he would have known who and what sort of woman this is who is touching him, for she is a sinner [whose touch defiles]." And Jesus answering said to him, "Simon, I have something to say to you." And he answered, "What is it, Teacher?" "A certain creditor had two debtors; one owed five hundred denarii, and the other fifty. When they could not pay, he forgave them both. Now which of them will love him more?" Simon answered, "The one, I suppose, to whom he forgave more." And he said to him, "You have judged rightly." Then turning toward the woman he said to Simon, "Do you see this woman? I entered your house, you gave me no water for my feet [customary hospitality], but she has wet my feet with her tears and wiped them with her hair. You gave me no kiss, but from the time I came in she has not ceased to kiss my feet. You did not anoint my head with oil, but she has anointed my feet with ointment. Therefore I tell you, her sins, which are many, are forgiven, for she loved much; but he who is forgiven little, loves little." And he said to her, "Your sins are forgiven." Then those who were at table with him began to say among themselves, "Who is this, who even forgives sins?" And he said to the woman, "Your faith has saved you; go in peace." (Luke 7:37–50)

In these two scenes, from John and Luke, Jesus deals with a woman personally, intimately, and against the grain of prevailing male-female relations. The sister of Lazarus is a friend. Her grief is his grief. Her trust is a claim on his conscience. The woman who anoints his feet is a woman in need, a woman in distress. She honors him as a way of honoring the God he is preaching about, the God she feels she has offended. Although public opinion discounts her—she is considered a whore, if not a prostitute—Jesus takes her as she is. Women as much as men come into his vision as individuals, people who don't have to bear the burdens of stereotypes. If this was the way Jesus treated women, no wonder they flocked to him.

OTHER NEW TESTAMENT VIEWS

The most important feminist interpretation of New Testament views of women is Elisabeth Schüssler Fiorenza's *In Memory of Her*. For Schüssler Fiorenza, the movement of those whom Jesus attracted was radically egalitarian, and only when Christianity took over hierarchical schemes from the surrounding Hellenistic environment did women become second-class members of the Church. In the ministry of Jesus women, like other marginalized groups, were invited to experience how the Kingdom of God and divine Spirit overturned the classifications that had made women and the poor count less than men and the wealthy. The first generation of Christians seems to have remembered this egalitarian thrust, and Acts 12:12–13 suggests that in the first generation women headed house churches: "When he [Peter] realized this, he went to the house of Mary, the mother of John whose other name was Mark, where many were gathered together and praying."

Schüssler Fiorenza finds such Pauline texts as Romans 16:6 and 12 and Philippians 4:2–3 implying that women could be missionary workers on the same level as men. Acts 18:26 presents a couple, Priscilla and Aquila, correcting an eloquent new convert. Apparently they were a missionary couple who had gained considerable status in the young Church:

> Now a Jew named Apollos, a native of Alexandria, came to Ephesus. He was an eloquent man, well versed in the scriptures. He had been instructed in the way of the Lord; and being fervent in the spirit, he spoke and taught accurately the things concerning Jesus, though he knew only the baptism of John. He began to speak boldly in the synagogue; but when Priscilla and Aquila heard him, they took him and expounded to him the way of God more accurately. (Acts 18:24–26)

Another text which suggests that early Pauline Christianity accepted the radical egalitarianism of the Jesus movement is Galatians 3:27–29:

> For as many of you as were baptized into Christ have put on Christ. There is neither Jew nor Greek, there is neither slave nor free, there is neither male nor female; for you are all one in Christ Jesus. And if you are Christ's, then you are Abraham's offspring, heirs according to promise.

Here Paul has transformed the notion of the Kingdom of God into his own characteristic sense that believers make up one organism with Christ, the resurrected Jesus. Just as Jesus had suggested that the Kingdom or Reign of God was a new situation that did away with prior hierarchies and blessed the previously outcaste, so Paul suggests that Christian faith creates a new entity in which the old oppositions no longer obtain. To dissolve the distinctions between Jew and Gentile, slave and free person, and male and female was to postulate an entirely new social vision.

In fact, the Church did not accept this Pauline vision as intended to structure the Christian community on a completely egalitarian basis. Eventually one's ethnic background—Jewish or Gentile—faded from significance, but slaves were not automatically emancipated and men consolidated church power. What Schüssler Fiorenza calls "love patriarchalism" furnished a rationale for this stalled revolution. Spiritually, or in terms of love and affection, ethnic origin, sex, and degree of liberty were made matters of only second-rate importance. Before God, people were judged by the quality of their religious lives, not by extrinsic criteria. (This conviction persisted throughout Christian history: in the final analysis, only God knew what was in people's hearts and could judge their real worth.) But in social groups, where the Church felt it had to accommodate to the mores of Hellenistic society, the stratifications of Hellenistic society would be taken into account. So it did come to matter whether one was slave or free, male or female. The patriarchalism of both Judaism and Hellenistic culture entered into the Church's codes for family life and the maintenance of its own community order. Supposedly love would remove the sting of such patriarchal structures, but clearly both the Pauline vision and the teaching of Jesus about the Kingdom of God were significantly diluted.

In summarizing how Christianity stood prior to the establishment of house codes that internalized patriarchal rankings, Schüssler Fiorenza stresses the fusion of egalitarianism and a domestic, family conception of the local Christian community, thinking that the result was something distinctive:

> The early Christian vision of the discipleship of equals practiced in the house church attracted especially slaves and women to Christianity but also caused tensions and conflicts with the dominant cultural ethos of the patriarchal household. True, women as well as men, slaves as well as free, Asians as well as Greeks and Romans, participated fully in the cult of the Great Goddess; and in such a religious context the baptismal confession of Gal 3:28 was not utopian. However, in contrast to the public cult of the goddess, in the Christian context, the public religious sphere of the church and the private sphere of the patriarchal house were not clearly separated. Insofar as Christians understood themselves as the new family and expressed this self-understanding institutionally in the house church, the public-religious and private patriarchal spheres were no longer distinguished. In fact, it was the religious ethos—of equality—that was transferred to and came in conflict with the patriarchal ethos of the household. The Christian missionary movement thus provided an alternative vision and praxis to that of the dominant society and religion.[4]

In Colossians we see the effort of disciples of Paul to harmonize the original egalitarian vision with the subjection of women to men that prevailed in the typical Hellenistic household. First, when it restates the Pauline baptismal formula of Galatians 3:28, Colossians 3:11 both softens the previous tensions (between Jew and Greek, free and slave, male and female: hierarchical dyads) and omits women: "Here there cannot be Greek and Jew, circumcised and uncircumcised, barbarian, Scythian, slave, free man, but Christ is all, and in all." Second, when it comes to fashioning a code for how Christian households ought to work, Colossians 3:18–4:1 makes the spirit of love, forbearance, and forgiveness that it had previously lauded an inner disposition compatible with marked social statifications. This is love-patriarchalism: the old superior-inferior relations retained but humanized by the infusion of the spirit and love of the new faith:

> Wives, be subject to your husbands, as is fitting in the Lord. Husbands, love your wives, and do not be harsh with them. Children, obey your parents in everything, for this pleases the Lord. Fathers, do not provoke your children, lest they become discouraged. Slaves, obey in everything those who are your earthly masters, not with eye service, as men-pleasers, but in singleness of heart, fearing the Lord. Whatever your task, work heartily, as serving the Lord and not men, knowing that from the Lord you will receive the inheritance as your reward; you are serving the Lord Christ. For the wrongdoer will be paid back for the wrong he has done, and there is no partiality. Masters, treat your slaves justly and fairly, knowing that you also have a Master in heaven.

Certainly there are some fine sentiments in this code, but it accepts a hierarchial structure of the Christian family at odds with the radical vision of Jesus and Paul. One finds the same sort of shift in Ephesians 5, where husbands become the heads of their wives, as Christ is the head of the Church. By the time we get to I Timothy, another work by a disciple of Paul, love patriarchalism has forgotten some of its love and turned misogynistic. Not only are women not the equals of men in the new faith, they are dangerous:

> Let a woman learn in silence with all submissiveness. I permit no woman to teach or have authority over men; she is to keep silent. For Adam was formed first, then Eve; and Adam was not deceived, but the woman was deceived and became a transgressor. Yet woman will be saved through bearing children, if she continues in faith and love and holiness, with modesty. (I Timothy 2:11–15).

Women are now second class.[5]

THE PATRISTIC PERIOD

Women continued to be second-class citizens throughout the patristic era. Church fathers such as Tertullian, Chrysostom, Jerome, and Augustine inveighed against the problems women caused virtuous men. In part their difficulty was cultural: **Gnosticism** was in the air, arguing that the flesh and matter were ungodly and so could be ignored. The fathers who opposed Gnosticism wanted to maintain the goodness of creation, including sex and marriage, without agreeing to any libertine tendencies. Most of them were influenced by Hellenistic prejudices that made the spirit more important than the flesh and that considered freedom from desire the religious person's ideal.

Clement of Alexandria (ca 150–215), a cultured man who sought to make Christianity the fulfillment of Greek philosophy, wrote of desire as follows:

> The human ideal of continence, I mean that which is set forth by Greek philosophers, teaches that one should fight desire and not be subservient to it so as to bring it to practical effect. But our ideal is not to experience desire at all. Our aim is not that while a man feels desire he should get the better of it, but that he should be continent even respecting desire itself. This chastity cannot be attained in any other way except by God's grace . . . Whether a man becomes celibate or whether he joins himself in marriage with a woman for the sake of having children, his purpose ought to be to remain unyielding to what is inferior. If he can live a life of intense devotion, he will gain to himself great merit with God, since his continence is both pure and reasonable. But if he goes beyond the rule he has chosen to gain greater glory, there is a danger that he may lose hope.[6]

The quotation is typical of the fathers in fearing sexual desire and making no effort to solicit or imagine women's views.

The Latin father Jerome (ca 347–420), whose letters brim with struggles to control his own desires, strove with might and main to establish the superiority of virginity to marriage. He urged the many women he counseled to follow the ascetical life of virginity, prayer, and fasting, and he was glad to use any source that deprecated marriage and female sensuality. Thus he once quoted with satisfaction a passage from a book on marriage attributed to Theophrastus. Theophrastus had agreed that under certain conditions—a woman who is fair, of good character, of honest parents, and a husband in good health and having ample finances—a wise man may marry.

> But all these conditions are seldom satisfied in marriage. A wise man therefore must not take a wife. For in the first place his study of philosophy will be hindered, and it is impossible for anyone to attend to his books and his wife. Matrons want many things, costly dresses, gold jewels, great outlay, maidservants, all kinds of furniture, litters and gilded coaches. Then come curtainlectures the live-long night: she complains that one lady goes out better dressed than she, that another is looked up to by all: "I am a poor despised nobody at the ladies' assemblies." "Why did you ogle that creature next door?" . . . Notice, too, that in the case of a wife you cannot pick and choose: you must take her as you find her. If she has a bad temper, or is a fool, if she has a blemish, or is proud, or has bad breath, whatever her fault may be—all

this we learn after marriage. Horses, asses, cattle, even slaves of the smallest worth, clothes, kettles, wooden seats, cups, and earthenware pitchers, are first tried and then bought: a wife is the only thing that is not shown before she is married, for fear she may not give satisfaction . . . if a woman be fair, she soon finds lovers; if she is ugly, it is easy to be wanton. It is difficult to guard what many long for. It is annoying to have what no one thinks worth possessing.[7]

We have come a long way from Pauline egalitarianism. Wives are now little better than chattel.

One woman from the patristic age who fared well in later Christian memory was Monica, the mother of Augustine. Because Augustine (354–430) became the foremost father of the Western church, laying down the theological foundations on which medievals such as Thomas Aquinas built, the picture he gave of Monica in his *Confessions* stimulated great veneration of her. Augustine attributed his conversion to his mother's prayers. Just as she had given him physical birth, so she gave him the spiritual birth of faith and grace. Thus Monica became for Augustine a figure for the Church, which also labors to bring lost sons back into the fold, corrects the recalcitrant, nourishes the feeble, and educates the immature. Because of his sense of his mother's prayers on his behalf, Augustine thought of divine grace as a motherly persuasion or compulsion.

If the Monica of the *Confessions* is all tears and handwringings, the Monica who appears in some of Augustine's letters is a fuller personality. After his conversion, Augustine established a monastic community dedicated to prayer and study. Monica joined their discussions and made them forget her sex. Indeed, they came to think of her as a great man in their midst, so affecting was her wisdom. When she remarked on the unusualness of her inclusion, Augustine replied that talent and character were the important things, not status. Augustine was a creative writer, more interested in stirring faith than in narrating history. Under his literary molding Monica came to symbolize the uneducated Christian whose simple faith proved more valuable than philosophical learning. She had mystical experiences, and through them Augustine himself was drawn up to divine wisdom.

In the Middle ages Monica functioned as a prototype of the holy mother and was venerated whenever women were struggling to stabilize their children in faith. Thus saints such as Birgitta and Jane Francis de Chantal looked to Monica as their model, as did the holy fifteenth-century Englishwoman Margery Kempe.[8]

Despite his reverence and appreciation for his mother, Augustine agreed with Clement and Jerome that marital sexuality was bothersome. His experiences with concubinage had made him think of sexual love as a slavery, and when he speculated about the original sin that had brought humanity to its present, low estate, he made sexual intercourse the means through which it was transmitted generation after generation. All this did little for either Christian marriage or Christian women.

I have mentioned the opposition to Gnosticism that fueled Clement of Alexandria. Another influential early father, Tertullian (ca 155–220), was incensed that Gnostic women presumed to prophesy and teach. Apparently he had forgotten the first generation of Christian women. Moreover, Tertullian thought that a failing in chastity was one of the worst of sins, and he called woman "the devil's gateway," "the first deserter of the divine law," the one because of whom "even the Son of God had to die."[9] Although Tertullian himself was married, he thought that widows who remarried would "harvest fruits well fitting these last days, dripping breasts, stinking wombs, crying babies."[10]

Because of this patristic view of sex and femininity, women who gained sanctity through either monastic asceticism or martyrdom regularly were described in male terms. To become holy, worthy of union with God, they had to change their sex. Thus Perpetua, a twenty-two-year-old married woman and prophetess, supposedly had a vision, before her martyrdom, in which she was stripped and became a man, without, somehow, ceasing to be a woman. John Chrysostom, a very influential Greek father, laid the foundation for sentiments such as these in Eastern Orthodox Christianity. He urged virginity because marriage was only for procreation, the world already was filled, and marriage therefore tended to function as a concession to sin. A first marriage was better than visiting prostitutes, but remarriage indicated stupidity. The widow who remarried would never be happy, because men like what no one else has owned and used. Chrysostom blamed women for the sins of David and Solomon, and he did not scruple to describe women as storehouses of spittle and phlegm. One sees, therefore, that the golden age of patristic literature was a bad time for women and healthy sexual love.[11]

THE MEDIEVAL PERIOD

The rise of monasticism in the patristic period meant that women had a reputable option besides marriage. They could consecrate their lives to religious service and virginity. Usually women's monastic establishments were controlled by men, either male members of the order to which the women belonged and whose rule they followed or the local bishop, who numbered them among his flock. During the medieval period female heads of monasteries—abbesses—occasionally controlled men as well as women, and regularly religious women (those who had taken the three vows of poverty, chastity, and obedience) managed their day-to-day affairs. Nonetheless, the Church that sanctioned their religious lives, East and West, was ruled by men: popes, patriarchs, and bishops.

Despite their official subordination to a male-dominated Church, medieval religious women often exercised considerable power, especially that generated by the freedom their service of God, in contrast to man-made orders, gave them. Eleanor McLaughlin has argued that however unusable present-day feminists may initially find the example of medieval religious women, closer inspection suggests that a millennium ago outstanding women were accomplishing things we would do well to study. McLaughlin's argument proceeds by way of concrete examples, and her first study, of an Anglo-Saxon nun named Lioba, is worth citing:

> Saint Lioba was an Anglo-Saxon nun of good Wessex family, a scholar, an abbess, a missionary in the wilds of Germany. She became the spiritual friend and confidante of Saint Boniface, bishop and Anglo-Saxon missionary to the Germans, who called her and a number of other women from the abbey at Wimborne to minister among the heathen of Saxony. Lioba's *Life*, written half a century after her death in 779, was intended to edify, like all hagiography, but we can glean from its pages a sense of the strength and influence available to a woman within the eighth-century ideal of holiness . . . Rudolf's *Life of Saint Lioba* begins with childhood. We see her mother sending the child, a miraculous birth of her old age, to be trained as a religious at Wimborne, where under Mother Tetta she was taught the sacred sciences. The translator records, ". . . she [Lioba's mother] gave her her freedom"— that is, to live for God alone as a nun was to be freed of family under whom all women of that day lived as in bondage, to father, brother or uncle. The way in which the religious life transcended biological bonds is also symbolized by the observation that it was Lioba's wide reputation for learning and holiness which caused Boniface to summon her to work with him in Germany, not his blood relationship to her mother. There is a self-conscious opposition between the bonds of sanctity and family which we will see repeated in later Christian literature. Also explicit is the wholly female context of Lioba's education. Mother Tetta was her intellectual and spiritual mentor, and Tetta herself, we are told, possessed the gift of prophecy as well as scholarship. Lioba also learned from her community of sisters.[12]

Much as Buddhist nuns found monastic life a haven from the oppressions of patriarchal family life, so many Christian religious women were freer to develop their talents in the monastery than they would have been in family life. Many medieval religious women in fact became renowned as mystics and sources of social betterment: help for the poor, succor of the suffering. A Catherine of Siena had the courage and reputation to rebuke the pope when she thought he was erring. A Joan of Arc obviously fit another profile, but she was like Catherine in claiming the inspiration of God for her bold acts.

However, perhaps the most important feminine figure of medieval times, again East and West, was the Virgin Mary. In the East, where iconography was the mainspring of popular piety, Byzantine painters regularly rendered what doctrinally was known as the *theotokos*: Mary as the God-bearer. If Christ was the *pantokrator*, the ruler of all, Mary was the Mother who humanized his power, whose embrace of him when he was a small child suggested she would intercede with him on sinner's behalf. For example, a twelfth-century Greek mosaic of the Virgin and child presents her in typical iconographic garb: a black mantle that comes down well over her forehead, covering her hair, and gold decorations that change its sobriety to regality; she may be in mourning for the fate the child will undergo, but she is a queen, the mother of God's little prince. Both mother and child have the nimbus that indicates sanctity. The child has hold of the mother's mantle, both to steady himself in her arms and to indicate their bond. The Virgin's right hand is at her breast, in another gesture of feeling. It is a splendid, elegant hand—the long, tapered fingers of a noble lady. In counterpoint to the emotion suggested by both the hand at her breast and the red spots at her cheeks (probably the blush of feeling rather than youth), the Virgin's countenance is somber and sad. She has a long, oval face, a long straight nose, large dark eyes, and impressive black brows. Her chin is round and full, her mouth small and red. She is a beautiful woman with complete feminine grace and not a hint of sensuality.[13]

Western medieval art also celebrated the Madonna and child. In the West, as in the East, church art served the common people as a visual catechism. Many women who had little or no access to religious literature learned about Jesus, Mary, and the saints from the scenes painted on church walls. In fourteenth-century Tuscan painting, which probably we should regard as late medieval art, a painter such as Giotto put into visual form the piety found in such contemporary devotional writings as *The Meditations on the Life of Christ*. Margaret R. Miles, interested for feminist reasons in retrieving the impact of Western religious art, has commented on a crucifixion scene of Giotto by explicitly linking it to Marian sentiments:

> Giotto's Crucifixion, in Santa Maria Novella, has been called the first fully realistic portrayal of the crucifixion of Christ in the history of western painting. In this depiction, Christ's dead body is pulled downward by its own gravity and is given naturalistic flesh tones and shadings. The centuries that separate the viewer from the event are obliterated, and the viewer is made a spectator at the cross; the viewer sees the scene that he had visualized while hearing a recitation from the *Meditations* of the passion story as seen through the eyes of the Virgin: "Behold, then, the Lord hangs dead on the cross; the whole multitude departs. . . . But you, if you will contemplate your Lord well, will consider that from the sole of His foot to the crown of His head there is no health in Him; there is not one member or bodily sense that has not left total affliction or passion. . . . Study devotedly, faithfully, and solicitously to meditate on all this."[14]

The sensate, grief-centered piety of the late medieval period, perhaps most classically expressed in *The Imitation of Christ* attributed to Thomas à Kempis, used the Virgin as the most exquisite, refined locus of sorrow. She above all was the mother who had watched her son die on the cross and had received his dead body into her arms—the devastated Pietá. In her women could see religious emotion at its most feminine and profound. Balancing the Virgin was the Magdalene, who regularly appeared with flaming red hair. She was the converted sinner, the woman of passion who finally had found an object worthy of her ardor. Because she had loved so much, her many sins had been forgiven her. In her medieval women could find the sensuality lacking in most iconography of the Virgin. Where the Virgin usually was composed, dignified, a visual lesson in the strength God gave to endure the worst evils of a short and brutal human life, the Magdalene had license to be unbridled, even histrionic. Together they furnished medieval women a remarkably full instruction in the love of Christ. Together they gave the lie to such esteemed teaching as that of Saint Thomas Aquinas, who followed Aristotle in judging female nature defective—misbegotten manhood.[15]

Nonetheless, we should not forget that, despite the symbolic influence of the Virgin and the Magdalene, and despite the achievements of exceptional nuns, the lot of the average Christian woman throughout medieval times could be quite grim. Daughter of Eve, she was always liable to be blamed for the woes of the human condition. If she ventured outside the roles approved by the Church, or if she showed interest in the pre-Christian European religious traditions of worship and healing, she might well be stigmatized as a witch. At the end of the medieval period and the beginning of the Renaissance and Reformation, witch burning in fact became such a craze that thousands of women were burned.

Moreover, for every woman in the convent freed to study and create, there were probably a thousand constrained by church laws and prevailing social customs to be less than their talents might have made them. For every woman idolized by a chivalrous knight, there were probably a thousand battered as a matter of course by brutish husbands. The possibilities held out by the best of medieval Christian culture were actualized in relatively few lives. As has been true for most other historical eras and religious traditions, the possibilities kept the darkness from totally prevailing, but they failed to establish good news in the lives of the majority.

REFORMATION THEMES

Although there had been significant movements for Church reform in the fourteenth and fifteenth centuries, the Protestant reformation of the early sixteenth century was the wave that broke the dam. George Tavard, surveying the history of women's treatment in Christian tradition, finds Martin Luther's views paradoxical. On the one hand, Luther's general intent was to restore to all Christians the liberty of the gospel. Insofar as women as well as men were images of God, they shared the basic capacities and rights related to this liberty. On the other hand, for Luther

> The natural order does not assign woman any other function than what corresponds to her sexual and procreative organs. Luther's commentary on Gen-

esis identifies mankind with Adam the male, seeing woman as adjunct to him for the sake of procreation: "Man is a more excellent creature than heaven and earth and everything that is in them. But Moses [whom Luther considered the author of Genesis] wanted to point out in a special way that the other part of humanity, the woman, was created by a unique counsel of God in order to show that this sex too is suited for the kind of life which Adam was expecting and that this sex was to be useful for procreation."[16]

Indeed, Luther's reading of the Bible led him to think that if there had been no fall, woman would have been the equal of man. However, in paradise Adam would have only needed Eve for procreation. After the fall, men need women not only for offspring but also for companionship and household management. Women serve as medicine for sexual desire—marital intercourse is the way men may avoid sins of unchastity. Following Augustine (to whose religious order he had belonged), Luther thought that the intrinsic connection between sex and sin meant that all children were born in sin (inherited the disorder that affected Adam and Eve after the fall). So since the fall, marriage has had something shameful about it. It has been and remains a remedy for concupiscence—untoward desire. Commentators have taxed Luther with fixating on the genital aspects of marital love, and feminists certainly should tax him with **androcentrism**—blissful unconcern for women's views. Indeed, because of his attitudes toward marriage, he was lenient about bigamy, polygamy, and adultery (in each case from a male point of view).

Finally, Luther taught that God had laid on women a greater share of the curse that came with original sin than was laid on men. Men had to earn their bread by the sweat of their brow, but women's bondage to childbearing implied the further bondages of submission to male rule and restriction to the domestic sphere:

> The rule remains with the husband, and the wife is compelled to obey him by God's command. He rules the home and the state, wages war, defends his possessions, tills the soil, builds, plants, etc. The woman on the other hand is like a nail driven into the wall. She sits at home. . . . Just as the snail carries its house with it, so the wife should stay at home and look after the affairs of the household, as one who has been deprived of the duty of administering those affairs that are outside and that concern the state. She does not go beyond her most personal duties.[17]

Luther did note that although this was God's will for women, many women either tried to revolt against it or grumbled constantly.

Today it seems clear that Luther and the other fathers of traditional Protestant theology were most handicapped by their limited approach to the Bible. Because they took the Bible as God's only sure channel of revelation and were leery of Church tradition, the patriarchal biblical world dominated their horizon. Moreover, because of the androcentrism of their cultural upbringing, they were little inclined to develop women's share in the biblical warrants for freedom. Feminist biblical scholars therefore have come to realize that no adequate liberation for women will come from the scriptures until women's views are fully represented in the interpretational frameworks biblical exegetes use.[18]

John Calvin dealt with women and marriage more delicately than the sometimes crude Luther, and insofar as he stressed the refining impact of femininity, he has been read as a great appreciator of women. However, cultural historians know the dangers in making women the naturally moral sex, the keepers of virtue and beauty. At the least, that usually places women on the margins of politics and business, cut off from the arenas in which public history is made. Public history becomes dirty and women become split into two great camps: innocent but not very interesting paragons of domestic virtue and ladies of pleasure. Calvin followed Luther in reading Genesis and the fall as entailing the subordination of women to men, but he was clearer than Luther that women provide men not only procreation but companionship. Without Eve, Adam is not fully human, and the union of man and woman ought to extend beyond their bodies and penetrate their souls. So strongly did Calvin insist on the subordination of women to men and women's restriction to the domestic sphere that he blamed Dina, the daughter of Jacob, for the kidnap and rape she suffered: if she had stayed at home where she belonged, it would not have happened. As well, Calvin justified the biblical double standard, finding it correct that adulterous women were to be stoned while unfaithful husbands were not subjected to capital punishment. At the wellsprings of Protestant theology, therefore, women continued to be as unequal to men as they had been in patristic and medieval theology.

We shall deal later with American women who took advantage of left-wing Protestant theology to achieve more individual fulfillment and public influence than the Lutheran and Calvinistic theologies would have allowed. An interesting example of the freedom European women found in left-wing Protestant churches is Jane Lead (1624–1704), who came under the influence of the mystical writings of the German Jacob Boehme (1575–1624). Lead was widowed in 1670, when she was forty-six. Thereafter her emotional and intellectual life deepened, as she followed the lead of ecstatic trances she had long experienced. Eventually she became a Boehmean prophet, writer, and principal founder of the Philadelphian Society which promoted Boehme's thought. Boehme had spoken of the cosmos in terms of a pervasive sexual imagery:

> But what effects has that thought had on the imaginations of little known women such as Jane Lead? Most immediately, its Inner Light theology offered utterance to her spiritual crisis. Lead probably viewed her writing largely as passionate religious witness. She was, after all, an ecstatic who thought of herself as a prophet. Yet, modern readers observant of her imaginative processes and her expression as well as her religious statement can rec-

ognize the outlines of an implicit visionary feminism. Here is a gynocentric vision that perceives universal spiritual transformation, modeled on her own, in predominantly female, not male, terms. Inherited ideas of the primacy of one's own "inner light" and the femaleness of the soul fused with Lead's fantasies and her social experiences as a woman to produce an intriguing form of apocalyptic literature.[19]

It would not be hard to find other women indebted to left-wing Protestant thought, Pietism, and continental spiritualist movements who broke out of the patriarchal constraints of mainstream Christian tradition and fashioned pathways more congenial to their mystical or social instincts. Similarly, the Catholic Reformation was fertile in new women's religious orders that pioneered a new spirituality suited for active apostolic work (teaching, nursing, social work) as well as prayer. These new orders regularly had to fight Roman resistance and the desire of church authorities to keep women cloistered, but slowly they won the right to serve the Church in nonmonastic, active working arrangements. Eastern Christianity generally abhorred the Protestant Reformation, as though preferring the Catholic devil it knew to the new adversary arising on the continent, while Orthodox traditionalism meant no break with patriarchal theology.

MODERN THEMES

In the seventeenth century one of the most influential Protestant developments was Puritanism, an English and American reform movement much influenced by Calvinist theology. Among the Puritan spokesman John Milton stands out, for his views on marriage were very influential. For Milton marriage was the place where the romance heralded in the tradition of courtly love might be purified and given its proper institutional form. Marital relations ought to be romantic: a union of man and woman for companionship, conversation, and love rather than for sexual congress and procreation. In his desire to promote individual freedom, Milton propagandized for both a free press and liberal divorce laws. Apparently his own marriage was unhappy, and he also sought freer divorce for personal reasons. When he analyzed marriage, Milton found that the worst failing was not adultery but what he called "idolatry": a rejection of the spiritual companionship he considered the heart of the marital compact.

However, although in some ways Milton's views might have served feminist ends, the underlying assumptions of his theology of marriage remained patriarchal: in marriage there ought to be a proper hierarchy, such that the wife would be the subject of the husband. Milton saw this hierarchy encoded in the creation of the two sexes. Where men had been created for God only, women had been created for the divinity in their men. For a wife to have a will different from her husband's would be a wrong greater than adultery. Finding such an unconjugal mind in his wife, a man would be obliged to divorce her. On the other hand, since a man could not be subject to his wife, he could not commit idolatry by having a will apart from hers. Thus she could not initiate divorce against him. Even should a believing woman be married to an unbeliever, she should try to minimize their discord, following the Pauline injunction (I Corinthians 7:13) that by her endurance and good example she might change his heart.[20]

In the eighteenth century the Shaker leader Anne Lee (1736–1784) demonstrated the religious creativity modern women could exercise. Her movement opposed the sexual relations then prevailing in industrial England, tedious religious practices, and warfare. Born into a poor family in Manchester, she received no education and worked in the clothing industry and as a cook. She came in contact with charismatic Shaking Quakers and at age twenty-six married a blacksmith. He never understood her religious interests, and after thirteen years of marriage, including four children who all died in infancy, she separated from him. Lee interpreted the deaths of her children as God's judgment on her concupiscence and strove to deny herself all carnal satisfactions. After being imprisoned with other Shakers in 1773–1774, she proclaimed that she had received a vision of the Garden of Eden that had made it plain sexual intercourse was the cause of humanity's separation from God. From sexual intercourse came the rest of humanity's woes: war, poverty, slavery, disease, and the inequality of men and women. Lee now felt herself married to Christ, and she urged her hearers to follow her example, avoiding carnal marriage and marrying Christ. In 1774 she and a few faithful followers went to New York to open this gospel to America. There she founded a celibate community that became famous not only for its exuberant religious singing and dancing but also for its crafts and furniture. Lee's theology was distinctive for criticizing the "mannish" character of received Christianity, postulating that God was both a Father and a Mother, and correlatively seeing the need for two Messiahs, Jesus Christ and herself.[21]

In the eighteenth and nineteenth centuries Christianity had to contend with an aggressive, sometimes atheistic humanism. As expressed in the Enlightenment and the French Revolution, it sought the emancipation of the individual from religious mythology and of the lower classes from the hierarchical social structures that had been oppressing them. On both counts, the humanists often took aim at the established churches and Christian morality. Even when they did not single out specifically religious causes, the humanistic reformers implicitly criticized the historical evolution that had brought conditions to their present pass.

One such humanistic critic and social reformer was Flora Tristan (1803–1844), a French socialist who linked egalitarian progress with the emancipation of women. In 1843 she published an appeal to the workers of France that had the following objectives:

(1) To constitute the working class by setting up a compact, solid, and indissoluble union. (2) The workers' union to choose and pay a defender who shall represent the working class before the nation [workers were without the voting franchise because of the 200-franc tax requirement], so as to establish universal acceptance of this class' right to exist [as an organization]. (3) To proclaim the legitimacy of hands (*bras*) as property, 25 million French workers having no property other than their hands. (4) To secure the recognition of every man and woman's right to work. (5) To secure the recognition of every man and woman's right to moral, intellectual, and vocational training. (6) To examine the possibilities of organizing the labor force in present social conditions. (7) To construct workers' union buildings in every department of France which shall provide intellectual and vocational training for working-class children and admit working men and women who have been disabled on the job or are sick or old. (8) To proclaim the urgent necessity of giving working-class women moral, intellectual, and vocational training so that they may improve the morals of men. (9) To proclaim the fact that juridical equality between men and women is the only means of achieving the unity of humanity.[22]

Tristan devoted herself to studying the condition of working-class people, especially working-class women, and doing what she could to improve their often wretched situations. She died in 1844 at the age of forty-one, worn out by sickness, hard work, and the opposition she had encountered (from working-class people themselves, as well as from the French authorities).

A final feature of the modern period germane to our interests was the revival in the nineteenth century of the Roman Catholic devotion to the Virgin Mary. Between 1850 and 1950 the cultus of the Virgin was a prime focus of Catholic devotion. In 1854 the papacy promulgated as dogma (formally defined doctrine) the **Immaculate Conception**: Mary's having been conceived without original sin. In 1950 the papacy promulgated as dogma the bodily assumption of Mary into heaven. Another aspect of the rise in Marian devotion was the many apparitions of the Virgin, most of which resulted in establishing local shrines such as those at Lourdes in France and Fatima in Portugal. Such shrines regularly became pilgrimage sites and focused the prayers of the faithful on the Virgin. Whether it was curing hopeless illness (Lourdes) or achieving the conve   on of Russia (Fatima), the devotions associated with such apparations o   ie Virgin dominated popular Catholic piety.

In assessing the significance of this Marian period, Barbara Corrado Pope has offered the following observations: the Marian devotions may be considered a softening or feminization of religious symbolism, but it is important to remember that throughout men exercised official control and that the distance of the Virgin from ordinary women furnished the celibate male clergy a safe object of contemplation. Women did respond to Mary, taking her as a role model and focus of devotion, but the fact that the Virgin had no connection with active sexuality limited her utility for women. The Mary who appeared at various sites was regal and certain—not the human figure, young and full of doubts, who appears on the pages of the Bible. Finally, the message of the Virgin contained no call for the transformation of unjust social structures, being limited to private conversion. Thus most Marian devotion supported conservative views of women.[23]

CONTEMPORARY CHRISTIAN FEMINISM

The majority of Christian feminists nowadays come from the white middle class, but certainly the consciousness of injustice on which they draw is at least as available to women of other social classes. For example, Maria, a Pueblo woman living in New Mexico, realized while quite young that she could not accept the patterns of her mother's life:

> My mother is a believing Catholic. I have never agreed with her on the subject of sex. I loved that talk with her—hearing from her own lips what she believed. But I knew that would be not only the first but the last real talk we'd have. She kept touching my arm and telling me not to "worry" because the blood would only come for a day or two, and about as often as a full moon. I wasn't "worried"; I was interested in what my life would be like, later on. My mother had the answer for me: a Pueblo man like my father would be my life! But my father was always telling me to behave myself, and stop running away to the mesa! I was not his favorite; the boys were! I almost asked my mother why she let my father be so unfair with his attention, but I couldn't get the words out of my mouth. I saw the answer in her eyes: don't ask me, because once I start asking myself a landslide will begin, and I won't be fast enough to get out of the way! As I sat there, glad to have a chance at least to be alone with my mother, I remembered the time I saw the rocks falling down off the mountains nearby, and the poor goats trying to escape. The birds were safe! I've wanted all my life to be a bird, the next time around—if there will be another chance![24]

The landslide of insight, realization, certainly is dangerous, but throughout contemporary societies women like Maria are risking it, for the sake of honoring their experience. If there is one common characteristic uniting current Christian feminist theologians and bringing them into potential conflict with the past, male-dominated orthodoxies, it is their insistence on the primacy of experience. They are tired of having men tell them what they should be feeling and thinking, what it means to be Christian women, how God works in their lives, and what God's plan is for them. Increasingly, they are defining fidelity to God as keeping faith with what they know firsthand, from their lived experience of what it means to be women struggling to make sense of their lives and the world through Christian faith.

The pioneer and most influential laborer in this vineyard of Christian feminist theology beyond doubt has been Rosemary Radford Ruether. In both historical work that has retrieved the past experience of women and constructive work that has pondered what a rethought, feminist Christian view of reality ought to include, Ruether has combined learning and a passionate concern for social justice. Like many feminists, her instincts are holistic: one should not separate the domination that has twisted the lives of women from the domination that has twisted the lives of blacks and is threatening the ecosphere. The problems we suffer tend to be connected. The blind spots begetting these problems tend to reduce to a similar disregard of creatures one can dominate, to a similar will to power. Ruether therefore has challenged Christian power bearers to rethink their faith. Can it be authentic if it is supporting unjust social structures, if it is oppressing the majority sex and abetting the sufferings of children?

Grounding this social criticism is Ruether's development of a divinity as viable for women as for men. In speaking of this divinity, the God/ess, Ruether has concluded:

> God/ess as once and future *Shalom* [Peace] of being, however, is *not* the creator, founder, or sanctioner of patriarchal-hierarchical society. This world arises in revolt against God/ess and in alienation from nature. It erects a false system of alienated dualisms modeled on its distorted and oppressive social relationships. God/ess liberates us from this false and alienated world, not by an endless continuation of the same trajectory of alienation, but as a constant breakthrough that points us to new possibilities that are, at the same time, the regrounding of ourselves in the primordial matrix, the original harmony. The liberating encounter with God/ess is always an encounter with our authentic selves resurrected from underneath the alienated self. It is not experienced against, but in and through relationships, healing our broken relations with our bodies, with other people, with nature. We have no adequate name for the true God/ess, the "I am who I shall become." Intimations of Her/His name will appear as we emerge from false naming of God/ess modeled on patriarchal alienation.[25]

The alienation fostered by patriarchal religious structures has shaped not only social relations but also peoples' selves. Feminists dealing with this fact frequently find themselves calling for a new spirituality. By this they mean a personal prayer and commitment to social justice that would heal women from within. Insofar as it were drawn from Christian sources, it would be an extension of the faith begun with Jesus of Nazareth. Insofar as it overcame the debilities women have suffered by having their patterns of psychological development ignored and their Christian autonomy retarded, it might answer the charges of antireligious feminists by demonstrating—proving through practice—that the Christian tradition can serve women's growth.

In dealing with the problems feminists now tend to have with most of what passed for Christian spirituality until recently, Joann Wolski Conn has stressed how Christian religious advice has retarded women's maturation:

Christian teaching and practice, instead of promoting women's maturity, has significantly contributed to its restriction. Women have consistently been taught to value only one type of religious development—self-denial and sacrifice of one's own needs for the sake of others. Whereas men have been taught to couple self-denial with prophetic courage to resist unjust authority, women have been taught to see all male authority as God-given and to judge that assertion of their own desires was a sign of selfishness and pride. The problem lies not so much with the model of religious development as with its application. For example, to encourage self-denial without attention to the way women are prevented from having a self (i.e., sufficient self-direction, autonomy) is, in effect, simply to promote conformity to a male-approved role.[26]

Two further voices now swelling the chorus of feminist Christian theology come from the experience of black and lesbian women. On the contribution of black experience Cheryl Townsend Gilkes has written,

Indeed, some of the best feminist scholars have yet to come to terms with their own racism, and their work continues to analyze and respond to black women's experience with velvet covered versions of the sexualized racism that has dogged the black experience. One image in particular—"the *unnatural* superiority of black women"—always gnaws at my consciousness as I confront the vicious lie that racism has damaged and hurt black men more than it has damaged and hurt black women. The fact that some white women reside all too comfortably in the master's house is brought home whenever their attention is turned to black women's experience.[27]

Of Lesbian experience Carter Heyward and Mary E. Hunt have written,

A quantum leap in feminist theory has taken place in the last five years due to the insights of such writers as Audre Lorde, Adrienne Rich, Barbara Smith, and Charlotte Bunch, women who have written about their lesbian feminist experience. A number of lesbian feminists in religion have begun to reflect on being lesbian in the context of harsh patriarchal sanctions against celebrating women's bodies—our own or those of others. As two such theologians, we have come to believe that the significance of lesbianism warrants critical attention by *all* feminist theologians.[28]

Overall, then, contemporary Christian feminism is assembling its mosaic from many different women's religious experience. The common denominator is honoring what women know and need.

DISCUSSION QUESTIONS

1. What sort of paradigm did the Virgin Mary offer medieval Christian women?
2. What was novel in Jesus's attitude toward women such as the woman who anointed his feet?
3. How did love-patriarchalism blunt the force of Pauline egalitarianism?

4.   What were the implications for women of the church fathers' worries about sexual desire?

5.   How did religious life offer a woman such as Lioba unusual freedom?

6.   Why did Martin Luther speak of woman as like a nail driven into the wall?

7.   Why did Anne Lee think there was need of a female messiah?

8.   How does experience function in the theology of present-day Christian feminists?

NOTES

[1]See Jaroslav Pelikan et al., "Christianity," in *The Encyclopedia of Religion*, Vol. 3, ed. Mircea Eliade (New York: Macmillan, 1987), pp. 348–431; also Williston Walker et al., *A History of the Christian Church*, 4th ed. (New York: Charles Scribner's Sons, 1985).

[2]See *1987 Britannica Book of the Year* (Chicago: Encyclopaedia Britannica, 1987), p. 338.

[3]Ben Witherington III, *Women in the Ministry of Jesus* (Cambridge: Cambridge University Press, 1984), p. 127.

[4]Elisabeth Schüssler Fiorenza, *In Memory of Her* (New York: Crossroad, 1983), p. 251.

[5]See Bernadette J. Brooten, "Paul's Views on the Nature of Women and Female Homoeroticism," in *Immaculate and Powerful*, ed. C. Atkinson, C. Buchanan, and M. Miles (Boston: Beacon, 1985), pp. 61–87.

[6]Elizabeth Clark and Herbert Richardson, eds., *Women and Religion: A Feminist Sourcebook of Christian Thought* (New York: Harper & Row, 1977), pp. 46–47.

[7]Ibid., pp. 66–67.

[8]See Clarissa W. Atkinson, " 'Your Servant, My Mother': The Figure of Saint Monica in the Ideology of Christian Motherhood," in *Immaculate and Powerful*, pp. 139–172.

[9]*De Cult. Fem.*, 1:1.

[10]*De Monog.*, 16.

[11]See Rosemary Radford Ruether, "Misogynism and Virginal Feminism in the Fathers of the Church," in *Religion and Sexism*, ed. Rosemary Radford Ruether (New York: Simon & Schuster, 1974), pp. 150–183; also see her "Mothers of the Church: Ascetic Women in the Late Patristic Age," in *Women of Spirit*, ed. Rosemary Ruether and Eleanor McLaughlin (New York: Simon & Schuster, 1979), pp. 71–98.

[12]Eleanor McLaughlin, "Women, Power and the Pursuit of Holiness in Medieval Christianity," in *Women of Spirit*, pp. 103–104.

[13]See Kurt Weitzmann et al., *The Icon* (New York: Alfred A. Knopf, 1982), pp. 146–147.

[14]Margaret R. Miles, *Image as Insight* (Boston: Beacon, 1985), pp. 72–73.

[15]On Thomas Aquinas, see Clark and Richardson, eds., *Women and Religion*, pp. 78–101. For more on the depiction of female sanctity in Western art, see Jane Dillenberger, "The Magdalene: Reflections on the Image of the Saint and Sinner in Christian Art," in *Women, Religion and Social Change*, eds. Y. Y. Haddad and E. B. Findly (Albany: State University of New York Press, 1985), pp. 115–145.

[16]George H. Tavard, *Women in Christian Tradition* (Notre Dame, Ind.: University of Notre Dame Press, 1973), p. 172.

[17]Ibid., p. 174, drawing on *Lectures on Genesis*.

[18]See Elisabeth Schussler Fiorenza, *Bread Not Stone: The Challenge of Feminist Biblical Interpretation* (Boston: Beacon, 1984).

[19]Catherine F. Smith, "Jane Lead: The Feminist Mind and Art of a Seventeenth-Century Protestant Mystic," in *Women of Spirit*, p. 190.

[20]See Clark and Richardson, eds., *Women and Religion*, pp. 149–152.

[21]See ibid., pp. 161–164.

[22]Julia O'Faolain and Lauro Martines, eds., *Not in God's Image: Women in History from the Greeks to the Victorians* (New York: Harper Torchbooks, 1973), p. 310.

[23]See Barbara Corrado Pope, "Immaculate and Powerful: The Marian Revival in the Nineteenth Century," in *Immaculate and Powerful*, pp. 192–196.

[24]Robert Coles and Jane Hallowell Coles, *Women of Crisis II* + r(New York: Delta/Seymour Lawrence, 1980), pp. 162–163.

[25]Rosemary Radford Ruether, *Sexism and God-Talk: Toward a Feminist Theology* (Boston: Beacon, 1983), p. 71.

[26]Joann Wolski Conn, "Introduction," in *Women's Spirtuality: Resources for Christian Development*, ed. Joann Wolski Conn (New York: Paulist, 1986), p. 4.

[27]Cheryl Townsend Gilkes, "Roundtable Discussion: On Feminist Methodology," *Journal of Feminist Studies in Religion*, 1, no. 2 (Fall 1985), p. 81.

[28]Carter Heyward and Mary E. Hunt, "Roundtable Discussion: Lesbianism and Feminist Theology," *Journal of Feminist Studies in Religion*, 2, no. 2 (Fall 1986), p. 95.

CHAPTER NINE

Islamic Women

OVERVIEW

Islam arose from the revelatory experiences of the prophet Muhammad (570–632 C.E.). Although Muhammad and the people to whom he preached had been influenced by Jewish and Christian ideas, Muslims stress the eternal character of Islamic religion (its creation by God), and many scholars of Islam stress the Arab origins of the religious complex that Muhammad created. Indeed, although Jews and Christians had tried to convert the people of Mecca, Muhammad's home city, they had not succeeded, probably because the Meccans wanted a religion distinctively their own. The Qur'an (35:42, 6:157) suggests this state of affairs.

Still, the Meccans had learned much about Judaism and Christianity from their contact with these traditions, and they also had native traditions that verged on monotheism. The problem was the popular devotion to "intermediary gods" and spirits and the lack of any profound devotion to the One God. Mecca in fact was a center of polytheistic business.

A further motive for making a new religious start, using Jewish and Christian ideas but resetting them in an Arab configuration, was to overcome the great disparity between the rich and the poor. Mecca had come to prosper as a commercial center, and Muhammad was appalled by the neglect of the poor. So, most scholars now are of the opinion that native Arab needs and circumstances were the main forces shaping the rise of Islam.[1] Of course we can assume that these general social factors, as well as the Jewish and Christian ideas influencing the rise of Islam, impinged upon women as well as men.

When he was about forty years old, Muhammad used to withdraw into solitude to meditate. He began receiving revelations, which initially he discredited but eventually came to consider information and calls to repentance given him by God for the sake of his fellow citizens. Muhammad had been orphaned at an early age, raised by a minor Arab tribe, and married to the widow Khadija, whose trading company he managed. Khadija and other members of his family persuaded him to take the revelations seriously, and so they qualify as the first Muslims—the first "submitters" to the Qur'anic word of God.

For the twenty years or so between the inception of the revelations and his death, Muhammad continued to receive disclosures he attributed to Allah. Although initially his preaching won little acceptance from his fellow Meccans (in good part because its monotheism threatened the business associated with the polytheistic cults centered at Mecca), Muhammad established himself as the head man in nearby Medina and then returned to conquer Mecca in 630. Although he only lived two more years, he set in process a Muslim conquest that quickly spread out to dominate the entire Middle East. The Qur'an (Recital) composed from the various revelations Muhammad had received became the Scripture of Islam, and ever since the death of Muhammad Muslims have looked to his revelations and example for the wellsprings of their faith.

Within twenty-five years of Muhammad's death Islam dominated the eastern half of the southern Mediterranean shore. It had conquered Egypt, the entire Arabian peninsula, Iran, and Khorasan. It was powerful from the Persian Gulf to the Black and Caspian seas, its armies sweeping all opposition before them. (In fact, little opposed Islam: a power vacuum lay ready to be filled.) In two centuries Muslims extended Islam to the Atlantic edge of the Mediterranean, the Iberian peninsula, southern France, and northern India. All this expansion was military, religious, and cultural in one. Spreading the Qur'anic faith was the inner spiritual impulse, while gaining greater economic and military power proved a powerful ancillary motive. Islam sponsored a high culture of literature, science, law, philosophy, and the crafts. It allowed conquered peoples who did not convert to continue their own religious traditions, although usually they were second-class citizens. For women it provided considerable improvement over their situation in pre-Islamic Arab culture, while continuing the patriarchal patterns that prevailed in the Middle East. (We shall pay considerable attention to what the Qur'an has to say about women.)

From the eleventh century, Christian Europe began to win back lands it had ceded to Islam, and by 1492 Muslims had lost their last European stronghold in Spain. Islam continued strong in India until the early eighteenth century, when the British supplanted the Mogul rulers. In modern times Britain and France controlled much of the Middle East and Islam was on the cultural defensive, trying to accommodate to Western science, technology, and political institutions. Since the creation of the state of Israel in 1948 Muslims have had a rallying point, and recent decades have witnessed a resurgence of traditionalist Muslim views and Islamic nationalism, most notably in Iran. Presently Islam is highly influential in Africa and has a growing population in both the Soviet Union and China.

The Umayyadid dynasty that arose in 661 in effect divided Muslims into two camps. The Sunnis were those who followed the Umayyadids and linked Muslim rule to pre-Muslim Arab tribal patterns. The Shiites were those who claimed that leadership in the community ought to be in the hands of blood descendants of Muhammad. Despite this difference in political outlook and differences in religious style, both branches of Islam have accepted the Qur'an and the same general *Shariah* (law, guidance), and so both have looked upon women in essentially the same way.

In terms of religious doctrine and practice, the key ingredients for all Muslims have been summarized in what came to be known as the Five Pillars. The first pillar is a summary of faith: There is no God but Allah and Muhammad is his prophet. This implies a strict monotheism: no rivals to Allah, no lesser objects of worship. The greatest sin in the Muslim catalogue is idolatry, and the great divide among human beings is that between believers in Allah and unbelievers. Believers will go to the Garden (paradise) while unbelievers will go to the Fire (hell). God will render Judgment on all people, according to their faith, and Muhammad preached that such Judgment was very near. In proclaiming Muhammad the prophet of Allah, Islam has understood him to be the seal, the consummation, of a line that began with Adam and Abraham. Moses and Jesus were great predecessors of Muhammad, and Islam honors them, as well as Mary, the mother of Jesus. It disagrees with Christians about the divinity of Jesus, however; there is no way Allah could have a Son. Similarly, it disagrees with the Christian view that God is a trinity of divine persons. Summarily, then, the first pillar corrects the religious thrust begun with prior biblical revelation and asserts that in Muhammad and the Qur'an Allah has provided a definitive blueprint of the divine nature and intentions.

The second pillar counsels Muslims to pray five times a day, and the tradition is that this prayer should be made bowing low and facing Mecca. The third pillar prescribes a strict fast during the daylight hours of the lunar month of Ramadan. The fourth pillar is the pilgrimage to Mecca: if they possibly can, all Muslims are to go to Mecca at the time of pilgrimage at least once during their lifetime. The fifth pillar is almsgiving: giving over a definite portion (often computed at about 2 percent of one's income) for the sake of the poor. Muslim women have not always been held to these precepts as strictly as men, but certainly they have been held to the monotheism of the first pillar and generally the other pillars also have structured their lives.

Nowadays there are about 237 million Muslims in Africa, 24 million in East Asia, 9 million in Europe, 625,000 in Latin America, 2 million, 675,000 in North America, 95,000 in Oceania, 535 million in South Asia, and 31.5 million in the Soviet Union. This makes a worldwide total of about 840 million, which means that about 17 percent of the world's population is Muslim (about one person in six).[2]

MUHAMMAD

The Qur'an is emphatic that God is the sole divinity and that God has never taken a divine son. Although this assertion was aimed against the Christian view of the Incarnation, it has functioned throughout Muslim history to block any tendency to divinize Muhammad. However high the Prophet stood in Muslim veneration and the Islamic sense of God's plan, he always remained fully human, a creature and no part of the divinity. On the other hand, Muslim esteem for Muhammad is hard to overestimate. He has functioned as the ideal Muslim, the prototype for all later believers. Not only did the Qur'an come from his mouth, his example became a key factor in Muslim law. Through the *hadith* (traditions) about Muhammad, Islam has formed much of its sense of how faith ought to be lived out in daily affairs.

For our purposes, the image of Muhammad as a family man is most pertinent. The following sketch is gleaned from the comprehensive work *The Cultural Atlas of Islam*, by the late Isma'il and Lois al Faruqi. Muhammad did not consider marrying until he was twenty-five, mainly because he was quite poor. Unlike the majority of Meccan young men, he did not frequent the bars and flirt with the barmaids. For the last two years of his bachelorhood, he worked for the merchant widow Khadija, increasingly gaining her confidence as a trusted and skillful agent. Much to Muhammad's surprise, a mutual friend proposed to arrange his marriage to Khadija. They married and Khadija bore Muhammad all of his children who survived to adulthood, including his daughter Fatima. Muhammad's two sons Qasim and Tahir died in infancy, while his three daughters Zaynab, Ruqayyah, and Umm Kulthum all married and died without children prior to the Prophet's conquest of Mecca in 630. Only through Fatima did Muhammad have grandsons, Hasan and Husayn. Until Khadija died in 621, she was Muhammad's only wife.

From Khadija Muhammad received wealth sufficient to free him from working for a living. Indeed, it probably was due to his leisure that he became interested in deeper questions about the meaning of life and was able to pursue his lengthy meditations. When Muhammad first started receiving revelations, he thought himself demented. It was Khadija who encouraged him and made credible the notion that God wanted him to be a prophet. Khadija not only offered her own faith, she secured the advice of her uncle Waraqah, a man reputed to have great religious wisdom. Waraqah found Muhammad's visions compelling and judged him to be the successor of Moses destined to be the prophet of the Arab people. Muhammad deeply loved Khadija, cried when she died, and kept her memory vivid. Later his youngest wife A'ishah remarked that she found herself envious of Khadija, even though Khadija was long dead.

> Though Muhammad married eight times after the death of Khadija, only one of them was a real marriage. That was his marriage to A'ishah, daughter of his closest companion, Abu Bakr. The others were marriages for political or social reasons. The Prophet entered into them as an exemplification of a new value Islam taught. A few examples will illustrate. Zaynab bint Jahsh, a cousin of his whom Muhammad knew well, was given by him in marriage to Zayd ibn Harithah, Khadija's slave whom Muhammad had manumitted. Incompatibility of the spouses made them miserable, and the marriage broke down. This was a double tragedy, since Arab custom made the divorced wife of a slave a social pariah, forever unmarriable. Although this custom was abolished by Islam, no Muslim would condescend to marry the woman despite her young age. To raise her status and teach the Arabs a lesson against social stratification, Muhammad took her in marriage. Hafsah was a widowed daughter of Umar ibn al Khattab, a close companion of the Prophet. She was in her forties and was poor. Her father was even poorer. He offered her to a number of friends and acquaintances, but all declined. It grieved him deeply that his daughter was homeless, unprotected, and liable to fall into trouble. To uplift them both and teach the Muslims that it is necessary for them to give the needed protection to their single women, especially the widows, the Prophet joined her to his household as his wife.[3]

If we pause momentarily, we note that in Muhammad's time women obviously were under the control of men, who arranged their marriages. Thus fathers arranged the marriage of their daughters and owners arranged the marriages of slaves. In the case of his cousin Zaynab bint Jahsh, Muhammad probably was the most influential male in her family, so to him fell arranging her marriage. Further, we note that multiple marriages—polygamy—apparently was the Arab custom. We shall see that the Qur'an allows a man up to four wives, as long as he can provide for them, and that both the Qur'an and latter Muslim custom prefer monogamy. Muhammad's marriage to Khadija therefore serves as the ideal part of his marital profile, while his multiple latter marriages are interpreted as contracted mainly from motives of compassion and giving good example. As with many other traditional religions, we find the widowed or unmarried woman marginal to mainstream society and so a cause of concern. Polygamy allows a people to care for these women and give them the chance to bear children (which traditional societies often consider their prime desire and function).

Another of Muhammad's wives, Sawdah, was a convert whose entry into Islam alienated her from her family. When her husband died, Muhammad married her both to protect her from the vengeance of her family and to show other Muslims that Islam would take care of those who joined its cause. His wife Juwayriyyah was a widow who came to Muhammad as booty in war. He freed her for the sake of her father, a tribal chief Muhammad wished to please, and offered to marry her. The father left the choice to her, and she agreed to marry Muhammad and embrace Islam, thereby preserving her honor. Within a few months of her marriage to Muhammad she had converted her entire family to Islam.

The wives of Muhammad became "mothers of the believers" and served the cause of the growing Muslim movement in diverse important ways. One of the main social goals Muhammad pursued was dissolving the old tribal ties and creating a more democratic society based on the primacy of all Muslims' allegiance to Islam. The old tribal allegiances had both spurred many divisive tendencies, including blood feuds, and allowed people who were not affiliated with a prosperous tribe to languish in poverty. Widows and orphans were especially vulnerable to neglect: they could be construed as belonging to no one. Muhammad's newly formed people were to consider all believers members of their family, brothers and sisters deserving care. The alms required of believers was a practical expression of this viewpoint, while the universal application of the basic formula of faith, the responsibility of praying five times each day, the obligation of fasting during Ramadan, and the pilgrimage to Mecca further established an Islamic democracy. On pilgrimage, for example, people were to wear the same simple garb, thereby downplaying their differences in wealth, social status, place of origin, and even (to a lesser extent) sex.

The Faruqis note that prior to Muhammad's reform and example of marrying vulnerable women Arabs tended to regard girls as threats to the family honor and so often buried unwanted female children alive. When a female became an adult, she could be bought, sold, or inherited—she was a sex object. In Islam a woman became capable of owning, buying, selling, and inheriting. She had to give her consent to any marriage arranged for her, and under stipulated conditions she could obtain a divorce. In the beginning women had the same religious obligations as men, and Islam strove to protect the family by making adultery a capital crime. Islam also obliged men to support women financially and strove to protect women from having to earn their livelihood (thereby freeing them for child rearing). Women could receive as much alms as they could give and were to be treated kindly.

THE SURAH ON WOMEN

Muslims revere the Qur'an as the Word of God, and the Qur'an is the first authority in Islamic life. Consequently, what the Qur'an has to say about women has greatly influenced how women have been regarded and treated. Surah (chapter) 4 of the Qur'an traditionally has had the title "Women," because matters pertaining to women are its main interest. Mohammed Marmaduke Pickthall, whose translations we follow in this section, thinks that the revelation of this surah occurred in the fourth year of Muhammad's stay in Medina (622 c.e.). The first three verses of this surah both suggest the Qur'anic style and contain some important theses for the Muslim view of women:

> O mankind! Be careful of your duty to your Lord Who created you from a single soul and from it created its mate and from them twain hath spread abroad a multitude of men and women. Be careful of your duty toward Allah in Whom ye claim (your rights) of one another, and toward the wombs (that bare you). Lo! Allah hath been a Watcher over you. Give unto orphans their wealth. Exchange not the good for the bad (in your management thereof) nor absorb their wealth into your own wealth. Lo! that would be a great sin. And if ye fear that ye will not deal fairly by the orphans, marry of the women, who seem good to you, two or three or four; and if ye fear that ye cannot do justice (to so many) then one (only) or (the captives) that your right hands possess. Thus it is more likely that ye will not do injustice.[4]

The Qur'anic style is elevated and poetic. Indeed, Muslims have made the Arabic of the Qur'an the standard of stylistic purity, arguing that its beauty proves its divine origin. So the words that one finds in the Qur'an are proclaimed and recited rather than simply read out. They are meant to have an impact that can only come from wholehearted hearing. In the first verse of Surah 4, the hearers are reminded of their duty to God concerning sex. The first Muslim duty is always to remember God and be mindful of the divine presence. God is the supreme, one might say the overpowering reality, so to forget God or consider a given matter without being mindful of God is to ensure that one will fall into error. The implication of the description of creation given here is like the implication of the account in Genesis: God began with the first man and made him a female companion. From these two the rest of humanity has derived, so the two-sexed character of humankind is by divine design (as is the subordination of women to men). Moreover, sexual relations (presumably both intercourse and other dealings) involve rights that repose in Allah.

In their dealings with one another, Muslim men and women are to make Allah the context, and so presumably their relations ought to unfold with gratitude, as do relations with one's mother. The conduct of child to mother, like the conduct of spouse to spouse, occurs within the outlines of the divine plan. The final thought of verse 1, that Allah is a Watcher over human beings, underscores the whole thrust of the verse and is typical of Islamic spirituality. All that human beings do is patent to God, completely open to the divine scrutiny. Those who remember this are not likely to sin.

In the society of Muhammad's day widows and orphans posed a considerable problem. Pickthall reminds us that at the probable time of this surah the followers of Muhammad had suffered many losses in battle, so it is likely that caring for widows and orphans was even more pressing than usual. Those who take over the care of orphans are reminded that to arrogate the orphan's wealth to the caretaker's own fortune would be a great abuse. Although females did not have as full inheritance rights as males, female orphans could hold title to wealth and so needed protection against "caretaking" that would have robbed them.

Verse 3 provides a scriptural justification for polygyny. As we have seen in the sketch of the Prophet's own example of being married to several wives at the same time, the motive can be to provide protection to women (here orphans) who otherwise would be vulnerable. The upper limit given is four wives, and the verse makes the important qualification that if one would not be able to do justice to so many wives, then only one wife should be taken. This qualification buttressed the usual Islamic preference for monogamy, just as the license given to take up to four wives became a sanction for polygyny among the wealthy.

Commenting on this matter of Muslim polygyny, Jane I. Smith has noted that while Muslim men may marry several sorts of women—Muslim, Jewish, Christian, or slave—Muslim women may marry only one man and he must be a Muslim. The Muslim wife has legal rights, for marriage is considered a contract (and not a sacrament). She can dictate the terms of her agreement and receive the dowry involved. Smith further notes that the percentage of Muslims having more than one wife is very small and that countries such as Turkey and Tunisia have outlawed multiple marriages.[5]

Surah 4 explores the whole question of inheritance in some detail, one of its key provisions being that a male heir should get the equivalent of two female portions (4:11). Women guilty of a lewdness confirmed by four witnesses may be confined to the house until death. A couple committing fornication should both be punished. If they then repent and improve their conduct, they should be let be, because of God's mercy. Marrying a woman married to one's father is considered a lewdness, abomination, and evil way (4:22). Sex with family relations—mothers, daughters, sisters, aunts, nieces, foster female relatives, mothers-in-law, step-daughters, daughters-in-law—is forbidden (4:23). So is sex with married women, except those captured in war. Compared to pre-Muslim Arab society, these injunctions represented considerable progress in women's rights and restraint of male desire.

Another key text for the traditional foundation of Muslim views of women is 4:34:

> Men are in charge of women, because Allah hath made the one of them to excel the other, and because they spend of their property (for the support of women). So good women are the obedient, guarding in secret that which Allah hath guarded. As for those from whom ye fear rebellion, admonish them and banish them to beds apart, and scourge them. Then if they obey you, seek not a way against them. Lo! Allah is ever High Exalted, Great.

This is as clear a statement of male supremacy as one would need to establish a two-tiered society. The text does not say just how Allah has made men to excel women, but it does say that by spending money on women's support men have earned control over women. The implication for women is that their first duty toward men is obedience. Indeed, when Muslim authors try to picture the Day of Judgment and those condemned to the Fire, they frequently imagine a large number of women (more than men). The usual sin of such women has been disobedience to their husbands.[6] Before such final punishment, disobedient women may be subject to banishment from the marital bed and to beating. If this makes them docile, a husband should not divorce them.

Muslim apologists take the understandable position that the overall treatment of women in the Qur'an and Muslim tradition is concerned with their welfare and grants them many rights. Properly understood, the Qur'anic injunctions ought to produce a household in which love and respect make legalistic severities unnecessary. In fact, apologists are apt to charge that Western permissiveness is much more harmful to marriage than traditional Islamic constraints. So, for example, when treating of Muslim strictures against infidelity, Lois al Faruqi has written:

> We do not have to surmise about the effect on women that this innovation [casualness about infidelity] might have, for a living example is available in Western society. The consequences are already glaringly apparent. The increased sexual dispensability of the wife which this new promiscuity produces is one of the factors leading to the increased divorce rate. It also has drastically adverse effects on . . . middle-aged and older women.[7]

TRADITIONAL VIEWS

From the Qur'an, the sayings and example of the Prophet, the law codes that developed, other sources of authority in the Muslim community, and informal traditions, such customs as keeping women veiled, greatly stressing their obedience and chastity and identifying their main value with procreation became pervasive throughout Muslim lands. Sometimes the impact of such overall tradition is revealed more accurately in folk literature and what anthropologists call "the little tradition" than in the formal law codes, so let us consider the portrait of the ideal woman that the common people have tended to receive from listening to popular stories. (As a highly oral culture, Islam has laid great stress on both recitals of the Qur'an and story telling.)

In one Moroccan folk tale, a Bedouin prince rich in camels and gold had a daughter named Hamda. When the girl reached maturity, the father pitched a tent for her apart from the rest of the tribe, to hide her from the sight of men. He also built a closed litter for her, so that she might travel in seclusion. One day the girl fell asleep in her litter and her camel wandered away from the rest of the caravan. When she awoke she found herself far from her own people and among strangers. The prince of these strangers was taken with her beauty and so asked to marry her. Hamda replied that this would be fitting, if the prince could raise the high bride price that she knew her father would have asked. The prince moved mountains to get the many camels required, and the marriage went forward.

As the story unfolds we witness the prince at the peak of contentment, because he has made the ideal match, with a woman beautiful, noble in lineage, and noble in character:

> So Hamda was made the wife of Prince Mohammed, and the prayer was spoken and the nights of gladness kept according to custom. When the prince entered the marriage tent, he found a pearl without price. In Hamda beauty reached perfection and modesty was its match. If love had seized the prince before, now he could not endure an hour away from Hamda's side. He forgot the two kinswomen he had married before and sent them away with their sons. And when Hamda's belly swelled and at the sum of her months she gave birth to a boy, his loved for her was doubled by love for her son. He called the child Faris, for he was strong and well made like a hero of the tales. When the other children were walking, Faris was running, following his father wherever he went, even into the guest tent to sit with the men.[8]

Needless to say, this beatitude does not endure, for the prior wives who have been shunted aside get their revenge on Hamda and Faris. But in the sketch of her beauty, modesty, and fertility, the author captures the heart of the traditional feminine ideal. One might add that she also would have to be obedient, but the rest of the story makes it plain that she was. Obviously such an ideal represents male fantasy and advantage, but women were bound to be shaped by it, since men had Qur'anic authority to hold sway in the Muslim household.

Insofar as women accepted their traditional obligations to modesty, obedience, and fertility as instituted by God, many no doubt tried to carry them out with a sense of peace and satisfaction. For example, they could find considerable traditional support for thinking that motherhood was a lofty vocation, deserving respect from all Muslims and central to God's plans for sanctifying human beings. Thus Saadia Khawar Khan Chishti, a

Pakistani woman prominent in education, has recently said in an article on female spirituality in Islam:

> It is an instinctive part of a female's spiritual role to provide for the needs of her offspring, for the newborn's nourishment is a symbol of Divine Providence. It is a living testimony of God's Attributes as the Provider or Sustainer that the nourishment for the baby comes from the mother's breasts in the form needed by the baby's digestive system for the normal growth and development of the body. In other words, the mother (human as well as the animal) functions as a means for Divine Provision for creatures of the Creator.
>
> Moreover, a spiritual mother nurtures the soul of her child with the powerful effect of the recitation of the *Shahadah* [profession of faith], the oft-repeated prayer [opening chapter of the Qur'an] . . . , and the beautiful Names or Attributes of God by singing them as a lullaby for putting the child to sleep or for comforting a wailing or a disturbed child. In doing so, the mother makes her contribution in permeating the very being of the child with the most powerful words of the Qur'an.
>
> If the mother performs her spiritual role with a sincere intention to please God (to Whom she belongs and to Whom is her return according to the Qur'an) then the *rahmah* [mercy] of God descends on her and she herself attains proximity to the Divine. Histories of the lives of spiritual adepts or saints frequently reveal that their mothers played a vital role in leading them toward the spiritual path.[9]

As in most other religious traditions, this positive view of women's vocation has not been the whole story. In both *hadith* (sayings) attributed to the Prophet and discourses by influential Muslim authors, female nature has been deprecated as untrustworthy and always needing careful control. Thus Ibn Khaldun (died 1406), a prominent authority writing on how Muslim rulers ought to comport themselves, says in passing,

> One of the things disliked in a ruler is excessive inclination to women. To consult them in affairs is to induce inefficiency, and an indication of weakness of judgement. As the Prophet—peace be upon him—said, "Consult them and do the opposite."[10]

Muhammad Ibn Abdun, writing on the proper implementation of Muslim law around 1100 c.e., was concerned about lewdness occurring in cemeteries:

> The worst thing about the cemeteries, and one much blamed by the people of our city, is that people go there among the tombs to drink wine and even commit debauchery. One must not allow any tradesman there, because they see the women who come to mourn (with bare faces), and also not allow any young men to sit in the ways so as to encounter the women. The muhtasib [ruler] must be careful to forbid that. It is necessary to forbid the storytellers and reciters of romances to be alone with women in the tents (they pitch nearby) to tell stories in, for they do it to seduce or rob them, and only loose women go to them anyway. If the storytellers stay at home and the women go there to hear them, that must be forbidden too, for it is worse than the first

case. One must always maintain close control of these people, for they are profligates.[11]

As we shall see, the control of women, by veiling, chaperoning, and other means, has continued to be a major factor in Islamic society to the present day. Women generally have been thought dangerous—both liable to draw improper attentions from men and prone to succumb. The modesty commanded by the Qur'an can have the positive overtones of being pure in the divine sight, but it can also have the negative overtones of being bent and so needing special controls.

Other important factors in the lives of traditional Muslim women have included their having few options other than marriage, their being married at an early age (sometimes betrothal was before puberty), their marriages being arranged by their male relatives (sometimes with great pressure, despite the Qur'an's stipulation that both parties to a marriage enter freely), and their not seeing their husbands until the wedding day. Generally Islamic religious leaders have frowned on birth control and have forbidden both sterilization and abortion, although in recent years family planning has spread. The Prophet is said to have detested divorce, but in most times and places men have been able to divorce their wives quite easily, almost at whim, while women's rights to divorce have been quite circumscribed. After divorce custody of the children usually would go to the father once the children had reached age seven.[12]

FEMALE SAINTS

Although Islam propounds a strict monotheism, allowing nothing created to partake of the divine being, it has fostered many saints whose cult has been an important part of Muslim devotional life. On a level all his own is the Prophet, Muhammad, whom all branches of Islam venerate as the perfect exemplar of true religion, the compleat Muslim. Especially praised in the Qur'an are Jesus and Mary who, unlike Muhammad, were sinless. Both Sunni and Shiite Muslims venerate the first four caliphs who succeeded Muhammad as leaders of the Islamic community, calling them "rightly guided," and most Shiite Muslims venerate the twelve **imams** (leaders), blood descendants of the Prophet, who functioned as infallible guides for their times. As well, Shiite Muslims remember the martyrdom of Husain, the grandson of Muhammad, making this commemoration the emotional highpoint of their ceremonial year. Finally, we may note that many Muslim countries are dotted with the tombs of local saints, women as well as men, which the faithful venerate as holy places.

Among the saints venerated as "mothers" of Islam and especially powerful models of the Muslim life are three female contemporaries of the Prophet. First, there is his wife Khadija, who welcomed the revelations given him by God and supported him at the beginning of his prophetic career. Second, there is his beloved youngest wife A'ishah. She entered the family of the Prophet as a little girl, held him in her arms when he died, and became a main source of the Prophet's sayings that greatly shaped later Islamic thought and practice. She lived nearly fifty years after Muhammad's death, through the eras of the four rightly guided caliphs, and even in her own day she was venerated as a great model of the religious way the Prophet had opened. Third, the Prophet's daughter Fatima, born of Khadija, has also been considered a mother of Islam. She married Ali, the fourth caliph, and became the mother of Hasan and Husain, both of whom were slain for their faith. (Shiites consider both to be imams.) Fatima was active in the Muslim community and won great respect not only because she was the daughter of the Prophet (he had no sons who survived to adulthood) but also because of her own religious gifts.

In the following description, one glimpses the respect in which she continues to be held:

> Fatimah, also called . . . (the best of women in all the worlds), was the blessed daughter of the Prophet of Islam who became the wife of Ali. She was declared by the Prophet as one who served as the gate to the citadel of spiritual knowledge. She was the mother of Imam Hasan and Imam Husayn, who both won the coveted crown of martyrdom. She was also the mother of Zaynab, who was the spiritual heroine of the battle of Karbala and who played the role of a veritable princess of female spirituality in Islam. Although fourteen centuries have elapsed since her departure from this stage of life, Sayyidah Fatimah and her family are continually remembered both in the prose and in the poetry of Muslims throughout the world. The Muslims unanimously recognize her as the fountainhead of female spirituality in Islam, because she occupied herself with the purity of the Oneness and Unity of God and was confirmed in her absolute sincerity in the practice of the beliefs and tenets of Islam.[13]

In addition to the mothers of the first generation of Islam, other outstanding female Muslims who have served the faithful as models of sanctity include Zubaydah, queen of Harun al-Rashid, a leader of the Abbasid Dynasty centered in Baghdad, and Rabi'ah, a famous mystical poet. Zubayah gave Islam a model of how piety could flourish in the midst of palatial surroundings. She was known for her strong interior life, and for her calm in the midst of warfare and court turmoil, which included the assassination of her princely son. By not seeking vengeance, she helped Baghdad avoid disastrous strife.

Rabi'ah (about 717–801) is the more famous figure, because she lived a life of great simplicity and was one of the first to stress ardent love of God, a theme that became immensely important in Sufi mysticism. Much is not known about her life, but the best conjecture is that she was born the fourth daughter of a poor family. She worked as a servant for some years in Basra, a city of southern Iraq, but her master released her from bondage because of her obvious piety. Thereafter she lived in solitary retirement, practicing various austerities and devoting herself to prayer. Her reputation for sanctity grew and so she drew many visitors seeking prayers or instruction. Where previously the usual Muslim stress had been on serving God with the devotion and obedience of a slave, Rabi'ah raised the possibility of approaching God like a lover.

As a saint, Rabi'ah generated many legends. For example, it is said that when she went on the pilgrimage to Mecca and visited the Ka'ba, the central shrine, it moved forward to greet her. It also is said that her donkey, which had died on the road, came back to life. Yet Rabi'ah is reported to have rejected these stories and denied that she could accomplish miracles. She feared hellfire for failing her Lord and so considered the miracles temptations of Satan.

In her love-centered piety, Rabi'ah especially drew on the Qur'anic verse (5:59) that seems to sanction speaking of affection between God and human beings.:

> O believers, whosoever of you turns from his religion, God will assuredly bring a people He loves and who love Him, humble towards the believers, disdainful towards the unbelievers, men who struggle in the path of God, not fearing the reproach of any reproacher. That is God's bounty; He give it unto whom He will; and God is All-embracing, All-knowing.[14]

Rabi'ah would spend whole nights in prayer, sometimes expressing her love of God in short poems and beautiful prayers. She would feel remorse whenever her heart strayed from God, and God so absorbed her that she did not concern herself very much with developing a special love of the Prophet.

Because of her desire to love only God, she eventually wanted to downplay the significance of heaven and hell, which she saw could dilute the purity of desiring to please God for God's own sake. Annemarie Schimmel has mentioned in this context what is perhaps the best known legend about Rabi'ah:

> Having been seen carrying a flaming torch in one hand and a pitcher of water in the other, she explained that this symbolic act meant that she would set Paradise on fire and pour water into Hell, "so that these two veils may disappear and nobody worship God out of fear of Hell or hope for Paradise, but solely for his own beauty." This tale, which reached Europe in the early fourteenth century, is the basis of several short stories, mystical and otherwise, in Western literature.[15]

Rabi'ah entered the lists of the leading Muslim saints, for example being included in a famous thirteenth-century collection of biographies of the saints. Although the story of her rejecting marriage to the contemporary saint Hasan of Basra probably is a pious invention, Rabi'ah was remembered as having made marriage quite secondary to living for God:

The contract of marriage is for those who have a phenomenal [this-worldly] existence. But in my case, there is no such existence, for I have ceased to exist and have passed out of self. I exist in God and am altogether His. I live in the shadow of His command. The marriage contract must be asked from Him, not from me.[16]

In perhaps her most famous poem, one included in many anthologies of Sufi literature, Rabi'ah speaks of two ways of love. The first is selfish, the second is worthy of God. In the first, selfish love, Rabi'ah does nothing but think about God. In the second love God raises the veil usually obscuring the divine presence and gives her full access. But whether her love be mottled with the impurity bound to attend anything achieved by her own efforts, or pure because directed by the divinity itself, neither redounds to her praise. For Rabi'ah all praise belongs only to God. Thus she has been a great model of pure devotion emptied of all self-concern.

WOMEN IN IRAN

In 1980 Nancy Falk and Rita Gross edited a collection of studies on the religious lives of women in non-Western cultures. Many of the studies were anthropological in character and so rendered the texture, the living feel, of everyday life. Two such studies focused on the religion of Iranian women, prior to the revolution that brought the Ayatollah Khomeini to power. What they reveal about women's experience of Islam no doubt now would require some modification, because of the return of a fundamentalist religious regime. On the other hand, the way these women lived already was quite conservative, quite untouched by the modernizations attempted by the Shah, so the patterns they reveal may well continue today. At the least, they provide one provocative sketch of what Islam has tended to mean for ordinary Iranian women for hundreds of years.

The first study concentrates on urban Muslim women and was carried out between 1974 and 1976. The author begins by noting that although the rituals of Muslim women have received little attention, in addition to the formal obligations women have to pray and make the pilgrimage to Mecca, they participate in marriage ceremonies, funerals, local pilgrimages, and ceremonies involving vows. It is this last preoccupation, with vows, that drew the reporter's special attention.

In contrast to men's religion, which was centered in the mosque, the religious activities of the women of Shiraz tended to occur in private homes, news of an event circulating through informal oral networks. Although most Iranian women had not received much formal religious education, by 1976 schools for women were imparting religious instruction and women could attend the theological center in the city of Qom. Women who, from whatever training, could read and explain the Qur'an often would conduct informal classes in the home. Concerning this sort of service, as well as any leadership of women's prayers and rituals, Iranian women tended to avoid publicity and wear no distinguishing clothing. They did not want to draw attention to themselves, probably because that might invite male control.

One Shiite ritual of great importance to the reporter's informants was the *rowzeh*, a gathering focused on a sermon and mourning in memory of slain members of the Prophet's family. Having recalled a tragic event such as the slaying of the imam Husain at the battle of Karbala, both women and men (sometimes the *rowzeh* would be a single-sex affair and sometimes mixed) would weep, beat themselves, and cry out to the suffering heroes. The women usually were the more demonstrative, sobbing and thrashing themselves.

In connection with the women's *rowzeh* a practice of making vows had arisen. For example, a woman wanting God's help for a child injured in a car accident might vow to sponsor a religious ceremony (perhaps another *rowzeh*) if the child recovered. The criticism this practice had drawn from both men and educated women was that it ran the danger of making religion a business affair—bartering with God. Another sort of vow associated with the *rowzeh* was that if the woman's petition were granted, she would sponsor a dinner in honor of one of the most approachable Shiite saints, *Abbas*. While this might seem quite legitimate on the surface, critics charged that too often the meal degenerated into unseemly partying. Indeed, the meal sometimes became an occasion for showing off colorful clothing frowned upon by traditionalist Islam. The serving of food could become quite lavish, and people sometimes spent more on such a meal than they could afford. Still, even religious Iranian women sometimes defended the meals with passion, which led the anthropologist studying this phenomenon to suggest that they played an important social role. Iranian women tended to be somewhat isolated and limited in their opportunities to attend public happenings. The meals furnished a chance to enjoy the company of other women, so they were precious highlights in many women's lives.[17]

Among rural Iranian women, social opportunities tended to be more frequent. The practice of wealthy men having a **harem** never had taken hold in the rural villages as it had in Iranian cities and many women had to be mobile to do their work in the fields. Often rural people were loosely organized along tribal lines and women would go about in colorful clothing, not even veiled. Rural women had little official power, the leadership positions being in the hands of men, but in fact many exerted considerable influence. For all these reasons rural Iranian women tended to be looked down upon by religious conservatives, who considered their relatively free ways immoral.

The field work for the description of rural Iranian women in the volume edited by Falk and Gross occurred between 1965 and 1976. It focused on a tribal area in southwest Iran in the southern part of the Zagros mountains. The author's close contact with the people drew her to study how they communicated their religious values through ceremonies, discussion of ordinary moral decisions, and folk literature (using proverbs and tales). The village on which she concentrated traditionally had supported itself by raising sheep and goats and farming. In recent years, however, it had lost its self-sufficiency, with the result that many men were away for significant periods of time, earning money outside. This produced a cultural cleavage, because the men were coming in contact with a much wider range of ideas than the women, who stayed home in the village. The women therefore were more conservative and traditional than the men.

In addition, older and middle-aged women were 100 percent illiterate, while about 20 percent of the younger women had learned to read (schooling for women had just become popular). Because Islam makes so much of reading the Qur'an, their illiteracy had greatly handicapped the village women. Fewer men were illiterate, and sometimes the author would see women listening to their children read religious stories from their schoolbooks. From time to time women would hear sermons from a *mullah* (preacher), either the one resident at the village mosque or a visitor, but generally the mullahs considered women unfit for theological instruction and paid little attention to their special needs. More popular with the women therefore were the itinerant preachers and snake handlers who from time to time would perform in the village, dramatizing the lives of the saints.

Few women attended the mosque regularly, although in theory they had the right. While the men tended to ascribe the women's staying away to a lack of interest in religion, the women themselves explained that they were forbidden attendance when they were ritually unclean (for example, menstruating) and that usually they had to care for the children, whom they could not bring into the mosque. Even when they would attend, they would find themselves put in a separate room, unable to see the preacher, and excluded from the distribution of tea and food. When it came time for Shiite ceremonies out of doors, as was the case with memorials of martyrs, many women would watch from their rooftops. But even though such observance was supposed to be meritorious, women could be criticized as only interested in man watching and tending to make the young men show off. At funerals the women had a sanctioned role as mourners, crying and singing around the body while the men dug the grave, but once the prayers began they had to leave.

So the religious lives of these women focused on magical rites concerned with healing, on visits to the shrines of saints who might help with daily problems, and on making vows to the saints. The saints clearly drew much of the women's emotional interest, no doubt because they seemed approachable, useful, and possibly interested in what concerned the women. The women were held to a stricter moral code than the men. They learned from the folk literature that they were less intelligent than men and morally weaker. As girls they usually only received a commonsensical religious instruction that explained such things as the ablutions to be made before prayers. In most ways, therefore, they were second class.[18]

WOMEN OF MOROCCO AND INDIA

We can gain further insight into how Muslim women actually have lived from studies of how they have been assigned social status and how ritual has affected them. In one study of a large Moroccan village, for example, what constituted a moral character for women was different from what constituted a moral character for men. Both sexes were honored for kindness, verbal skills, and a sense of humor, but men of good repute above all were honest or straight in their dealings, supported their families well, and did not gamble, drink, or visit prostitutes excessively.

> A respectable woman promotes the welfare of her family as a good wife and mother, is an excellent and thrifty housekeeper . . . , and keeps her family's honor pure by never interacting with strange men, staying inside, and not spreading the affairs of the family around the village. One gossips, of course, but about *others*, while keeping family problems out of the public realm.[19]

Perhaps the prime moral responsibility that a young woman of this village bore was not to discredit her family by becoming pregnant while unmarried or by having an affair after her marriage. The woman herself would suffer the greatest injury from such behavior, but the whole family would become grist for the mills of gossip that turned continually. Even small infractions of the ideal of modesty would set the wheels spinning, so a woman out on the street in the midafternoon would take pains to make it clear that she was on her way to see the doctor or was engaged in some other unavoidable errand. Still, what was permitted women somewhat depended on their station in life. While a new bride was expected to be shy, demure, and slow to speak, a postmenopausal woman could interact with men and be raucous or bawdy. Similarly, a new bride could not address her father-in-law but his wife could interact with him freely, making earthy jokes.

Another interesting difference between men and women focused on magic. Men affected to have little to do with it, expressing their interest in the supernatural through orthodox Islamic channels. Women showed much more interest in magic, and they feared the local sorceress less than men did. The main use women made of the sorceress was to obtain spells and potions to revive their husbands' interest in them, luring him away from female competitors. In effect the women played on the men's fear of sorcery to push them toward marital fidelity.

Overall, the reporter studying these Moroccan village women found them more able to change their status in their groups than men could in men's groups. This was because the main determinants of status—perception of their character, control of information, and recourse to magic—all were under their control. Women with experience and skill at manipulating gossip, for example, could raise their own standing and lower that of their rivals. Still, most women always had to keep an eye out for their reputation or that of their daughters. They had, for example, to make sure that the superintendent of the women's bath or the seamstress—people who came in contact with many other women—did not spread bad estimates. If a young girl of marriageable age were to be stigmatized by such an influential source as too free with men, she would immediately become less desirable in the sight of the parents of young men looking for brides.

Muslims in India have inherited centuries of tensions between Hindus and Muslims. Presently they are a minority existing within a secular state with a strong Hindu majority. And while Hindus apportion status mainly on the basis of caste, Muslims in India have developed more fluid determinants of status. For them economic and political standing is as important as religious standing. Muslim women of Bengal, however, are also apt to be ranked according to their ritualistic activities: how immersed they are in rituals venerating the saints and concerned with the life cycle. While women have virtually no part in the major Islamic feasts, these being controlled by men, they have a ritualistic domain all their own.

Women are excluded from the major feasts, and so the formal sphere of religious life, because secluding his wife and daughters brings a Muslim man prestige. On the other hand, if his women were to make a public appearance the man would be shamed. Within the sphere assigned to them, however, Bengali Muslim women are honored by other women for public devotion. This sphere mainly consists of devotions at the tombs of local saints and at local rivers and ponds, where spiritual forces (both helpful and hurtful) are thought to dwell. What women do in this sphere does not have an impact on the prestige of their husbands. It is considered a realm apart. The only problems come when women are perceived as divinizing the saints and spirits, which runs counter to orthodox Muslim monotheism and so offends traditionalists.

Nonetheless,

> For rural Muslim women [of the Bengal area], *pir* [saint] worship and reverence constitute a most important part of their life. It is the women who perform the rites and cook the food offering for the saints; it is they who visit and plead with the saint, intervening on behalf of their brothers, fathers, hus-

bands, or children. The women draw up a contractual agreement with the saint, whereby only after the saint has fulfilled his or her part does the woman then fulfill her promise to the saint.[20]

Concerning rituals for the life cycle, the two that most involve women are marriage and birth. Women also favor religious practices designed to express and placate their everyday concerns: fear of illness, widowhood, barrenness, the coming of a second wife, and poverty. The more women are dominated by these fears and elaborate ritualistic devotions to the saints, the lower they sink in official (orthodox) religious status.

The saints frequently are paired, as hot and cold or male and female. Here the influence of Hindu interest in androgyny and complementarity seems to have penetrated folk Islam. So, for instance, the mythical pair Khidr and Olaii Bibi are, respectively, a passive male saint and an awesome, powerful female saint sometimes considered his wife. Depending on their temperaments, the saints will be petitioned for different favors. Thus one would want a hot saint to help with childbearing or curing small pox. Olaii Bibi would be more desirable than Khidr. But for something like protecting seafarers, Khidr (who is associated with the cool waters) would serve very well.

It would take considerable space to sort out all the elements of such a complex scheme, but we can see the main lines of its impact. In exporting itself to foreign cultures such as the Hindu culture of India, Islam has nearly inevitably had to contend with native traditions. So, in addition to the segregation of the sexes and the different religious roles assigned them by Islam, rural Muslims of Bengal have worked with Hindu ideas about rituals specific to women. Women have been assigned or have generated practices focused on the saints, who are relatively marginal in orthodox Muslim theology, because this left the mainstream Muslim devotions—the Qur'anic religion centered in the mosque—in the hands of men. As well, many women apparently have found the saints more responsive to their needs as wives and mothers.

If we generalize from what we have seen of women's religious lives in Iran, Morocco, and India, we can underscore the folk character that women's Islam often has assumed. Devotion to the saints, concern with spells, making vows—these have been the great preoccupations. Probably most such Muslim women would not deny the great truths of orthodox Islam— the oneness of God, the significance of the Prophet, the revealed character of the Qur'an—but frequently they have wanted something more practical. As well, they have had to develop a sphere of their own, because official religion largely shunted them to the sidelines. There are strong parallels, of course, in other religious traditions, Christianity and Judaism among them. The little, folkloric religion of concern with saints, with officially minor devotions, and with protection against domestic misfortunes virtually everywhere has had a female majority.

MODERN DEVELOPMENTS

Despite the resurgence of fundamentalism in Iran and other Muslim lands, modern trends have continued to have an impact on the laws governing women and their daily lives. Under the influence of Western law codes, Muslim lands such as Pakistan have reconsidered their family law, a central part of the *Shariah* or overall Islamic Guidance. How to update the tradition, in view of outside angles of vision that suggested women were suffering injustices, divided reformers and conservatives in many lands. What usually had to happen was for reformers to find within the tradition bases from which to reason to changes. That way they could defend themselves against the charge that they were taking on the untraditional, even godless ways of outsiders.

As the editors of a recent collection of essays by Muslim reformers have put it,

> The two major purposes of Muslim family law reforms have been 1) to improve the status of women and 2) to strengthen the rights of nuclear family members vis-á-vis those of the more distant male members of the extended family. Reforms have occurred in three areas: marriage, divorce, and inheritance.
>
> Among the more significant changes in marriage laws are the discouragement of child marriages and the restriction of polygamy. The latter has been effected by such measures as requiring that a husband obtain judicial permission to take an additional wife and permitting a woman to include a stipulation in her marriage contract that gives her the right to divorce should her husband subsequently take another wife.
>
> Divorce was perhaps the most crucial area of legal reform. Among the principal changes legislated were an expansion of the grounds upon which a woman may obtain a divorce and the restriction of the male's unilateral right of divorce.[21]

Pakistan offers a good example of the debates that reform of Muslim family law engendered. In the late 1950s fierce debates raged, and the new ordinance issued in 1961 only emerged after having passed through their fiery furnace. The majority tried to justify their proposed changes as natural developments from the basic principles of the Qur'an and the tradition. For example, they interpreted the Qur'an as not enjoining polygamy, not permitting it without conditions, and not encouraging it. Further, they suggested that the practice of polygamy usually was motivated by baser instincts and resulted in many injustices. Thus, they concluded,

> It is thoroughly irrational to allow individuals to enter into second marriages whenever they please and then demand *post facto* that if they are unjust to the first wife and children, the wife and children should seek a remedy in a court of law. This is like allowing a preventible epidemic to devastate human health and existence and offering advice to human beings to resort to the medical profession for attempting a cure.[22]

Speaking for the minority, one author lamented the lack of expertise in traditional Islamic science found among members of the Commission that was proposing the changes. He then attributed the positions taken by the Commission to a combination of ignorance and disrespect for the Qu-r'an and feelings of inferiority when encountering Western opinion. While in both societies, the Western and the Islamic, men experienced a lack of contentment with one woman, Islamic society had the advantage of granting the second woman full legal rights. Western society, in contrast, simply sanctioned adultery and abused second women outside the marital bond. In conclusion, the author of the minority report found the traditional permission for polygamy sound and blasted those who wanted to depart from it:

> In short, we have not the slightest excuse for imitating the ways of a people with a social setup and a legal system which tolerates sexual satisfaction by means other than marriage. It is hard indeed to imagine a worse type of blind imitation than the one we find in the present case wherein the women who have kicked up so much dust on the question of polygamy and the Commission which has supported their views have not chosen to utter a word against adultery or recommend it to be declared a penal offense, although this form of vice not only means a flagrant violation of the rights of the lawfully wedded wife but also constitutes a deprecation committed on the chastity of others.[23]

In a fine overall study of how recent social changes have influenced the lives of Muslim women, Yvonne Yazbeck Haddad has underscored the centrality of women's issues to the battles about change that have polarized liberals and conservatives within Islam. The debate about polygamy that we have just seen dividing Pakistanis was typical of many Muslim societies. Because Muslim men had so much pride invested in control of women, anything touching traditional sex roles made seismic ripples. From the beginning of the twentieth-century women from the educated and wealthier classes had pressed for greater educational opportunities for women and for opening to women such careers as medicine and government service. They also had attacked the traditional laws about family matters such as marriage and divorce as impeding women's development and denying Islamic countries the contributions that women's talents could have made. A major symbol of the liberation that such reformers wanted was throwing off the veil. Only if women were not secluded from public life, only if they could study and work in the mainstream without all the restraints the prior passion for their chastity had imposed, would they be able to meet the challenges of current history and prove that Islam was not a backward tradition but one capable of adaptation. Thus the leading Muslim feminists tended to put aside the veil and adopt Western dress, much to the outrage of traditionalist religious leaders.

In recent decades, countries that seemed to be following programs of secularization in pursuit of a Western-style economic and political progress have run afoul of a growing conservative backlash. Iran is only the most prominent example. The result has been great stresses for women who have wanted to enjoy the manifest benefits of increased opportunities in education and the workplace without suffering the charge of having been corrupted by Western values. Once again dress and the veil have become the leading symbols of where a given woman stands. In some cases women have little choice, of course, since new conservative governments have made wearing the veil and traditional, wrap-around clothing mandatory. In the recent environment women once again frequently have been perceived as the inner bastion that Islam has to defend against Western corruption.

To get some sense of how Muslim women themselves were coping with the new strains, between 1980 and 1984 Haddad conducted numerous interviews with women from Egypt, Jordan, Oman, Kuwait, and the United States who had redonned the veil, trying to understand their motivation. It proved to be complex. Some had acted from quite purely religious reasons, thinking that God required veiling. Others had stressed psychological factors that boiled down to finding a way to go back to their roots, to the authentic wellsprings of their culture. A third motive that surfaced was disenchantment with the prevailing political order—a sense that modernization Western-style wasn't achieving the sort of society they wished. A fourth, sometimes related reason was to express identification with Islamic revolutionary forces bent on restoring traditional ways.

Interesting, a fifth motive that surfaced was using the veil to proclaim that one was affluent, a lady of leisure who did not have to bend to the ways of the work world. Sixth, some respondents saw the veil as a way of proclaiming that they did not want to be taken as sex objects. Other motives that interlocutors offered for resuming the veil included seeing it as a sign of urbanization, reducing the amount of time and money that had to be spent on clothes, and keeping the domestic peace (avoiding fights with family males who insisted on veiling). Of course, not all Muslim women have resumed wearing the veil, just as not all ever dropped it, but the motives of those who have epitomize current complexities.[24]

DISCUSSION QUESTIONS

1. Briefly describe the Five Pillars of Islam.
2. How did Islam improve the lot of Arab women?
3. What were your impressions when reading the surah on women?
4. Explain the spiritual potential Islam has seen in motherhood.
5. What does the veneration of Rabi'ah suggest about Muslim ideas of sanctity?
6. Why might women of rural Iran feel unwelcome in the mosque?
7. How has the need for a chaste reputation impinged on Muslim women?
8. Why has the veil become so important a symbol?

NOTES

[1]For general background about Islam, see Fazlur Rahman et al., "Islam," in *The Encyclopedia of Religion*, Vol. 7, ed. Mircea Eliade, (New York: Macmillan, 1987), pp. 303–446; Isma'il R. al Faruqi and Lois Lamya' al Faruqi, *The Cultural Atlas of Islam* (New York: Macmillan, 1986); Frederick Mathewson Denny, *An Introduction to Islam* (New York: Macmillan 1985); Maxime Rodinson, *The Arabs* (Chicago: University of Chicago Press, 1981); and The Editors of Encyclopaedia Britannica, *The Arabs* (New York: Bantam, 1978).

[2]See Daphne Daume and Louise Watson, eds., *1987 Britannica Book of the Year* (Chicago: Encyclopaedia Britannica, 1987), p. 338.

[3]Faruqi and Faruqi, *The Cultural Atlas of Islam*, p. 123.

[4]Mohammed Marmaduke Pickthall, *The Meaning of the Glorious Koran* (New York: Mentor, 1953), p. 79.

[5]See Jane I. Smith, "Islam," in *Women in World Religions*, ed. Arvind Sharma (Albany: State University of New York Press, 1987), p. 237. See also her "Women, Religion and Social Change in Early Islam," in *Women, Religion, and Social Change*, ed. Y.Y. Haddad and E.B. Findly (Albany: State University of New York Press, 1985), pp. 19–35.

[6]See Jane I. Smith and Yvonne Haddad, "Women in the Afterlife: The Islamic View as Seen from Qur'an and Tradition," *Journal of the American Academy of Religion*, 47, no. 1 (Spring 1975), pp. 39–50.

[7]Lois Lamya' Ibsen al Faruqi, "Marriage in Islam," *Journal of Ecumenical Studies*, 22, no. 1 (Winter 1985), p. 68.

[8]Inea Bushnaq, ed., *Arab Folktales* (New York: Pantheon, 1986), p. 21.

[9]Saadia Khawar Khan Chishti, "Female Spirituality in Islam," in *Islamic Spirituality: Foundations*, ed. S. H. Nasr (New York: Crossroad, 1987), pp. 204–205.

[10]John Alden Williams, ed., *Themes of Islamic Civilization* (Berkeley: University of California Press, 1982), p. 113.

[11]Ibid., p. 157.

[12]See Smith, "Islam," pp. 238–239.

[13]Chishti, "Female Spirituality in Islam," p. 207.

[14]A. J. Arberry, *The Koran Interpreted*, Vol. 1 (New York: Macmillan, 1956), p. 127.

[15]Annemarie Schimmel, "Rabi'ah Al-'Adawiyah," in *The Encyclopedia of Religion*, Vol. 12, p. 193.

[16]A. J. Arberry, *Sufism* (New York: Harper Torchbooks, 1970), p. 42.

[17]See Anne H. Betteridge, "The Controversial Vows of Urban Muslim Women in Iran," in *Unspoken Worlds: Women's Religious Lives in Non-Western Cultures*, ed. N. A. Falk and R. M. Gross (San Francisco: Harper & Row, 1980), pp. 141–155.

[18]See Erika Friedl, "Islam and Tribal Women in a Village in Iran," in ibid., pp. 159–173.

[19]Susan Schaefer Davis, "The Determinants of Social Position Among Rural Moroccan Women," in Jane I. Smith, ed., *Women in Contemporary Muslim Societies* (Lewisburg, Pa.: Bucknell University Press, 1980), p. 92.

[20]Lina M. Fruzzetti, "Ritual Status of Muslim Women in Rural India," in ibid., p. 193.

[21]John J. Donohue and John L. Esposito, eds., *Islam in Transition: Muslim Perspectives* (New York: Oxford University Press, 1982), p. 200.

[22]Ibid., p. 204.

[23]Ibid., p. 208.

[24]Yvonne Yazbeck Haddad, "Islam, Women and Revolution in Twentieth Century Arab Thought," in *Women, Religion and Social Change*, pp. 275–306.

CHAPTER TEN

American Women

THE COLONIAL PERIOD

In previous chapters we have dealt with American women from time to time, and many of the feminist scholars on whom we have drawn have been American women, but this chapter affords us the chance to consider the story of American women's religious experience as a whole. The main assumptions of those who fashioned this story are familiar from our prior studies, especially those of Jewish and Christian women's religious experience. American women inherited a status by many titles second rate. Biblical religion, both Jewish and Christian, had granted women equal access to God and salvation, but it had shown more fear of female nature than of male and had denied women equal access to power and leadership in the religious community. As we shall see, some sectarian groups were more egalitarian, but the mainstream Christian story, as played out in Protestant, Catholic, and Orthodox churches, and the mainstream Jewish story, as played out in Orthodoxy and Conservatism, made masculine humanity the norm. In addition, women's access to civil rights and power—the vote, elected office, positions of leadership in business, education, the military, and other critical zones of American culture—was severely limited. Only in the twentieth century did women become anything like fully enfranchised

Americans, and feminists usually judge that women still have a long way to go before they will feel they are half the American people.

Prior to the advent of settlers from Europe and the naming of the two continents of the new world "the Americas," there of course were native Indians whose women shared in their different tribal religions. As we have noted, American Indian women generally were honored for their power to bring forth new life. This power was in polar tension with men's power to kill, so much of native American religion sought a proper harmony between male and female power, as well as harmony with nature and the spirits. In a tribe such as the Oglala Sioux, the traditional rites were considered gifts of the Buffalo Maiden, a lovely goddess concerned for the tribe's well-being. She instructed the people in such matters as how to care for the soul of a deceased person and how to celebrate a girl's accession to womanhood. As well, she spoke of the pipe through which tribal members could communicate with the Great Spirit, Wakantanka, and of the sweatlodge they could use to purify both body and soul. Such things pertained to women as well as men, giving women means to consecrate and purify their stipulated work of child rearing, preparing the food, sewing the clothes, and the like.[1]

American Indian women sometimes had influential roles as curers or diviners, and sometimes they had to assent to important tribal decisions. Nonetheless, in most tribes men tended to hold most of the leadership roles, both religious and political. One example would be the religion of Huron tribes in the seventeenth century, as this was perceived by Jesuit missionaries. As Annemarie Shimony recently has summarized this perception, most religious and ceremonial matters were a male domain. Such concerns as funeral rites, the interpretation of dreams, cures for illnesses attributed to malign spirits, and protection against witchcraft usually were handled by men. Women would participate in such rites as the *ononharoia*, a feature of the annual winter festival, when Hurons would act as though mad to purge themselves of upsetting desires. The shamans who interpreted tribal members' dreams were always men, but women with spiritual powers might divine. Women also had the right to have their dreams interpreted and were credited with access to the supernatural realm.[2]

Among the white women of colonial America, one of the most interesting early figures certainly was Anne Hutchinson (1591–1643). Her experience shows what could happen to women of spirit who did not hew to the submissive line thought proper for their sex. In 1637 Hutchinson was put on trial for her deviances. Specifically, she was thought to have challenged such articles of Massachusetts Puritan faith as the belief that good works were a sign of salvation, that the Holy Spirit did not directly inspire individual believers, and that ministers had a monopoly on biblical interpretation. As Edwin S. Gaustad has summarized it,

> Anne Hutchinson presumed too much, talked too much, knew too much; in short, she did things "not fitting for your sex." In a trial that verged on a

farce, this mother, wife, midwife, and theologian was examined in November of 1637; to the surprise of few, she was found guilty. Like Roger Williams, she fled for refuge to Rhode Island, later to Long Island where she and several young children were slain by Indians.[3]

Mary Dyer (d. 1660) suffered a similar fate. Witnessing the trials of Anne Hutchinson, she also moved to Rhode Island, and then to England. In England she encountered the Quakers, who so impressed her that she returned to Boston in 1657 to preach with Quaker enthusiasm. This brought her afoul of the authorities, and when jailing, expulsion, and repeated warnings did not bridle her, she was finally hanged. In her address to the General Court of Massachusetts after the death sentence had been passed, Mary Dyer said in part,

> Whereas I am by many charged with the Guiltiness of my own Blood; if you mean, in my coming to Boston, I am therein clear, and justified by the Lord, in whose Will I came, who will require my Blood of you, be sure, who have made a Law to take away the Lives of the Innocent Servants of God, if they come among you, who are called by you, *Cursed Quakers*; altho' I say, and am a living Witness for them and the Lord, that he hath Blessed them, and sent them unto you: Therefore be not found Fighters against God, but let my Counsel and Request be accepted with you, To Repeal all such Laws, that the Truth and Servants of the Lord may have free Passage among you, and you be kept from shedding innocent Blood, which I know there are many among you would not do, if they knew it so to be.[4]

If the poet Anne Bradstreet is representative, Massachusetts women who were able to accept the Puritan orthodoxy apparently could have a happy enough life. In 1678, after her death, a poem entitled "To My Dear and Loving Husband" appeared singing of a love that apparently entirely fulfilled her. Although the poem makes few explicitly religious allusions, it is somewhat reminiscent of the mutuality of the biblical Song of Songs:

> If ever two were one, then surely we.
> If ever man were loved by wife, then thee;
> If ever wife was happy in a man,
> Compare with me ye women if you can.
> I prize thy love more than whole mines of gold,
> Or all the riches that the East doth hold.
> My love is such that rivers cannot quench,
> Nor ought but love from thee, give recompense.
> Thy love is such I can no way repay.
> The heavens reward thee manifold I pray.
> Then while we live, in love let's so persevere,
> That when we live no more, we may live ever.[5]

In the American colonies, then, women probably tended to be content in the measure they could accept the way of life dominated by male religious leaders. Certainly religion differed from area to area, Massachusetts being a bastion of Puritan orthodoxy (the Salem witch trials of 1692 caused nineteen women to be hanged as witches), Rhode Island becoming a haven for dissidents, the Middle Colonies harboring such Dutch groups as the Quakers, Maryland being founded by Roman Catholics, and the southern colonies feeling much loyalty to the Church of England. However, probably the predominant influence was the Puritanism of those British believers who had emigrated to American to enjoy religious liberty. As historian Sydney Ahlstrom has put it, "It was only in a series of almost accidental colonial commonwealths strung along the North American seaboard, however, that the distilled essence of this Puritan Revolution could manifest its full historical significance."[6] If not a Puritan, then, a colonial woman could be in big trouble.

THE EIGHTEENTH CENTURY

The later part of the prerevolutionary, colonial period continued the pattern of an established church confining the faith and morals of all citizens to what it deemed orthodoxy. For the Catholics of Maryland the late seventeenth and early eighteenth centuries were times when they were wise to keep their religious observance muted and private. The historian Jay Dolan has stressed that seventeenth-century Catholic religion largely centered in the home:

> For Maryland Catholics, religion remained a private affair, centered around the home and the family, principally because of the precedent for this in England, but also because clergy were few and churches were scarce. Reflecting this domestic character of seventeenth-century religion, the Catholic rites of passage took place within the home. Children were baptized at home, and the priests frequently recorded the number in their annual reports. If the priest was not available, most often the parents or the midwife baptized the newborn infants. Marriage was a very informal ritual, with the vows often exchanged at home without the benefit of clergy.[7]

Such a domestic focus obviously brought religion closer to women's domain, and the severe anti-Catholic legislation of the early eighteenth century reinforced it. In 1704 the Maryland legislators, reacting to successes of Jesuit proselytizing in the seventeenth century, passed "An Act to prevent the Growth of Popery within this Province." Among other things this act forbade conversion to the Church of Rome and outlawed priests' saying Mass or exercising other sacramental functions. The penalty for second offenders could be banishment to England. Catholic protest modified this legislation, but the legal redress offered Catholics in 1707 provided only for private worship. Thus the pattern of focusing religious life in the home was reinforced.

No doubt many religious women of the early eighteenth century made their mark, both inside their families and outside, but the first stand-out, feminist personality one encounters in most anthologies is Abigail Adams, who was writing about the time of the Revolution of 1776. Her letter to her husband John Adams, written while he was engaged in what became the declaration of independence and revolution, is famous for its plea that he not forget the female half of the population. While Abigail may be twitting John in places, she was underscoring views of the sexes that not only prevailed in eighteenth-century America but claimed a biblical sanction:

> I long to hear that you have declared an independency—and by the way in the new Code of Laws which I suppose it will be necessary for you to make I desire you would Remember the Ladies, and be more generous and favourable to them than your ancestors. Do not put such unlimited power into the hands of the Husbands. Remember all Men would be tyrants if they could. If peculiar care and attention is not paid to the Ladies we are determined to foment a Rebelion, and will not hold ourselves bound by any Laws in which we have no voice, or Representation. That your sex are Naturally Tyranical is a Truth so thoroughly established as to admit of no dispute, but such of you as wish to be happy willingly give up the harsh title of Master for the more tender and endearing one of Friend. Why, then, not put it out of the power of the vicious and the Lawless to use us with cruelty and indignity with impunity. Men of Sense in all Ages abhor those customs which treat us only as the vassals of your Sex. Regard us then as Being placed by providence under your protection and in immitation of the Supreem Being make use of that power only for our happiness.[8]

John Adams seems not to have taken Abigail fully seriously, choosing to stress the pertness of her letter rather than its radical implications:

> As to your extraordinary Code of Laws, I cannot but laugh. We have been told that our Struggle [against British rule] has loosened the bands of Government every where. That Children and Apprentices were disobedient—that schools and Colleges were grown turbulent—that Indians slighted their Guardians and Negroes grew insolent to their Masters. But your Letter was the first Intimation that another Tribe more numerous and powerful than all the rest were grown discontented.—This is rather too coarse a Compliment but you are so saucy, I wont blot it out. Depend on it, We know better than to repeal our Masculine systems. Altho they are in full Force, you know they are little more than Theory. We dare not exert our Power in its full Latitude. We are obliged to go fair, and softly, and in Practice you know We are the subjects. We have only the Name of Masters, and rather than give up this, which would compleatly subject Us to the Despotism of the Peticoat, I hope General Washington, and all our brave Heroes would fight.[9]

The rather bleak, Puritan view of human nature that Abigail Adams displayed in seeking protection for women against tyrannical husbands surfaced ten or so years later when she answered a request of Thomas Jefferson for information about Shay's Rebellion, an uprising in her native

Massachusetts (although she was residing in London at the time, apparently she was well informed of events back home):

> With regard to the tumults in my native state which you inquire about, I wish I could say that the report had exaggerated them. It is too true, sir, that they have been carried to so alarming a height as to stop the courts of justice in several counties. Ignorant, restless desperadoes, without conscience or principles, have led a deluded multitude to follow their standard, under pretense of grievances which have no existence but in their imaginations. Some of them were crying out for a paper currency, some for an equal distribution of property, some were for annihilating all debts, others complaining that the Senate was a useless branch of government, that the Court of Common Pleas was unnecessary, and that the sitting of the General Court in Boston was a grievance. By this list you will see the materials which compose this rebellion, and the necessity there is of the wisest and most vigorous measures to quell and suppress it. Instead of that laudable spirit which you approve, which makes a people watchful over their liberties and alert in the defense of them, these mobbish insurgents are for sapping the foundation, and destroying the whole fabric at once.[10]

Abigail Adams, of course, was atypical, not so much for her attitudes as for her access to the most powerful men of the nation. It is somewhat ironic that her soul could be composed of strong thrusts toward both liberty and law and order, although of course the two need not be contradictory. The religion of the more ordinary women of eighteenth-century America probably was less shaped by the influence of the European Enlightenment and more shaped by the religious feelings roused in such movements as the "Great Awakening" that flashed forth in New England during the 1730s. Prior to this there had been revivals on what were considered the colonial frontier, but the influence of Jonathan Edwards, a first-rate theologian, helped to accredit the New England phenomenon and make the experience of conversion a catalyst for changing Puritan patterns:

> The Great Awakening in New England was not essentially different from the "frontier revival" of the preceding decade; but it nevertheless bore certain distinguishing marks. Flamboyant and highly emotional preaching made its first widespread appearance in the Puritan churches (though by no means in all), and under its impact there was a great increase in the number and intensity of bodily effects of conversion—fainting, weeping, shrieking, etc. But we capture the meaning of the revival only if we remember that many congregations in New England were stirred from a staid and routine formalism in which experiential faith had been a reality to only a scattered few. . . . Preaching, praying, devotional reading, and individual "exhorting" took on a new life.[11]

Needless to say, women were doing little of the preaching in such churches, but they were doing much of the fainting and shrieking, in large part because females were judged the more emotional sex.

THE ANTEBELLUM PERIOD

The nineteenth century was the time when American religious women came into their own, taking leadership roles in sectarian Christian groups, fashioning new religions, championing the emancipation of black slaves, and beginning to agitate for women's rights to equal citizenship and dignity. As well, millions of immigrants swelled the nation's ranks, Jewish and Catholic groups prominent among them. The result was a welter of new movements, tendencies, and women's influences. On the whole, scholars speak of the feminization of religion during this time. As America became industrialized and the spheres of business and politics became less the province of leisured gentlemen and more the province of hard-driving seekers of power, religion and the home became considered clean havens from the dirty affairs of the men running the country. Women were honored for a motherhood and religiosity that might keep the nation from losing its soul. By their gentility and tender moral influence, they were supposed to keep bestial humanity from making public affairs totally a jungle. The result often was an evisceration of religion and a marginalizing of women that prettified both.

In part because religion had become a more feminine zone, women played leading roles in the sectarian movements of the first half of the nineteenth century. Such groups as the Quakers and the Shakers lay great stress on inner, emotional experience, and this was considered an area congenial to feminine sensitivities. We have mentioned Mary Dyer, the seventeenth-century Quaker martyr. The eighteenth-century Shaker founder Anne Lee not only started one of the sectarian groups most interesting in the nineteenth century but was instrumental in getting it to incorporate a feminine principle into the Christian Godhead. For the Shakers God was Mother as much as Father, while Anne Lee herself stood alongside her bridegroom Jesus Christ as half of the earthly reflection of the two-fold heavenly deity. Mary Baker Eddy (1821–1910), whose work only came into its own after the Civil War, founded Christian Science, a movement often more influential than its limited number of members would suggest.[12]

Women also played important roles in the revivalism, utopianism, movements for social reform, and adaptations of European immigrants that were distinctive, sometimes bewildering features of nineteenth-century American religious life.[13] In evangelical circles women gave much of the impetus to the Holiness Movement. Indeed, one study of such impetus begins,

> On May 21, 1835, at 2:30 P.M., Sarah Worrall Lankford experienced assurance of entire sanctification. In August she consolidated the prayer groups she attended at both the Allen Street and Mulberry Street Methodist churches in New York City into one meeting held at 54 Rivington Street, the home she and her merchant husband, Thomas, shared with her sister Phoebe

and her sister's husband, Walter Palmer, a physician. That prayer meeting, known around the world as the "Tuesday Meeting for the Promotion of Holiness," continued for more than sixty years.

Although Phoebe was a member of the prayer circle, she herself did not experience sanctification until after an experience "on the evening of July 26th, 1837, between the hours of eight and nine o'clock," when "the Lord gave me such a view of my utter pollution and helplessness, apart from the cleansing, energizing influences of the purifying blood of Jesus, and the quickening aids of the Holy Spirit, that I have ever since retained a vivid realization of the fact."[14]

Thereafter Phoebe became the more famous sister and her writings became a mainstay of the Holiness Movement. (It is hard to say whether Pheobe's dismal view of herself as polluted was simply an expression of a mainstream Protestant position about human nature generally or represents an internalization of the special worthlessness that patriarchy often has projected onto women. My guess is the former.)

While some of the women who experienced inner transformations favored a removal from wicked society, many others sought to combine their experiences of spiritual power into a force for social betterment. Prominent among this latter group were the Grimke sisters, who became leading figures in the abolitionist movement and then spokeswomen for women's suffrage and civil equality with men. Because of their interests in both the abolition of slavery and nonsexist marriage, the sisters studied the Bible and sought to justify their positions by what today would be called a liberationist exegesis. Thus Angelina Grimke, writing in 1836, appealed to the Christian women of the South in terms of seven propositions.

She proposed, first, that slavery was contrary to women's declaring their own independence. Second, she found slavery contrary to the biblical covenants between God and both Adam and Noah. Third, Grimke argued that since slavery had been criticized by the prophets, slave dealers had no excuse for maintaining it. Fourth, in Grimke's opinion there was no slavery in the time of the patriarchs and matriarchs (which implied that current times were a decline from a prior time of virtue). Fifth, she believed that slavery had never existed under Jewish dispensation (probably she had in mind only biblical times), when every servant had protection under the law and society was concerned to prevent both voluntary and involuntary servitude. Sixth, American slavery reduced human beings to mere property, "chattel personal," robbing them of their human rights, fettering their minds and bodies, giving masters an unnatural and irrational power, and casting slaves outside the pale of the protection of the law. Seventh and last in Grimke's list of propositions to Christian women of the South was that slavery contradicted both the examples and the commands of Christ and the apostles.

But perhaps you will be ready to query, why appeal to *women* on this subject? *We* do not make the laws which perpetuate slavery. *No* legislative power is vested in *us*; *we* can do nothing to overthrow the system, even if we wished to do so. To this I reply, I know you do not make the laws, but I also know that *you are the wives and mothers, the sisters and daughters of those who do*; and if you really suppose *you* can do nothing to overthrow slavery, you are greatly mistaken.[15]

What practical conclusions did Grimke draw for women's action? She urged four responses, all of which she thought all women could muster to fight slavery. All could read, pray, speak, and join themselves to specific causes. Following her own advice, both Angelina and her sister Sarah became leaders in the abolitionist movement.

Women in antebellum America also contributed to pacifist thought, which frequently they linked with feminist instincts.[16] Perhaps the most poignant symbol of feminist social force in the mid-nineteenth century, however, was the black abolitionist Sojourner Truth, who became famous for her powerful, effective oratory. A description of her effectiveness in Iowa in 1863 captures something of her appearance, style, and impact:

> The graphic sketch of her by the author of "Uncle Tom's Cabin" has doubtless been read with interest by thousands. No pen, however, can give an adequate idea of Sojourner Truth. This unlearned African woman, with her deep religious and trustful nature burning in her soul like fire, has a magnetic power over an audience perfectly astounding. I was once present in a religious meeting where some speaker had alluded to the government of the United States, and had uttered sentiments in favor of its Constitution. Sojourner stood, erect and tall, with her white turban on her head, and in a low and subdued tone of voice began by saying: 'Children, I talks to God and God talks to me. I goes out and talks to God in de field and de woods. [The weevil had destroyed thousands of acres of wheat in the West that year.] Dis morning I was walking out, and I got over de fence. I saw de wheat a holding up its head, looking very big. I goes and takes holt ob it. You b'lieve it, there was *no* wheat dare? I says, God (speaking the name in a voice of reverence peculiar to herself), what *is* de matter wid *dis* wheat? and he says to me, 'Sojourner, dere is a little weasel in it.' Now I hears talkin' about de Constitution and de rights of man. I come up and I takes hold of dis Constitution. It looks *mighty big*, and I feels for *my* rights, but der aint any dare. Den I says, God, what *ails* dis Constitution? He says to me, 'Sojourner, dere is a little *weasel* in it.'" The effect upon the multitude was irresistible.[17]

Prior to the Civil War, then, many religious women sought to use their moral influence to remove the curse of slavery.

FROM THE CIVIL WAR TO WORLD WAR I

The latter part of the nineteenth century and the early part of the twentieth century were times when American women continued to play key roles in religious movements. Many of these roles concerned the adaptation of immigrants to their new surroundings or the aspiration of women to suffrage and civil equality. Some of the proportions of the emigrations from Europe that swelled the American population in the nineteenth century are suggested by the case of Jewish newcomers. Although Jews had been present in America since 1654, when 23 had landed at New Amsterdam, as late as 1820 there probably were no more than 3,000 Jews in the United States. Yet between 1820 and 1880 the Jewish population grew to nearly 300,000, most of them Germans coming as a small portion of the 5 million German immigrants who arrived in that period. After 1880 still more Jews came from Russia and Eastern Europe, where they were suffering persecution. By the time this influx stopped in 1923, more than 3 million more Jews had immigrated.

The German Jews tended to adapt to their new circumstances and to be filled with ideas from the European Enlightenment. They were leaders in the movement to reform Judaism and free it from its strict adherence to Talmudic law. The Russian Jews tended to view such innovations as apostasies. For them freedom was freedom to live a fully Orthodox life. Jewish women also tended to divide into two groups, those who saw American culture as a chance to free themselves from the restrictions Orthodox Jewry placed on women and those who felt that wives and mothers had special responsibilities to preserve the old ways regarding kosher diet, observance of the Sabbath, and the like. Thus the *Occident*, a periodical concerned with reporting news about Jewish life in America, supported Jewish women who started a coeducational school in Charleston by writing,

> This sacred and laudable undertaking emanates from the mothers and daughters of Israel who are opposed to the innovations lately established in this congregation, and whose zeal and energies will be actively employed in impressing upon the tender minds of their pupils the *orthodox* tenets of our religion.[18]

The other end of the spectrum was represented by women like Mary Antin, who wrote a book hymning the praise of America entitled *The Promised Land* because America offered women escape from the backwardness imposed on them by traditional Judaism. Speaking of her sister's early marriage two years after the family had arrived in the United States, Antin lamented,

> Had she been two years younger she might have . . . evaded her Old-World fate. She would have gone to school and imbibed American ideas . . . it has always seemed to me a pitiful accident that my sister should have come so near and missed by so little the fulfillment of my country's promise to women.[19]

Much of the adaptation of Roman Catholicism to America lay in the hands of the nuns who came to the United States to minister to the various ethnic groups, often by running schools. In the early nineteenth century they regularly suffered attacks by bigots, and quite often the support promised them by the Catholic bishops who had sought their help never materialized.

Concerning the bigotry, the first half of the nineteenth century was an especially dark time:

> When Catholic sisters first began to be seen in America in the first half of the nineteenth century, they were greeted with hostility and suspicion. Rumors of evil practices and women held by force in convents were circulated, and Protestant ministers argued against Catholicism from their pulpits, directing their attacks particularly against nuns. Nuns were frequently insulted or pelted in the streets. Occasionally riots broke out, and mobs pillaged and burned the convents. One of the most famous such cases was the burning of the Ursuline convent in Charlestown, Massachusetts, on August 11, 1834. . . . The mob looted the building and desecrated the chapel, even digging up the bodies of the sisters in the cemetery, before burning the convent and academy.[20]

In the second half of the nineteenth century and the first quarter of the twentieth century, residual antagonisms remained, but the Catholic authorities themselves curtailed the previously rather free-floating work of many religious women, tending to tie them to such institutions as grammar schools and hospitals. By 1900, for example, there were nearly 4,000 parish elementary schools serving over 850,000 students.[21]

Both Catholics and Jews were still outside the American mainstream, however, so not withstanding the fact that outstanding Jewish women such as Henrietta Szold and Catholic women such as Elizabeth Seton and Frances Cabrini became American exemplars of the best ideals of their traditions, it was Protestant women who led the religious feminists in their efforts to get women the vote and to emancipate them from their second-rate status. One of the most provocative such Protestant women was Elizabeth Cady Stanton. In 1848 she and the Quaker Lucretia Mott had organized a convention for women's rights at Seneca Falls, New York. Later, she worked with Susan B. Anthony for women's suffrage. In 1895, however, she published the first portion of her work *The Women's Bible*, having realized that a sacred scripture that seemed to relegate women to inferiority and dependency was a major impediment to women's equality. Stanton therefore proposed to take the Bible as a human work and edit it of its misogynism. Early in her venture she summarized the view of women set forth in the Bible, that all feminists might measure the scale of their foe:

> From the inauguration of the movement for women's emancipation the Bible has been used to hold her in the "divinely ordained sphere," prescribed in the Old and New Testaments. The canon and civil law; church and state; priests and legislators; all political parties and religious denominations have alike taught that woman was made after man, of man, and for man, an inferior being, subject to man. Creeds, codes, Scriptures and statutes, are all based on this idea. The fashions, forms, ceremonies and customs of society, church ordinances and discipline all grow out of this idea . . .

The Bible teaches that woman brought sin and death into the world, that she precipitated the fall of the race, that she was arraigned before the judgment seat of Heaven, tried, condemned, and sentenced. Marriage for her was to be a condition of bondage, maternity a period of suffering and anguish, and in silence and subjection, she was to play the role of a dependent on man's bounty for all her material wants, and for all the information she might desire on the vital questions of the hour, she was commanded to ask her husband at home. Here is the Bible position of woman briefly summed up.[22]

A final glimpse into the religious activities of women in the late nineteenth century comes from the labors of Frances Willard, leader of the Women's Christian Temperance Union. As part of a Plan of Work adopted in 1874 her followers fashioned a Pledge:

If nobody would drink, then nobody would sell. First, we urge the circulation of the total abstinence pledge as fast and as far as facilities permit, life signatures being sought, but names being taken for any length of time, however brief. Second, we have a special pledge for women, involving the instruction and pledging of themselves, their children, and as far as possible their households; banishing alcohol in all its forms from the sideboard and the kitchen, enjoining quiet, persistent work for temperance in their own social circles. Third, we earnestly recommend ladies to get permission to place a pledge-book in every church and Sabbath-school room, where it shall be kept perpetually open in a convenient place, indicated by a motto placed above it. . . . If we would have men forsake saloons, we must invite them to a better place, where they can find shelter, and food, and company. . . . We wage our peaceful war in loving expectation of that day when "all men's weal shall be each man's care," when "nothing shall hurt or destroy in all my holy mountain," saith the Lord.[23]

RECENT TRENDS

In the seventy-odd years since the end of World War I American women have undergone changes of consciousness that for many amount to a revolutionary new outlook. Women's participation in the national efforts necessary to wage two wars brought them more fully into factories, the military, and offices than they had been previously. Gaining the vote in 1920 opened the way to fuller participation in the nation's political processes. But it was only with the convergence of such social trends as the movement of the middle class to suburbia in the 1950s, the movement of blacks for civil rights in the 1960s, and the mobilization against American involvement in Vietnam in the 1970s that women started to consider themselves an oppressed bloc that might pull together for redress of the economic and social injustices it had been suffering. Relatedly, many women became involved in the family planning movement spearheaded by Margaret Sanger (1883–1966). Such organizations as Planned Parenthood and the National

Organization of Women, along with such periodicals as *MS* and *Signs*, provided forums for what was increasingly becoming a movement—a shift of consciousness that like a rolling ball of dough gathered more and more aspects of women's experience into itself.

For religious women such social change posed important questions about their traditions. Insofar as their theologies were based on the Bible, Protestant churches tended to assume that God had sanctioned the primacy of men in positions of power. Despite the history of women's leadership in the left-wing, sectarian, and spiritualist churches, usually only those Protestant churches that had accepted modern biblical criticism found ways of accommodating women's desires for ordination and liberation. The churches that maintained a premodern or fundamentalist reading of Scripture tended to brand feminism another of the Devil's many modern works.

Jewish women seeking liberation from traditional patterns of subjugation to men found more hope in Reform synagogues than in Orthodox or Conservative. Like their liberal Protestant sisters, Reformed Jewish women had tools for challenging the traditionally androcentric interpretation of the Bible and the Talmud, since Reform Judaism took such authorities as human works capable of being updated and supplanted. Synagogues in which the traditional authorities were considered virtually definitive precedents gave women little hope they could fully participate in religious services, study theology, or serve as rabbis.

For Roman Catholic women the watershed event was the Second Vatican Council of 1962–65. Although the Council said little explicitly that encouraged Catholic women's liberation, its key documents on the Church in the modern world and religious liberty implied that a more democratic, personal, and freer faith was in the offing. Through its ecumenism, the Roman Church was moving out of its religious ghetto. Through its stated desire for dialogue with the modern world, it was moving out of its intellectual ghetto. Its reforms in biblical interpretation and liturgical practice encouraged women of liberal persuasion to think that "the people of God," the Council's preferred designation for the faithful, would have a bigger place for their contributions than the preconciliar Church had had.

In the last fifteen years or so American religious women with increasing momentum have dedicated themselves to creating new theologies and views of religious experience that might correct or supplant the male-dominated worldviews under which they used to suffer. Whereas women in conservative churches and synagogues have been prominent in the ranks of those opposing the Equal Rights Amendment and the movement for reproductive freedom, liberal and radical religious women have sought to fashion a new spirituality that would give primacy to women's own experience, both political and mystical. The nonreligious part of the movement for women's liberation often has written religion off as part of the patriarchal problem, implying or even declaring outright that one could not be a feminist and a member of a mainstream American religious group. But many mainstream religious women have disagreed, arguing that they will no more let secularists take away their faith than they will let male chauvinist religious leaders. Indeed, many women interested in religion have come to experience ministry as a fine vehicle for effecting feminist goals.

Currently leaders in American feminist theology and religious studies include such academic women as Rosemary Radford Ruether, Elisabeth Schüssler Fiorenza, Judith Plaskow, and Carol Christ. Rosemary Ruether has been the pioneer, the closest thing to a mother of contemporary American feminist theology. A prolific author and lecturer, she has offered both historical studies that have illumined women's past religious experience and constructive studies that have mapped out the new modes of thought and social organization that women's full equality with men postulates.[24]

Elisabeth Schüssler Fiorenza has specialized in New Testament topics, developing a feminist hermeneutic that breaks open the androcentrism of the biblical materials and suggests how women were equal sharers in the founding of the Christian church.[25] Like Rosemary Ruether, she comes from a Roman Catholic background and is interested in the political implications of Christian faith. Both women favor socialist views that would be rooted in the freeing power of the gospel and divine grace. With Judith Plaskow, Schüssler Fiorenza edits the *Journal of Feminist Studies in Religion*, which has become a main forum for women's scholarship and reflection about religious experience.

Judith Plaskow comes from a Jewish background and has been interested in fashioning a theology rooted in women's experience. As well, she has been interested in developing new rituals for Jewish women that would give them feminist forms for expressing their faith. As is true of most feminist teachers, she has also sought pedagogical methods that invite women to share their experience and reflect together on its import more than most male-dominated pedagogical models, both academic and religious, have allowed. Finally, she has been interested in retelling traditional stories from a feminist point of view and in fashioning new tales that might bear today's women a mythic power.[26]

Our fourth representative figure, Carol Christ, edited with Judith Plaskow *Womanspirit Rising*, perhaps the most influential reader in feminist approaches to religion. Her special interests have included feminist literature and spirituality. Christ has found as much nourishment for these interests in the new feminist witchcraft as in the mainstream religious traditions, and she serves as a link between the academic religious community and women trying to create covens in which worship of the Goddess, special reverence for nature, and new ways of bonding might flourish.[27]

One could mention many other women whose studies in ethics, spirituality, history of religions, biblical materials, literature, and other areas now contribute to developing the consciousness of religious women.

Under the rubric of spirituality—heightened consciousness, better connection with all aspects of reality—secular feminists often find such work germane to their humanistic interests.[28] Key issues that continue to absorb the community of religious feminists include working for women's ordination in churches and Jewish bodies that still ordain only men (there has been progress in both traditions, but Roman Catholicism, Eastern Orthodox Christianity, and Orthodox Judaism still refuse women ordination) and working on the difficult question of abortion. Religious women in general and feminists in particular still debate such matters, most of them firmly advocating women's rights and sexual equality while recognizing that it is seldom certain just what are the best means to achieve such ends.[29] Recently lesbian religious feminists such as Carter Heyward and Mary Hunt have made important contributions to Christian theological reflection, while the work of Jewish feminists often incorporates reflection on the Holocaust and Zionism.[30] Black religious feminists are producing provocative studies of the implications of black women's experience, and original theoreticians such as Mary Daly are reworking such areas as the foundations of ethics and the philosophy of love.[31] All in all, then, American religious feminism presently is a pot vigorously bubbling.

DISCUSSION QUESTIONS

1.   Why were Anne Hutchinson and Mary Dyer considered deviant?

2.   How feminist is the letter of Abigail Adams to John Adams and how chauvinist is his reply?

3.   How should one evaluate Sojourner Truth's talking with God?

4.   Why did Elizabeth Cady Stanton feel free to criticize the Bible?

5.   Why have feminist theologians recently focused on women's experience and made it a prime theological source?

NOTES

[1]See Joseph Epes Brown, ed., *The Sacred Pipe* (Baltimore: Penguin, 1971).

[2]See Annemarie Shimony, "Iroquois Religion and Women in Historical Perspective," in *Women, Religion and Social Change*, ed. Y. Y. Haddad and E. B. Findly (Albany: State University of New York Press, 1985), p. 400.

[3]Edwin S. Gaustad, ed., *A Documentary History of Religion in America: To the Civil War* (Grand Rapids, Mich.: Eerdmans, 1982), p. 132.

[4]Ibid., pp. 134–135.

[5]Encyclopaedia Britannica, *Annals of America*, Vol. 1 (Chicago: Encyclopaedia Britannica, 1976), p. 198, quoted by permission.

[6]Sydney E. Ahlstrom, *A Religious History of the American People* (New Haven, Conn.: Yale University Press, 1972), p. 123.

[7]Jay P. Dolan, *The American Catholic Experience* (Garden City, N.Y.: Doubleday, 1985), pp. 83–84.

[8]Alice S. Rossi, ed., *The Feminist Papers* (New York: Columbia University Press, 1973), pp. 10–11.

[9]Ibid., p. 11.

[10]Encyclopaedia Britannica, *The Annals of America*, Vol. 3 p. 80.

[11]Ahlstrom, *A Religious History of the American People*, pp. 286–287.

[12]See Barbara Brown Zikmund, "The Feminist Thrust of Sectarian Christianity," in *Women of Spirit*, ed. R. R. Ruether and E. McLaughlin (New York: Simon & Schuster, 1979), pp. 205–224.

[13]See Rosemary Radford Ruether and Rosemary Skinner Keller, eds., *Women & Religion in America*, Vol. 1 (San Francisco: Harper & Row, 1981).

[14]Nancy Hardesty, Lucille Sider Dayton, and Donald W. Dayton, "Women in the Holiness Movement: Feminism in the Evangelical Tradition," in *Women of Spirit*, p. 226.

[15]Rossi, ed., *The Feminist Papers*, pp. 296–297.

[16]See Dorothy C. Bass, "In Christian Firmness and Christian Meekness: Feminism and Pacifism in Antebelllum America," in *Immaculate and Powerful: The Female in Sacred Image and Social Reality*, ed. C. Atkinson, C. Buchanan, and M. Miles (Boston: Beacon 1985), pp. 201–225.

[17]Gaustad, ed., *A Documentary History of Religion in America*, pp. 476–477.

[18]Anne Braude, "The Jewish Woman's Encounter with American Culture," in *Women and Religion in America*, Vol. 1, p. 156.

[19]Anne D. Braude, "Jewish Women in the Twentieth Century: Building a Life in America," in *Women and Religion in America*, Vol. 3, ed. R. R. Ruether and R. S. Keller (San Francisco: Harper & Row, 1986), pp. 133–134.

[20]Mary Ewens, O. P., " The Leadership of Nuns in Immigrant Catholicism," in *Women and Religion in America*, Vol. 1, p. 132.

[21]See Lorine M. Getz, "Women Struggle for an American Catholic Identity," in *Women and Religion in America*, Vol. 3, p. 178.

[22]Edwin S. Gaustad, ed., *A Documentary History of Religion in America: Since 1865* (Grand Rapids, Mich.: Eerdmans, 1983), p. 69.

[23]Ibid., pp. 66–67.

[24]For examples of Ruether's historical work, see her own contributions to *Women of Spirit* and *Women & Religion in America*. For her constructive work, see *Sexism & God-Talk* (Boston: Beacon, 1983).

[25]See Elisabeth Schüssler Fiorenza, *In Memory of Her* (New York: Crossroad, 1983), and *Bread Not Stone* (Boston: Beacon, 1984).

[26]See Judith Plaskow's contributions to *Womanspirit Rising*, ed. Carol Christ and Judith Plaskow (San Francisco: Harper & Row, 1979), and her *Sex, Sin and Grace* (Lanham, Md.: University Press of America, 1980).

[27]See Christ's contributions to *Womanspirit Rising*, and her *Diving Deep and Surfacing: Women Writers on Spiritual Quest* (Boston: Beacon, 1980).

[28]See, for example, *The Politics of Women's Spirituality*, ed. Charlene Spretnak (Garden City, N.Y.: Doubleday, 1982).

[29]For example, my own book *The Double Cross: Ordination, Abortion, and Catholic Feminism* (New York: Crossroad, 1986), is typical of many Catholic feminists in being for ordination but against abortion.

[30]See, for example, the issue of *Religion & Intellectual Life* dedicated to "Feminism and Religious Experience," iii, no. 2 (Winter, 1986), and the Spring 1987 issue of *Journal of Feminist Studies in Religion*, 3, no. 1.

[31]See Delores S. Williams, "Black Women's Literature and the Task of Feminist Theology," in *Immaculate and Powerful*, pp. 88–110; and Mary Daly, *Gyn/Ecology* (Boston: Beacon, 1978), and *Pure Lust* (Boston: Beacon 1984).

CHAPTER ELEVEN

Conclusion

PATTERNS OF OPPRESSION

Women's experience with the world religions has been varied and mixed, as one would expect such a central portion of the whole human story to be. In this section let us consider the dark chapters, the too many places where religions oppressed women—denied their full humanity and increased their sufferings.

Mary Daly's book *Gyn/Ecology* has spotlighted the most gruesome episodes: widow burning in India, foot binding in China, genital mutilation in Africa, witch burning in Europe. Indeed, she sees modern American medical practice regarding women as continuing the centuries' old horror tale.[1] And while scholars rightly debate just how widespread such abuses have been and just how validly we may take them as expressing a deep misogynism, there is no valid debate about either the fact that they happened or the pain they caused thousands of women.

When we investigate the rationale offered by the culture in question, usually we find that the abusive treatment merely exaggerates a pejorative view of female nature that the culture has assumed as part of its general worldview. Thus it made a certain perverse sense to pressure Hindu widows to mount the funeral pyre, because their husbands had given them most of their reason to exist. Similarly, insofar as Chinese women existed for the pleasure and service of Chinese men, it was logical to force them into a mincing gait, when that became the fancy of the male erotic spirit. The African women who suffered clitoridectomy were the victims of the judgment of African males that women would be better wives and mothers if deprived of sexual pleasure. Many of the European women harried and murdered for supposed witchcraft simply were nonconformists, women who refused to fall into line with the roles set for them by a Christian patriarchy. Finally, the American women who suffered unnecessary surgeries regularly were the victims of a patriarchal medical corps more concerned about its own profit and ease than about the pains peculiar to female bodies.

Concentrating on such atrocities has its drawbacks, however, and in extreme cases it can lead to a wholesale hatred of men. The fact is that patriarchy—rule by men—has been the main pattern throughout history and that in both its genesis and its maintenance the sexes have managed a complex causality.[2] Still, this does not deny the perhaps more pertinent fact that women have been the more overt victims, let alone justify blaming such victims for the abuses they have suffered. Because religion regularly functions as a sanction for the social relations in a given culture, religion has on its hands the stains of many women's blood and tears. By justifying patriarchy—saying it was something encoded in the plans by which the heavenly powers were running the earth—much civil religion (religion justifying present cultural patterns) the world over gave men the right to treat women as they wished. At the same time, such civil religion gave women the self-image of being something disposable, something untrustworthy, something made not for itself but for the pleasure, offspring, and work it could generate.

I repeat that this is the dark side of women's experience. We shall come to brighter aspects in the next section. But we should not miss the sharp edge of what the religions have connived with and abetted. At its worst, patriarchal theology East and West made women wonder whether they weren't hateful to the gods, weren't the portion of creation the Creator most regretted. It is hard to exaggerate the inner turmoil this wondering caused. While the mutilations of women's bodies—the murders, the rapes, the operations—rightly get the headlines, women's self-doubt, weakness, proneness to manipulation, and other sins lie heavily on religion's head. For freedom religion should have set women free (Galatians 5:1), but again and again women found their priests, religious lawgivers, monks, and pious family patriarchs their foremost enslavers.

Lest we get lost in a fog of generality, it will be well to tell a few stories and paint the patterns of oppression in primary colors. To begin with the psychic oppressions, the ways that harsh religions ruled by men robbed women of joy and happiness, we can quote Isabel Moore, the heroine of Mary Gordon's powerful novel *Final Payments*. Isabel has given the flower of her womanhood to caring for her bedridden father, the victim of a stroke. After his death she has bloomed, knowing a brief period of love and pleasure. But now her idyll has fallen apart and the hard old religion reaches up to snatch her heart, telling her that she must pay for her enjoyments, that real virtue is doing her duty, the more difficult the better:

> Pleasure. In the last few months I have enjoyed things immensely. But that was because I had been in error about myself, about the nature of things. I knew now that the truth of my life was that buzzing pain, black, purple, at the back of my skull; I was alone; my father was dead; I would never see him again . . . I knew that it was Margaret I must go to; only there would I be safe from Hugh, from Liz and Eleanor and their talk about "life." They did not understand my life, and they had caused me to misunderstand it. It was not possible for me to be like other people; I was not like other people. I was not satisfied with what they called "life."
>
> I would take care of Margaret; I would devote myself to the person I was least capable of loving. I would absorb myself in the suffering of someone I found unattractive. It would be a pure act, like the choice of a martyr's death which, we had been told in school, is the only inviolable guarantee of salvation. If you died for the faith you would be guaranteed salvation. And when Margaret died, I would simply go on to someone else. I would be the person I wanted to be, beyond loss, beyond reproach.[3]

This is religion as dehumanizing. It is religion as making virtue and the transcendence of God the enemy of people's happiness and fulfillment. No doubt Isabel Moore is an exceptional case, standing for only the few whose religion completely ate at their marrow. But myriad women have found that the wisdom their culture canonized as most holy more bruised their hearts than consoled them. The Islamic women told they were unclean and so unfit for the mosque; the medieval Christian women told their husbands could clout them for any impertinence; the Buddhist women told the Buddha had only taken women into the Sangha reluctantly and freely asking forgiveness for the sins that had caused them to be reborn as females; the Jewish women told they were unsuitable for studying Torah; the Japanese women kept out of business—all have felt, in ways both subtle and gross, the chill of rejection. From little girls wanting to serve at the altar and being told they could not, to Chinese and Muslim women being sent into harems, women the world over have found their native tradition ranged against their simple desire to be free, to grow, to create, to be valued for their own sakes, to hold up their own half of the sky.

Wendy Doniger O'Flaherty's balanced, insightful book *Women, Androgynes, and Other Mythical Beasts* suggests, largely from Indo-European examples, how much mythology has told women they were abnormal humanity, the deviant partner of the dyad. For example, Hindu sacrifice often stigmatized female nature as unholy:

> In Hinduism, especially on the royal level, the stallion remains a sacred animal: it is primarily a sacrificial animal, for horse sacrifices continued to be performed, albeit rarely, long after the general rule of noninjury to animals put an end to most Hindu animal sacrifices. The stallion also retains its conno-

> tations of fertility. The mare, by contrast, has taken on new, negative dimensions: she is erotic but not fertile . . . and not only is she not part of the sacrifice to the Vedic gods but, on the contrary, she is associated with demons and demonic destruction.[4]

Certainly women are not mares, and certainly Hindu theology had some positive symbols for female nature. But when stallions are fertile and mares are merely erotic, the mythology that it is proper to oppress women is knocking at the door.

PATTERNS OF RESILIENCE

Although there are many reasons to depict women as victims of traditional religions, there are also patterns across the world religions that show women to have bounced back, mustered true grit, and drawn from their traditions not only a grudging respect but downright admiration. So the Sufi saint Rabi'ah, who began as a household drudge, became one of the most influential exemplars of holiness. So the Chinese mythology that supported male supremacy was forced to make a place for women warriors. In Upanishadic India, where most of the sages were men, we meet Gargi Vacaknava, a woman who pushes the sage Yajnavalkya to the limit. In Talmudic Judaism we meet Beruriah, the exception proving the rule that study was only for men and so of course calling that rule into doubt. Although the Buddha is said not to have wanted women in the Sangha, he finally had to give in to the manifest sincerity of his aunt. Although Jesus apparently treated some women harshly, many persevered and won his admiration.

The gospel story of Jesus being bested by the Canaanite woman can stand not only for all the resolute women of the New Testament but also as a type of the resiliency women everywhere have shown:

> And Jesus went away from there and withdrew to the district of Tyre and Sidon. And behold, a Canaanite woman from that region came out and cried, "Have mercy on me, O Lord, Son of David; my daughter is severely possessed by a demon." But he did not answer her a word. And his disciples came and begged him, saying, "Send her away, for she is crying after us." He answered, "I was sent only to the lost sheep of the house of Israel." But she came and knelt before him, saying, "Lord, help me." And he answered, "It is not fair to take the children's bread and throw it to the dogs." She said, "Yes, Lord, yet even the dogs eat the crumbs that fall from their masters' table." Then Jesus answered her, "O woman, great is your faith! Be it done for you as you desire." And her daughter was healed instantly. (Matthew 15:21–28)

Several features of this story are worth noting, because they are typical of women's religion as a whole. First, the woman is a foreigner, someone whom orthodox Judaism considered unclean and so not to be dealt with. She forces Jesus to break with this rigidity, this legalism, refusing to play by the slanted rules a patriarchal structure had laid down. Second, when it comes to the needs of her child, the woman has no shame. If getting help requires that she grovel, grovel she will. The good of her child is far more important than fancy notions about honor. Honor is a luxury only the powerful and wealthy—most of whom are men—can afford. Third, the woman perseveres. One word of rejection hardly daunts her. She has learned that water wears down rock. Like her Eastern sisters, she is instinctly a Taoist. When Jesus, who has gained a great reputation as a healer, as a friend of the needy, rebuffs her, she undercuts him by reminding him of his vocation: "Help me." Last, the woman is more than able to hold her own when it comes to word play and wit. Jesus calls her a dog, as any rabbi of his day legitimately might have. She in effect barks: dogs too have a right to be fed. And so she wins. The Master's resistance, whether real or contrived to produce a demonstration of faith, is dashed by the admiration that waves out from him. The further implication of the story is that all believers would do well to deal with God as this woman has dealt with Jesus. All would do well to keep praying and never give up.

Again and again, we find women working, praying, and never giving up. We find black women singing that nobody knows the troubles they've seen and going home to slug along once again. We find indomitable spirits like Sojourner Truth, Elizabeth Cady Stanton, and nameless mothers the world over getting to the point where they know they have nothing to lose but the bedrock of their selves and so persisting fearlessly. In past ages such women would have been called saints: Catherine of Siena, fearlessly badgering the pope to reform himself and the church, Gargi Vacaknava, determined to keep questioning until she gets an answer that makes sense; women of the Jewish ghettoes wearing themselves out for their children and the poor of their neighborhoods. Today we have similar women fighting against drunk driving, fighting against drugs, fighting for gun control, prominent in the work to keep the earth green, passionate in their labors to avert nuclear holocaust. Equally, we have women persevering as grammar school teachers, though their communities despise their work by paying it only a pittance. We have women nursing the very poor, attending the mentally ill, doing 70 percent of society's scut work. Ultimately it doesn't matter whether they do such work because they want to or because they have no alternative. Either way, they are "manning" the last defenses of our society against total heartlessness, the last barriers to a full capitulation to utility and greed.

A lot of the resilience that women show, like a lot of the resilience that put-upon men show, amounts to moral victories. Consider the Chicana Teresa, who has had to struggle with the invitation of the dance-hall owner Peter Diaz to join his stable of hostesses:

> She grew stronger as hours, then days separated her from the dance hall, Peter Diaz, his fleet of Cadillacs and army of chauffeurs, handymen, sentinels, and henchmen. . . . She had been essentially correct. The priest told her what

he knew after she went to him with her confession. The priest had once approached Peter Diaz in an earnest and quiet effort to win him over—to no effect. Teresa was told at church that she had earned God's respect and affection. She had, most certainly, faced down the Devil himself. Surely her life would, as a consequence, begin to become favored, enriched. A year later she had ample cause to agree. She had fallen in love with a young man who was a cousin of one of her brothers-in-law. He worked as a busboy in a rather elegant San Antonio hotel. He had hopes of becoming, one day, a waiter. He managed to get her a job in the same hotel. She cleaned the rooms, changed the beds. Between the two of them, they were (by *barrio*) standards rather lucky: two reliable jobs—and in a completely air-conditioned building.[5]

Until we realize what a victory not taking the easy money that corrupts can be, we won't appreciate the valor of so many poor people, women and men alike. Until we can appreciate that having a reliable job in an air-conditioned building would be the outer portal of paradise for billions of people, we won't have a hint of what's really going on in the religious battles for people's souls. Women and men who say no to corruption do something saintly.

In her 1985 Madeleva Lecture in Spirituality, Monika Hellwig surveys the past conditions under which Christian women labored to love God and neighbor and then brings her survey to bear on present times:

> The all-important question, of course, is what inspiration and implications we might draw for our own times. A most significant conclusion is certainly that as long as women are systematically excluded from ordination and from the institutional positions of leadership and decision-making in the Church, this has some advantages as well as the more obvious disadvantages. To be deprived of the power of domination, to have little or no access to bullying power, to be unable to compel or persuade by threat or use of institutional sanctions, is necessarily to be thrown back on other resources. And that may well be to discover that divine power, the power of grace, is of a very different kind—freedom for self-transcendence, freedom for true community with others, freedom for God and for God's purposes in creation and history. On the other hand, to have access to bullying power is to be sorely tempted to use it. But it is not Christ's way. Because of our Church organization, Christ's way by empowerment of human freedom to transcend is likely to be more immediately apparent to women.[6]

We might say the same of Krishna's way of love, of the Buddha's way of renunciation, of the Tao that moves gently, of the Wisdom that played before God at creation.

THE BOTTOM LINE

How one finally evaluates the proportions between the patterns of oppression and the patterns of resilience greatly depends on one's own philosophy or theology. Where sin abounded, has grace abounded the more? Are weak human beings more to be despised or pitied? Does knowing much about the story of women's experience with the world religions mean forgiving more? What does God or the Buddha of Light see from heaven's vantage? These are questions that call into play one's basic horizon, the preunderstanding one brings to humanistic studies. That preunderstanding may have been imbibed with one's mother's milk, learned in a religious assembly, or taken in from the secular milieu. In it we live and move and have our judgmental being, so to it belongs the final say in many cases.

Nonetheless, it is possible to discuss what ought to go into judgments about the bottom line and so to render them less onesided, more rational and holistic. For example, there is the matter of survival. Despite all its barbarities, the human race to this point has survived. Against many evolutionary odds, it has kept reflective consciousness in the world for what probably amounts to millions of years. With reflective consciousness come understanding, freedom, and love. Because we can know that we know, we open onto realms of transcendence—heavens that exceed what we can measure, utopias that never will know bricks and mortar but endure as the soul's hometown. And the story of both our psychic survival and our penetration of the realms of transcendence cannot be told without central reference to religion. The modern delineation of a profane world capacious enough to make people think it can house homo sapiens is a historical aberration. For 99 percent of the world's ages people have lived as though thought and spirit mattered at least as much as stocks and weapons.

If one thinks that women are fully human beings, one has to make this human survival an important ingredient in one's estimate of how history and religion have treated women. Without backing away in any measure from the condemnation that each act of cruelty and injustice to women or men merits, one still has to admit that countless generations of women have lived, had the chance to bless the light of their eyes and the air they breathed, and made it possible for their daughters and sons to have the same chance.

Indeed, one has to admit that great numbers of such women have known wonder, insight, prayer, peace, creative work, love, a sense of purpose, gratitude before beauty, awe at the holiness of God. If these are the things of supreme moment, much more important than material possessions or social esteem, great numbers of women have had a fair chance to realize the heart of the human matter.

For all of us, life is short and we are not God. We are mortal, imperfect, limited through and through. Learning how to balance this truth with the equal truth that we have a reach that exceeds our grasp, a thirst for immortality, is a large part of becoming wise. Those who agree that all human lives are afflicted, including perhaps most poignantly the lives of those who think they have it all, will take a hard look at many denunciations of women's religious experience. If the denunciation is saying that women should not have had to suffer, it is risking childishness. All human beings have had to suffer. Suffering is built into being ignorant and bound for the grave. If the denunciation rather is saying that women have suffered more than their fair share, have often suffered needlessly, it gets closer to the bottom line. Yet many men also have suffered more than their fair share, because they came from the wrong race or spoke the wrong language or worshiped what others considered the wrong God. So the proper denunciation finally is quite restrained: women often have suffered for their sex and gender as men have not; women often have been sexual victims of men—the first strangers or aliens onto whom men projected their needs to dominate, boost their egos, and even inflict pain. So stated, the denunciation seems to me valid, and with it goes a valid criticism of the world religions, since most of the men who have victimized women throughout history have been helped by their religious traditions.

There are no remedies for the capacity of human beings to be cruel and sin, save conversion to better ways of love and grace. There are no shortcuts to wisdom and holiness, no detours that bypass suffering and disappointment. Only when he had confronted death, old age, and disease, did the future Buddha become serious about enlightenment. Only when he surrendered to his Father's will did Jesus enter the hour of Satan that proved to be his hour of victory. Everywhere the religious myths and symbols repeat the same lesson. The way up to the vision of God is the way down to a clear-eyed contemplation of human limitation. The way to resurrection passes through the cross. If you want to follow the Tao that gives all things their proportions, you have to endure the heat of summer and the winter's ice. For every time there is a purpose—if one is able to abide and endure the decrees of heaven, not running away into distraction, not indulging a facile hopelessness.

This is the coin the world's traditions about wisdom and salvation have minted. This is the sort of language that any people who want to sense the length and the breadth, the height and the depth, of the reality into which they have been placed (without their consent or understanding) have to decipher. And while women sometimes have been barred from the gnostic circles, the hermetic groups, that considered themselves the elect code crackers, the basic bibles and qur'ans have all been open to women. So we too have heard angelic voices saying, "Take and read," or "hear and ponder in your heart."

Sometimes we who teach religious studies do our students the double disservice of both downplaying the mysterious, sacramental character of the religions' traditional language and keeping silent about what is necessary if a student is fully to profit from the humanistic exposure our courses afford. The fact is that virtually all the people who have claimed to find light and strength, wisdom and salvation, in the world religions have pondered their scriptures deeply. The fact is that only contemplation and quite ordinary, practical love afford people the chance to become fully human.[7]

Have women, past and present, contemplative gifts, the capacity to-ponder in their hearts, to let go of egocentricity, to deal nakedly with the mystery of existence? Who could deny it? Not only does a cloud of feminine witnesses, a whole chorus of feminine saints, rise up to prove women's contemplative capacity, the very sufferings that women have undergone have tended to make them reflective–stereotypically more reflective than men, quicker to mature and sense the mysteries of love. Standing at the margins, women have tended to learn in their bones that much dogma is bunk, that most power is pocked, that life's great treasures are simple things like a decent home and large stores of affection. Dealing with children and the sick, women have learned experientially that the only fully effective power is gentle and patient. And all this holds true today. For any woman or man with eyes to see, ears to hear, the world and human nature both clamor for contemplation: reverent attention, regular and deep pondering. Before long, such contemplation becomes like the breathing of one's soul, the nourishment of one's truest self, as countless women, famous and anonymous, have realized.

The same with practical love, daily shouldering one's duties, a life of contribution and service rather than gilded leisure. One of the greatest perils of the religious life is not having the corrections, the humblings, the challenges of needing to earn one's living, cooperate with other people, unite oneself with collaborators to build something greater than what individuals alone ever could. Clearly most women have not had to worry about this peril. Clearly the calls on most women's time and love have been all too great, making most women's problem overextension, too much self-spending, rather than luxury and unreality. As long as women continue to be the majority of the world's poor, the challenges of practical love are sure to be with them. Certainly we should do all we can to get all poor people a decent standard of living, to remove the sufferings that ruin the body and sap the spirit. But on the way to this goal we ought not to miss the saintliness, the simple wisdom, that many wives and mothers, maids and clerks, develop.

Because these are the sorts of reflections to which my preunderstanding of the data of the world religions regarding women run, I find more meaning than futility, more heroism that villainy, more comedy than tragedy. As well, I think that what was in the past—the essential chance to become fully human—remains richly available to women today. So while I work and pray that patriarchy will fall, I remain convinced that patriarchy never has the last word. The last word belongs with the Prajnaparamita, the wisdom that has gone beyond all human partialities, and She is ever gracious.

DISCUSSION QUESTIONS

1. Why have the world religions so regularly made women the second sex, the weaker vessel?

2.   What does standing on the margins tend to teach people about the ways of the world and the ways of God?

3.   How does contemplation open a door to liberty of spirit?

4.   What are the typical fruits of practical love?

5.   On balance, how do you feel about women's experience with the world religions?

NOTES

[1]See Mary Daly, *Gyn/Ecology* (Boston: Beacon, 1978).

[2]See Gerda Lerner, *The Creation of Patriarchy* (New York: Oxford University Press, 1986).

[3]Mary Gordon, *Final Payments* (New York: Ballantine Books, 1979), pp. 248–249.

[4]Wendy Doniger O'Flaherty, *Women, Androgynes and Other Mythical Beasts* (Chicago: University of Chicago Press, 1980), p. 246.

[5]Robert Coles and Jane Hallowell Coles, *Women of Crisis: Lives of Struggle and Hope* (New York: Delta/Seymour Lawrence, 1978), pp. 168–169.

[6]Monika K. Hellwig, *Christian Women in a Troubled World* (New York: Paulist, 1985), pp. 25–26.

[7]On the pathology of uncontemplative modern thought, see Saul Bellow, *More Die of Heartbreak* (New York: William Morrow, 1987); for a *tour de force* on the spiritual life that both balances contemplation and active love and deals with many feminine symbols of key forces, see Anonymous, *Meditations on the Tarot* (Amity, N.Y.: Amity House, 1985).

Glossary

Androcentrism   centering on or in the male; the domination of or emphasis on male interests or points of view.

Androgynous   of, or belonging to, the state of being at once both male and female; hermaphroditic.

Bhakti   Hindu term for the devotional love of a devotee (bhakta) for a personal deity which leads to salvation (moksha).

Buddhanature   the essence of and ability to attain Buddhahood.

Canon   list or body of writings that are considered authoritative or scriptural.

Canonical   officially accredited or authoritative; entered on the list of approved and directive documents.

Celibacy   the state of not having a spouse; abstention from sexual intercourse; chastity, specifically the obligation (as of certain priests or religious) not to marry.

Covenant   the semicontractual bond between Israel and Yahweh such that Israel would be His people and He would be their God; a solemn contract pledging the partners to mutual rights and duties.

Desire   a conscious impulse toward an object or experience that promises enjoyment or satisfaction in its attainment. In Hinduism and Buddhism, desire is what ensnares one in samsara.

Dharma   the teaching of the Buddha; Buddhist doctrine and truth; in Hinduism, duty, responsible acceptance of one's social station (caste) and its implications.

Diaspora   the dispersion of Jews among the Gentiles after the Babylonian exile (586 B.C.E.) and after the Roman destruction of Jerusalem (70 C.E.).

Divination   the art of discerning future events.

Dream-time   the "original time" out of which came the ancestors (and all reality) and into which Australian aborigines believe they are initiated ever more deeply through their rites of passage, until, at death, they enter it fully.

Emptiness important concept in Mahayana Buddhist philosophy, stressing that no reality is substantial and that all reifying language is misleading.

Enlightenment Buddhist term for realization of the truth or attainment of the goal.

Exorcism process of trying to cast out evil spirits thought to have possessed the person.

Gnosticism a religious movement based on secret knowledge (gnosis) that contested with early Christianity.

Gynecocentrism state of being centered on or in the female; a dominance or emphasis on feminine interests or points of view.

Harem the practice of setting a part of the house aside for the exclusive use of the women of the family, their female attendants, and eunuchs. The system dates from pre-Islamic times and lasted (in its full form) until the second half of the twentieth century only among the more conservative elements of Arab society.

Heaven In Confucian thought, it is sometimes described as the impersonal force underlying the cosmos, the ultimate source of order and morality.

Hellenistic pertaining to the cultural ideals, derived from Alexander the Great, that dominated the Near East and Eastern Europe in the late centuries B.C.E. and the early centuries C.E..

Hermaphroditic of, or relating to, the state of being both male and female; androgynous.

Holism a theory according to which a whole cannot be analyzed without residue into the sum of its parts or reduced to discrete elements.

Iconography art representing religious or legendary subjects by conventional images and symbols.

Imams heads of the Muslim communities, leaders of prayers in the mosques. Among Sunnis imam was synonymous with caliph, that is, successor of Muhammad, who had administrative and political (but not religious) functions. Among Shiites, the imam became a figure of absolute spiritual authority.

Immaculate Conception Roman Catholic dogma, declared by Pius IX on December 8, 1854, that asserts that Mary, the mother of Jesus, was preserved from the effects of original sin from the first instant of her conception. This privilege was the result of God's grace and not due to any intrinsic merit on her part.

Karma the Indian moral law of cause and effect, such that past unenlightened actions keep beings in samsara (cycle of births and deaths).

Koan paradoxical saying or riddle (for example, "the sound of one hand clapping") used by Zen Buddhist masters as a prod to enlightenment.

Mahayana one of the three major divisions within Buddhism (Theravada and Vajrayana are the other two) which believes in the gradual attainment of salvation (Buddhahood) over many lifetimes aided by the spiritual assistance of bodhisattvas (individuals who gain Buddhahood but postpone entering nirvana until all creatures are saved).

Mantras Hindu and Buddhist term for sacred sounds thought to have mystical power and repeated as aids to meditation.

Manu mythological figure in Hinduism credited with authoring the Laws of Manu (which date from between 200 B.C.E. and 100 C.E.).

Matrilinear relating to, pertaining to, or based on tracing descent through the maternal line.

Medium a go-between, usually in the sense of the person who goes into a trance to transmit messages from the dead or intelligent spirits.

Mikvah a pool of natural water in which one bathes for the restoration of ritual purity. In modern times, only traditionally observant Jews use the mikvah: males each Friday and before major festivals, women before their wedding, after childbirth, and following menstruation.

Mishnah a code of Jewish law (interpretations of the oral Torah), based on the opinions of leading rabbis, as collected in the diaspora (i.e., after 70 C.E.) and promulgated around 200 C.E.

Misogyny hatred of women.

Moksha Hindu term for release, liberation, salvation; release from the tedious cycle of transmigration (rebirth).

Myths   storied forms of explanation, usually traditional, that may discard the limits of ordinary experience and portray divine or ultimate realities acting beyond the constraints of time and space.

Nazarene   An Israelite who vowed for a specific period to abstain from wine, cutting his hair, or touching a corpse.

Nirvana   the Buddhist term for the state of fulfillment and release from the bondage of worldly existence (samsara).

Patriarchal   of, or relating to, the manifestation and institutionalization of male dominance over women and children in the family and over women in society in general.

Patristic age   the era of Church history dominated by the writings of the Greek and Latin "fathers" (from the Latin *pater*). The literature of this period (excluding the New Testament) is usually dated from the first to the eight centuries and includes the writings of Clement of Rome, Justin Martyr, Origen, Tertullian, Eusebius, Athanasius, the Cappadocean Fathers, John Chrysostom, Cyril of Alexandria, Augustine, and others.

Pharisees   ancient Jews who defended the oral Torah.

Pollution   ritual uncleanness that renders the bearer unfit for contact with the holy until he or she has been purified. Nearly all religions have the concept of pollution; pollution need not imply moral guilt. For example, contact with the dead, with blood, or with a woman after childbirth can cause pollution.

Polygynous   relating to, practicing, or characterized by a man's having two or more wives at the same time.

Puja   Hindu term for ceremonial prayer or worship, especially that which occurs in the home or local temple.

Rites of passage   ceremonies in which one moves from one state to another, for example, from childhood to adulthood, or from life to death. Puberty, marriage, and death usually are celebrated by rites of passage.

Sacredness   holiness, that which is more real and significant than ordinary reality, purer and deserving purer handling.

Sacred thread   an investiture of Hindu boys of the upper three castes with a sacred thread conferred on them the status of "twice born," permitting them to hear (and study) the Vedas and participate in rites that would ensure immortality.

Samsara   the Hindu and Buddhist term for the state of continual rebirths that causes cosmic suffering.

Sar possession   a common North African Muslim belief that allows women to become "possessed" to gain leverage against their husbands' nearly total power and caprice. Exorcism involves giving the wives gifts or parties by which the spirits making them ill or unruly are driven out.

Sexism   the practice that defines the ideology of sexual supremacy, of male superiority and beliefs that support and sustain it.

Shame   a painful emotion caused by consciousness of guilt, shortcoming, or impropriety in one's own behavior or in the behavior or position of a closely associated person or group.

Sila   Buddhist term for morality; the ethical precepts binding on all Buddhists (for example, not to kill, lie, steal, fornicate, or drink intoxicants).

Taboo   Polynesian term used to designate some thing (or act) that one should avoid, because of its sacral or dangerous character.

Talmud   the main collection of Jewish law and rabbinic teaching, comprised of the Mishnah and the Gemara (commentary on the Mishnah) and promulgated around 500 C.E.

Theocracy   government by the immediate administration of God or by priests or clergy as representatives of God.

Torah   in the broadest sense, the whole of God's revealed teaching or guidance for humankind as revealed to the Jewish people. In the restricted meaning, it is the first five books of the Old Testament (the Law or the Pentateuch). Torah is also used to designate the entire Hebrew Bible or both the "oral Law" and the "written Law." Rabbinic commentaries and interpretations of both oral and written Law are also viewed by some as part of the Torah.

Transcendent going beyond this-worldly limits, ultimately into the limitless mystery of God.

Upanishads the final writings of the Vedas (Hindu scriptures) where the theme is the search for the ultimate principle explaining reality.

Vedas the four collections of Hindu sacred writings that represent the highest intuitive knowledge attained by the ancient rishis (holy seers).

Bibliography

GENERAL

The best general reference is Mircea Eliade, ed., *The Encyclopedia of Religion* (New York: Macmillan, 1987). The journals *Journal of Feminist Studies in Religion* and *History of Religions* are good sources of specialized studies. Books composed of studies that cut across several religious traditions include *Women in World Religions*, ed. Arvind Sharma (Albany: State University of New York Press, 1987); *Unspoken Worlds: Women's Lives in Non-Western Cultures*, ed. Nancy A. Falk and Rita M. Gross (San Francisco: Harper & Row, 1980); *The Book of the Goddess Past and Present*, ed. Carl Olsen (New York: Crossroad, 1983); *Women, Religion and Social Change*, ed. Yvonne Yazbeck Haddad and Ellison Banks Findly (Albany: State University of New York Press, 1985); *Immaculate and Powerful: The Female in Sacred Image and Social Reality*, ed. Clarissa Atkinson et al. (Boston: Beacon, 1985); and *Speaking of Faith: Global Perspectives on Women, Religion and Social Change*, ed. Diana L. Eck and Devaki Jain (Philadelphia: New Society, 1987).

CHAPTER ONE:
INTRODUCTION

BELENKY, MARY FIELD ET AL. *Women's Ways of Knowing: The Development of Self, Voice, and Mind.* New York: Basic Books, 1986.
DINNERSTEIN, DOROTHY. *The Mermaid and the Minotaur.* New York: Harper & Row, 1976.
MILES, MARGARET. *Image as Insight: Visual Understanding in Western Christianity and Secular Culture.* Boston: Beacon, 1985.

CHAPTER TWO:
WOMEN IN PRIMAL SOCIETIES

BROWN, JOSEPH EPES. *The Sacred Pipe*. Norman: University of Oklahoma Press, 1953.
DONNER, FLORINDA. *Shabono*. New York: Delacorte, 1982.
DOWNING, CHRISTINE. *The Goddess: Mythological Images of the Feminine*. New York: Crossroad, 1981.
GIMBUTAS, MARIJA. *The Goddesses and Gods of Old Europe*. Berkeley: University of California Press, 1982.
GRIFFIN, SUSAN. *Woman and Nature*. New York: Harper & Row, 1978.
HALIFAX, JOAN. *Shamanic Voices*. New York: E. P. Dutton, 1979.
PAUME, DENISE, ED. *Women of Tropical Africa*. Berkeley: University of California Press, 1971.
SPROUL, BARBARA. *Primal Myths: Creating the World*. San Francisco: Harper & Row, 1979.
STARHAWK, *The Spiral Dance: A Rebirth of the Ancient Religion of the Great Goddess*. San Francisco: Harper & Row, 1979.
TURNBULL, COLIN. *The Forest People*. New York: Simon & Schuster, 1962.
UNDERHILL, RUTH. *Red Man's Religion*. Chicago: University of Chicago Press, 1965.

CHAPTER THREE:
HINDU WOMEN

BERREMAN, GERALD D. *Hindus of the Himalayas: Ethnography and Change*, new ext. ed. Berkeley: University of California Press, 1974.
HAWLEY, JOHN STRATTON, AND DONNA MARIE WULFF, EDS., *The Divine Consort: Radha and the Goddess of India*. Boston: Beacon, 1986.
KAKAR, SUDHIR. *Shamans, Mystics and Doctors: A Psychological Inquiry into India and Its Healing Traditions*. New York: Alfred A. Knopf, 1982.
O'FLAHERTY, WENDY DONIGER, ED. *Karma and Rebirth in Classical Indian Traditions. Berkeley: University of California Press, 1980*.
PANIKKAR, RAIMUNDO. *The Vedic Experience: Mantramanjari*. Berkeley: University of California Press, 1977.
UPADHYAYA, BHAGWAT SARAN. *Women in Rgveda*. New Delhi: S. Chand 1974.

CHAPTER FOUR:
BUDDHIST WOMEN

BEYER, STEPHAN. *The Cult of Tara: Magic and Ritual in Tibet*. Berkeley: University of California Press, 1978.
CONZE, EDWARD. *Buddhist Meditation*. New York: Harper Torchbooks, 1969.
KAPLEAU, PHILIP. *The Three Pillars of Zen*. Boston: Beacon, 1965.
PAUL, DIANA Y. *Women in Buddhism*. Berkeley, Calif.: Asian Humanities Press, 1979.
PREBISH, CHARLES S. *American Buddhism*. North Scituate, Mass.: Duxbury, 1979.
SPIRO, MELFORD E. *Buddhism and Society: A Great Tradition and Its Burmese Vicissitudes*, 2nd exp. ed. Berkeley: University of California Press, 1982.
THOMAS, EDWARD J. *The History of Buddhist Thought*, 2nd ed. New York: Barnes and Noble, 1951.

CHAPTER FIVE:
CHINESE WOMEN

GERNET, JACQUES. *Daily Life in China on the Eve of the Mongol Invasion 1250–1276*. Stanford, Calif.: Stanford University Press, 1970.

GIUSSO, RICHARD, ED. *Women in China.* New York: Philo, 1981.
GRANET, MARCEL. *The Religion of the Chinese People.* New York: Harper Torchbooks, 1977.
KINGSTON, MAXINE HONG. *China Men.* New York: Alfred A. Knopf, 1980.
KINGSTON, MAXINE HONG. *The Woman Warrior: Memoirs of a Girlhood Among Ghosts.* New York: Alfred A. Knopf, 1977.
SPENCE, JONATHAN D. *The Gate of Heavenly Peace: The Chinese and Their Revolution 1895–1980.* New York: Viking, 1981.
YANG, C. K. *Religion in Chinese Society.* Berkeley: University of California Press, 1970.

CHAPTER SIX:
JAPANESE WOMEN

BLACKER, CARMEN. *The Catalpa Bow.* London: Allen & Unwin, 1975.
DALBY, LIZA CRIHFIELD. *Geisha.* Berkeley: University of California Press, 1983.
HORI, ICHIRO. *Folk Religion in Japan.* Chicago: University of Chicago Press, 1968.
KAWABATA, YASUNARI. *Beauty and Sadness.* Tokyo: Charles Tuttle, 1975.
NAKANE, CHIE. *Japanese Society.* Berkeley: University of California Press, 1972.
SUZUKI, SHUNRYU. *Zen Mind, Beginner's Mind.* New York: Weatherhill, 1970.

CHAPTER SEVEN:
JEWISH WOMEN

HARRIS, LIS. *Holy Days: The World of a Hasidic Family.* New York: Summit Books, 1985.
LERNER, GERDA. *The Creation of Patriarchy.* New York: Oxford University Press, 1986.
SWIDLER, LEONARD. *Women in Judaism.* Metuchen, N.J.: Scarecrow Press, 1976.
TERRIEN, SAMUEL. *Till the Heart Sings.* Philadelphia: Fortress, 1985.
TRIBLE, PHYLLIS. *God and the Rhetoric of Sexuality.* Philadelphia: Fortress, 1978.
TRIBLE, PHYLLIS. *Texts of Terror.* Philadelphia: Fortress, 1984.
ZBOROWSKI, MARK, AND ELIZABETH HERZOG. *Life is With People: The Culture of the Shtetl.* New York: Schocken, 1962.

CHAPTER EIGHT:
CHRISTIAN WOMEN

CLARK, ELIZABETH, AND HERBERT RICHARDSON, EDS. *Women and Religion: A Feminist Sourcebook of Christian Thought.* New York: Harper & Row, 1977.
CONN, JOANN WOLSKI, ED. *Women's Spirituality: Resources for Christian Development.* New York: Paulist, 1986.
RUETHER, ROSEMARY RADFORD, ED. *Religion and Sexism.* New York: Simon & Schuster, 1979.
RUETHER, ROSEMARY, AND ELEANOR MCLAUGHLIN, EDS. *Women of Spirit.* New York: Simon & Schuster, 1979.
SCHÜSSLER-FIORENZA, ELISABETH. *In Memory of Her.* New York: Crossroad, 1983.
TAVARD, GEORGE. *Women in Christian Tradition.* Notre Dame, Ind.: University of Notre Dame Press, 1985.
WITHERINGTON, BEN. *Women in the Ministry of Jesus.* Cambridge: Cambridge University Press, 1984.

CHAPTER NINE:
MUSLIM WOMEN

BUSHNAQ, INEA, ED. *Arab Folktales.* New York: Pantheon, 1986.
DONOHUE, JOHN J., AND JOHN L. ESPOSITO, EDS. *Islam in Transition: Muslim Perspectives.* New York: Oxford University Press, 1982.

FARUQI, ISMA'IL R. AL, AND LOIS LAMYA' AL FARUQI. *The Cultural Atlas of Islam*. New York: Macmillan 1986.

NASR, S. H., ED. *Islamic Spirituality: Foundations*. New York: Crossroad, 1987.

SMITH, JANE I., ED. *Women in Contemporary Muslim Societies*. Lewisburg, Penna.: Bucknell University Press, 1980.

WILLIAM, JOHN ALDEN, ED. *Themes of Islamic Civilization*. Berkeley: University of California Press, 1982.

CHAPTER TEN:
AMERICAN WOMEN

AHLSTROM, SYDNEY E. *A Religious History of the American People*. New Haven, Conn.: Yale University Press, 1972.

GAUSTAD, EDWIN S., ED. *A Documentary History of Religion in America*, 2 vols. Grand Rapids, Mich.: Eerdmans, 1982, 1983.

ROSSI, ALICE S., ED. *The Feminist Papers*. New York: Columbia University Press, 1973.

RUETHER, ROSEMARY RADFORD, AND ROSEMARY SKINNER KELLER, EDS. *Women & Religion in America*, 3 vols. San Francisco: Harper & Row, 1981ff.

SPRETNAK, CHARLENE, ED. *The Politics of Women's Spirituality*. Garden City, N.Y.: Doubleday, 1982.

CHAPTER ELEVEN:
CONCLUSION

COLES, ROBERT, AND JANE HALLOWELL COLES. *Women of Crisis: Lives of Struggle and Hope*, 2 vols. New York: Delta/Seymour Lawrence, 1978, 1981.

DALY, MARY. *Gyn/Ecology*. Boston: Beacon, 1978.

O'FLAHERTY, WENDY DONIGER. *Women, Androgynes and Other Mythical Beasts*. Chicago: University of Chicago Press, 1980.

Index

A